MISSION REVOLUTION

COLUMBIA STUDIES IN TERRORISM AND IRREGULAR WARFARE

COLUMBIA STUDIES IN TERRORISM AND IRREGULAR WARFARE

Bruce Hoffman, Series Editor

This series seeks to fill a conspicuous gap in the burgeoning literature on terrorism, guerrilla warfare, and insurgency. The series adheres to the highest standards of scholarship and discourse and publishes books that elucidate the strategy, operations, means, motivations, and effects posed by terrorist, guerrilla, and insurgent organizations and movements. It thereby provides a solid and increasingly expanding foundation of knowledge on these subjects for students, established scholars, and informed reading audiences alike.

Ami Pedahzur, *The Israeli Secret Services and the Struggle Against Terrorism*

Ami Pedahzur and Arie Perliger, *Jewish Terrorism in Israel*

Lorenzo Vidino, *The New Muslim Brotherhood in the West*

Erica Chenoweth and Maria J. Stephan, *Why Civil Resistance Works: The Strategic Logic of Nonviolent Resistance*

William C. Banks, *New Battlefields/Old Laws: Critical Debates on Asymmetric Warfare*

Blake W. Mobley, *Terrorist Group Counterintelligence*

Jennifer Morrison Taw

MISSION
REVOLUTION

THE U.S. MILITARY AND
STABILITY OPERATIONS

Columbia
University
Press ■
New York

Columbia University Press
Publishers Since 1893
New York   Chichester, West Sussex
cup.columbia.edu
Copyright © 2012 Columbia University Press
All rights reserved

Library of Congress Cataloging-in-Publication Data
Taw, Jennifer, M., 1964–
 Mission revolution : the U.S. military and stability operation / Jennifer
 Morrison Taw.
      p. cm.—(Columbia studies in terrorism and irregular warfare)
 Includes bibliographical references and index.
 ISBN 978-0-231-15324-9 (cloth : alk. paper)—ISBN 978-0-231-52682-1 (e-book)
 1. United States—Armed Forces—Stability operations. 2. Military doctrine—
 United States. 3. United States—Military policy. I. Title.
 UH723.T378 2012
    355.4—dc23
2012001235

Jacket image: Scott Nelson | Getty images
Jacket design: Thomas Beck Stvan

References to websites (URLs) were accurate at the time of writing. Neither the
author nor Columbia University Press is responsible for URLs that may have
expired or changed since the manuscript was prepared.

To my husband, Steve, and our three perfect kids:
  Emily, Max, and Keenan.

CONTENTS

ACKNOWLEDGMENTS

I am indebted to the many people who helped make this book possible. Bruce Hoffman, who invited me to participate in this book series, has been a staunch and deeply supportive mentor since I first crossed RAND's threshold more than twenty years ago. Maren Leed, Anna Simons, A. Heather Coyne, and John Nagl generously tapped their expansive networks of experts and got me great interviews with truly helpful people. Takako Mino, Victoria Din, and Kate Castenson contributed invaluable ideas and resources at different stages of research. I cannot thank Peter Austin and David Charters enough for their meticulous reviews of earlier drafts; the final reviewers also provided thoughtful and constructive feedback. I could not have written this book without all of this assistance. Any errors in fact or analysis are mine. Thanks are also due to those who enabled production: Anne Routon, Alison Alexanian, and Robert Fellman shepherded this book with patience and tenacity. Finally, I will always be grateful for how my family, friends, colleagues, and students have buoyed me with their warm-hearted encouragement and interest. And, of course, my biggest thanks go to my husband and kids—Steve, Emily, Max, and Keenan—both for giving me the time to research, write, and teach and for balancing those pursuits with the rich whirl of our family life.

ABBREVIATIONS

AAR	After Action Review/Report
ACDA	Arms Control and Disarmament Agency
ADT	Agribusiness Development Teams
AEF	Aerospace Expeditionary Force
AEI	American Enterprise Institute
AFDD	Air Force Doctrine Document
AFP	Air Force Pamphlet
AFRICOM	United States Africa Command
AFSOC	Air Force Special Operations Command
AFTTP	Air Force Tactics, Techniques, and Procedures
AH	Air Handler
ALB	Air Land Battle
ASETF	Air and Space Expeditionary Task Force
BC	Basic Combat
BCT	Brigade Combat Team
BCT-S	Brigade Combat Team—Stability
BTT	Border Transition Teams
CA	Civil Affairs
CAOCL	Center for Advanced Operational Culture Learning
CAS	Close Air Support
CBC	Canadian Broadcasting Corporation
CERP	Commander's Emergency Response Program
CH	Cargo Helicopter

ABBREVIATIONS

CIP	Center for International Policy
CIW	Marine Corps Center for Irregular Warfare
CIWAG	Center for Irregular Warfare and Armed Groups
CIWC	Coalition Irregular Warfare Center of Excellence
CJCS	Chairman of the Joint Chiefs of Staff
CNAS	Center for New American Security
COIN	Counterinsurgency Doctrine
CORDS	Civil Operations and Rural Development Support
CORM	Commission on the Roles and Missions of the Armed Forces
CRC	Civilian Response Corps
CRG	Contingency Response Groups
CRS	Congressional Research Service
CSIS	Center for Strategic and International Studies
CT	Counterterrorism
CTFP	Regional Defense Combating Terrorism Fellowship Program
CV	Combat Vehicle
DA	Direct Action
DCHA	Bureau for Democracy, Conflict, and Humanitarian Assistance (USAID)
DOD	Department of Defense
DODD	Department of Defense Directive
DST	District Support Teams
EFV	Expeditionary Fighting Vehicle
EOD	Explosive Ordinance Disposal
EPRT	Embedded Provincial Reconstruction Team
EXTAC	Experimental Tactic
FCS	Future Combat System
FID	Foreign Internal Defense
FM	Field Manual
FMF	Foreign Military Financing
FMFM	Fleet Marine Force Manual
FPC	Force Planning Construct

ABBREVIATIONS

FY	Fiscal Year
GAO	Government Accountability Office
GCC	Geographic Combatant Commands
GCV	Ground Combat Vehicle
GI	General Infantry
HA/DR	Humanitarian Assistance/Disaster Relief
ICRC	International Committee of the Red Cross
IDAD	Internal Defense and Development
IED	Improvised Explosive Devices
ILE	Intermediate-Level Education
IMET	International Military Education and Training
IO	Information Operations
ISAF	International Security Assistance Force
IW	Irregular Warfare
JDPC	Joint Doctrine Planning Conference
JFCOM	Joint Warfare Command
JHSV	Joint High-Speed Vessel
JIW	Joint Irregular Warfare Center
JOC	Joint Operating Concept
JP	Joint Publication
JPME	Joint Professional Military Education
LCS	Littoral Combat Ships
LIC	Low-Intensity Conflict
LMI	Logistics Management Institute
MAGTF	Marine Air-Ground Task Force
MAGTFTC	Marine Air-Ground Task Force Training Command
MARSOC	Marines Special Operations Command
MCWP	Marine Corps Warfighting Publication
MDCP	Marine Corps Decision Coordinating Paper
MEB	Marine Expeditionary Brigades
MEF	Marine Expeditionary Forces
MESF	Maritime Expeditionary Security Force
MEU	Marine Expeditionary Units
MH	Medium Helicopter

ABBREVIATIONS

MISO	Military Information Support Operations
MNF	Multinational Force
MOOTW	Military Operations Other Than War
MOS	Military Occupation Specialties
MOSW	Military Operations Short of War
MPLA	Movimento Popular de Libertação de Angola (People's Movement for the Liberation of Angola)
MRAP	Mine Resistant Ambush Protected
MTT	Military Transition Teams
NAVMC	Navy Marine Corps
NDAA	National Defense Authorization Act
NDIA	National Defense Industry Association
NDP	Naval Doctrine Publication
NECC	Navy Expeditionary Combat Command
NGO	Nongovernmental Organization
NSAM	National Security Action Memorandum
NSC	National Security Council
NSPD	National Security Presidential Directive
NTC	National Training Center
NWC	National War College
NWDC	Navy Warfare Development Command
TACMEMO	Tactical Memorandum
ODA	Operational Detachment A
OMA	Office of Military Affairs (U.S. CIA)
OOTW	Operations Other Than War
OPTEMPO	Operations Tempo
ORHA	Office of Reconstruction and Humanitarian Assistance
OSD	Office of the Secretary of Defense
PDD	Presidential Decision Directive
PKSOI	Peacekeeping and Stability Operations Institute
PLO	Palestine Liberation Organization
PME	Professional Military Education
PRT	Provincial Reconstruction Team
PSYOP	Psychological Operations

ABBREVIATIONS

PTT	Police Transition Teams
QDDR	Quadrennial Diplomacy and Development Review
QDR	Quadrennial Defense Review
QIP	Quick Impact Projects
RMA	Revolution in Military Affairs
ROVER	Remotely Operated Video Enhanced Receiver
S&R	Search and Rescue
S/CRS	State Department's Office of the Coordinator for Reconstruction and Stabilization
SA	System Administrator
SBCT	Stryker Brigade Combat Team
SEAL	Sea, Air, and Land
SF	Special Forces
SFA	Special Force Assistance
SLAMRAAM	Surface-Launched Advanced Medium Range Air-to-Air Missile
SOCOM	Special Operations Command
SOF	Special Operations Forces
SOS	Special Operations Squadron
SOUTHCOM	United States Southern Command
SR	Special Reconnaissance
SSTR	Stability, Security, Transition, and Reconstruction Operations
STOVL	Short Take-Off Vertical Landing
TTP	Tactics, Techniques, and Procedures
UAV	Unmanned Aerial Vehicle
UH	Utility Helicopter
UNDP	United Nations Development Programme
UNITA	União Nacional para a Independência Total de Angola (National Union for the Total Independence of Angola)
USAF	United States Air Force
USAFRICOM	United States Africa Command
USAID	United States Agency for International Development
USASOC	United States Army Special Operations Command

ABBREVIATIONS

USASOF	United States Air Force Special Operations Forces
USAWC	United States Army War College
USIA	United States Information Agency
USIP	United States Institute of Peace
USJFCOM	United States Joint Forces Command
FEA	Front-End Analysis
USMC	United States Marine Corps
USSOCOM	U.S. Special Operations Command
UW	Unconventional Warfare
WIN-T	Warfighter Information Network (Tactical)

MISSION REVOLUTION

INTRODUCTION
MISSION CREEP WRIT LARGE

The U.S. Military's Embrace of Stability Operations

You must know something about strategy and tactics and logistics, but also economics and politics and diplomacy and history. You must know everything you can know about military power, and you must also understand the limits of military power. You must understand that few of the important problems of our time have, in the final analysis, been finally solved by military power alone.

—President John F. Kennedy, remarks to the graduating class of the U.S. Naval Academy,
Annapolis, Maryland, June 7, 1961

The mission of the Department of Defense is to protect the American people and advance our nation's interests. . . . The U.S. military must therefore be prepared to support broad national goals of promoting stability in key regions, providing assistance to nations in need, and promoting the common good.

—*Quadrennial Defense Review Report* (2010), U.S. Department of Defense

On November 28, 2005, the U.S. Department of Defense released Directive Number 3000.05,[1] which requires stability operations to be treated on par with offense and defense in every aspect of military preparation. In its directive, the Pentagon offered only a very general characterization of stability operations: "Military and civilian activities conducted across the spectrum from peace to conflict to establish or maintain order in States and regions." Notably, the mission includes civilians, involves the establishment and maintenance of order, and applies equally in peacetime and in conflict.

Stability operations also represent the U.S. armed forces' nascent steps into more traditionally civilian territory. Although conducted in support of and in cooperation with civilian authorities, the military's objectives in stability operations differ dramatically from defense, deterrence, or victory:

> Stability operations are conducted to help establish order that advances U.S. interests and values. The immediate goal often is to provide the local populace with security, restore essential services, and meet humanitarian needs. The long-term goal is to help develop indigenous capacity for securing essential services, a viable market economy, rule of law, democratic institutions, and a robust civil society.[2]

Stability operations are thus readily differentiated from the armed forces' traditional offensive and defensive missions and represent a dramatic change in the military's perception of its role and responsibilities. This is the armed forces' most fundamental adjustment since the establishment of the Department of Defense in 1947, and it is arguably more foundational than the 1986 Goldwater-Nichols reorganization.[3] Military leaders are touting this as a revolution, and it is playing out in doctrine and in changes to training, force structure, and procurement. Military leaders now are calling for U.S. forces to be prepared for "full-spectrum operations" entailing "the application of combat power through simultaneous and continuous combinations of four elements: offense, defense, stability, and civil support."[4]

Despite being so recent, moreover, the change is wholehearted, with a fully developed legitimizing logic that goes something like this: The military has a surplus of conventional capabilities but a deficit for conducting the kinds of operations being undertaken in Iraq and Afghanistan. As these kinds of operations have predominated since the end of the Cold War and, arguably, even during the Cold War—the military must adapt. It must be ready for operations "in a complex era of persistent conflict," terminology that shows up in some form or another in working papers, articles, and new doctrine and that indicates that the change is in response to a new and challenging strategic environment.[5]

The shift in priorities is even evident in word choice. In the 2006 Quadrennial Defense Review (QDR), stability operations were described as a subset of irregular warfare (IW), a broad category of operations including counterinsurgency (COIN), counterterrorism (CT), unconventional warfare (UW), and foreign internal defense (FID).[6] In the 2010 QDR, however, all references to IW were dropped in favor of more specific references to each of the components of the category.[7] This change was made in part to allay confusion; including stability operations with the other components of IW made little sense, since stability operations can include any military or civilian effort to establish order and can take place simultaneously with— indeed, can play a prominent and necessary role in—any of the other elements of IW. Stability operations, moreover, can also be undertaken during peacetime or as a part of conventional war. In peacetime, stability operations involve efforts to shape host nations' environments, with the goal of helping to prevent tensions and reduce the likelihood of conflict. Where conflicts have arisen, stability operations are intended to promote room for negotiations and reduce the causes of strife. In war, stability operations are supposed to mitigate the negative and long-term effects of combat on civilian populations and address underlying causes of tension. As war winds down, stability operations are used in an effort to create opportunities for accords, begin processes of rebuilding, and limit the likelihood of renewed violence.[8]

By elevating stability operations—of all the IW components—to a primary mission alongside offense and defense, the DOD has signaled that the military's job has expanded. It is not only to win battles, defeat enemy forces, and deter aggressors but actively, alongside civilian counterparts, to promote stability through the provision of controlled and nonviolent environments, improved governance, and economic growth. This unprecedented emphasis on stability operations thus effectively represents a new raison d'être for the U.S. military.

The U.S. operations in Iraq precisely mirror the swing from emphasizing fighting and winning the nation's wars to the embrace of stability operations. In fact, Secretary of Defense Donald Rumsfeld's vision of the war in Iraq was as a showcase for the then-current Revolution in Military Affairs (RMA), which he championed in the Pentagon. The RMA was intended

3

to bring conventional warfare into the twenty-first century, emphasizing speed, lethality, accuracy, flexibility, and information dominance, all rooted in state-of-the-art technology. The military was to be a dominant, highly professional, and efficient fighting force. Nation building was anathema to this view, and Rumsfeld often stated that he opposed using U.S. forces for such tasks, including for postcombat reestablishment of peace.[9] Thus, the secretary of defense expected the war in Iraq to be a rapid, overwhelming defeat of Saddam Hussein's forces, followed by the withdrawal of American troops. When asked in 2003, before the war began, how long it might last, he responded: "It could last six days, six weeks. I doubt six months."[10] And he was right—if the war's duration is measured by the time between the first deployment of U.S. forces and the declaration of victory, if the end of the war was the defeat of Saddam's military and the toppling of his government.[11] But well over six years, billions of dollars, thousands of casualties, and one "surge" later, American troops were still in Iraq, conducting counterinsurgency and nation building, the kind of slow, manpower-intensive, low-tech operations that Rumsfeld particularly despised and that the military more generally had always undertaken as a sideline to the main event.

As will be discussed in chapter 2, responding to the conflicts in Iraq and Afghanistan, in 2006 the Army and the Marine Corps together published new counterinsurgency doctrine, emphasizing the importance of stability operations for success in COIN. Less than two years later, the Army published a new version of capstone doctrine, Field Manual (FM) 3-0, *Operations*, which included stability operations' new elevated role, and a keystone stability operations manual, FM-07, *Stability Operations*.

There have thus been two transformations in the past ten years, the much-touted and oft-debated RMA and the quieter but arguably more significant elevation of stability operations. Arguably rooted in weapons systems that began development in the 1970s, the RMA accelerated with the end of the Cold War and the consequent drawdown in U.S. military forces, the advent of new technologies (especially information technologies), and lessons from the 1991 Gulf War. But even as the military implemented the RMA, troops were being deployed in increasing numbers to a different kind of battlefield, one on which these new capabilities were only marginally useful. Peace operations, counterdrug ventures, counterinsurgency efforts, and ultimately stability and reconstruction missions could not be conducted as stand-off operations. They required large numbers of troops rather than the RMA's preferred small footprint and were far more dependent on elusive human intelligence than the kinds of electronic, satellite, and signal intelligence that underpinned information supremacy in the RMA. Just as the "lessons learned" from the Gulf War reinforced the RMA, the "lessons learned" from the OOTW of the immediate post–Cold War period and the recent and challenging operations in Afghanistan and Iraq are the roots of the military's current transformation.

Questions inevitably arise from this dramatic adjustment to the military's mission and the concomitant changes in organization, doctrine, and training. The first: Is this shift as radical as it appears? DODD 3000.05, FM 3-0, the new U.S. Army-Marine Corps counterinsurgency (COIN) field manual, and incipient joint doctrine seem to represent a sea change in how the military perceives both threats and its own role.[12] Yet some argue that this has been more evolutionary than revolutionary and reflects not a dramatic departure but rational next steps in the military's development. The military has always undertaken stability operations: reconstruction after the American Civil War entailed extensive nation building, as did the massive post–World War II efforts in both Europe and Japan, not to mention all the stability operations that have been conducted as elements of COIN, disaster relief, or peacekeeping. Thus, as a means of offering some context, this study begins in chapter 1 with a long view of the military's involvement in—and opinion of—stability operations. An overview of doctrinal development over the past twenty years in chapter 2 then provides some insight into how substantive a change has really taken place, as does the assessment in chapter 3 of the military's changing organization, force structure, education, and training.

The second question: If this is truly a new direction for the military, what led the infamously stubborn institution to change course so dramatically and in such a relatively short period of time? There have been many explanations offered for the new policy, but none of them satisfactorily explains the timing of DODD 3000.05. Chapter 4 offers a new approach to thinking about the political dynamics that resulted in the shift in the armed forces' mission.

Once the politics of change are scrutinized, it is useful to examine, as is done in chapter 5, the meaning of this much broader mission both in terms of military capabilities and as it affects policy options. Capabilities and policy are deeply interrelated, and changes in one affect the other. In terms of stability operations, military capabilities will be shaped by changes in training, force structure, and equipment that are a function of policy. Policy options will, in turn, be affected; the military's shift toward stability operations is intended to broaden the military's utility to civilians as they attempt to manage conflict, promote peace, and encourage democracy. Having these enhanced tools at their disposal may affect policy makers' calculations regarding foreign policy. It is likely to change the balance of responsibilities among domestic actors. The military's transformation and more expansive application will also change international perceptions of the U.S. military and U.S. foreign policy more generally, creating an unpredictable ripple effect as friends and opponents adjust to this change in the U.S. armed forces.

Finally, the assumption underlying the entire transformation needs further assessment to determine whether this shift in approach is a positive, visionary development or a potentially dangerous detour for both the military and the nation. Chapter 6 examines in conclusion whether the military is—or ever has been—the correct tool for addressing instability. While it seems that the lessons from Iraq and Afghanistan are that the military needs better preparation before conducting these kinds of operations, perhaps the lesson should instead be that we should avoid these kinds of operations altogether and seek more cost-effective, constructive, and long-term means of influencing the international environment in ways conducive to protecting American interests.

Overall, this book means to demonstrate that DOD 3000.05 represents a significant change from previous practices, to identify and examine the dynamics that led the Pentagon to adopt this new approach, and to consider the implications—for the military, for policy makers, and for U.S. interests more generally—of elevating stability operations to a primary mission.

ONE
STABILITY OPERATIONS IN CONTEXT

Stability operations are a core U.S. military mission that the Department of Defense shall be prepared to conduct and support. They shall be given priority comparable to combat operations and be explicitly addressed and integrated across all DOD activities including doctrine, organizations, training, education, exercises, materiel, leadership, personnel, facilities, and planning.

—Department of Defense Directive 3000.05

DEFINING STABILITY OPERATIONS

DOD Directive 3000.05, in elevating stability operations to the equivalent of combat operations, defines them as "military and civilian activities conducted across the spectrum from peace to conflict to establish or maintain order in States and regions."[1] This definition is broad enough, with the inclusion of "establish . . . order," that almost any military operation could fall within it. Joint doctrine's definition of stability operations is far more specific, though it still includes establishing a secure environment: "various military missions, tasks, and activities conducted outside the United States in coordination with other instruments of national power to maintain or establish a safe and secure environment, provide essential governmental services, emergency infrastructure reconstruction, and humanitarian relief."[2] FM 3-0, the Army's capstone doctrine, defines stability operations as efforts to "promote and protect US national interests by influencing the threat, political and information dimensions of the operational environment through a combination of peacetime developmental, cooperative activities and coercive actions in response to crisis."[3] Like the preceding definitions, this one leaves room for a wide range of military actions, as long as they are in the service of shaping the environment.

Ultimately, the term refers to the application of a group of operations in support of establishing and maintaining order. The group of operations includes most of the same tasks that fell under previous categories (such as LIC and OOTW), but by refining the way they are presented, specifically in the service of promoting stability, they become less a disparate bunch of unrelated undertakings and more a toolkit for a specific objective. They include:

- Peace operations, including peacekeeping and peace enforcement
- Humanitarian and civic assistance
- Noncombatant evacuations
- The broad subcategory of security assistance with foreign military sales, international military education and training, and more
- Shows of force
- Arms control
- Support to insurgencies
- Support to counterdrug operations
- Combating terrorism
- Support to domestic civilian authorities[4]

Each of these is a potential tool for the promotion or maintenance of order and thus can be considered a form of stability operation.

The relationship between COIN, FID, and stability operations is worth parsing in more detail, since the three are so closely connected, often overlap, and are sometimes, incorrectly, used interchangeably. FID refers to civilian and military efforts to help a host nation's government implement its internal defense and development (IDAD) strategy and thus comprises stability operations undertaken in support of a foreign administration. COIN is the full range of military and civilian efforts undertaken to combat an insurgency; U.S. forces' involvement in COIN can involve direct military engagement with insurgents, but it is usually focused on support for host nation governments' COIN efforts, including the provision of military training, materiel, and advice as well as development assistance and other stability operations. References to both FID and COIN inherently include reference to stability operations, since these comprise a huge portion of both efforts. Stability operations, however, are not restricted to either of these categories and can include everything from routine peacetime engagement, such as security assistance, to peacekeeping, and to stabilization and reconstruction efforts as a conventional war moves into its final phases.

Clearly adjusting terminology to emphasize stability operations rather than broad categories like OOTW or IW is more than simply semantic, even though stability operations often involve precisely the same tasks that fell under previous groupings. As "operations other than war," the tasks were defined by what they were not; as stability operations, they are defined as part of a larger strategic objective.[5] This change in nomenclature reflects the shift in priorities and in the perception of the military's appropriate role. Whereas these tasks were once considered distractions from war, they are now considered part of war itself, part of "full-spectrum operations," and as tasks often necessary simultaneously with combat. More importantly, they are also seen as valuable peacetime strategies and as required for successfully concluding conflict and creating lasting peace. Suddenly, American military leaders are taking Clausewitz's dictum that war is a continuation of politics by other means more to heart than ever before.[6]

Despite the new appreciation for such operations' significance, the very broadness of the concept of stability operations can have drawbacks. Stability operations can involve a wide variety of tasks that will be undertaken in varying circumstances; use different types, combinations, and numbers of troops and units; require different kinds of equipment; and rely on different forms of training. Some tasks are more akin to conventional combat operations or are more readily undertaken by personnel prepared for such contingencies:

- Shows of force
- Noncombatant evacuation operations
- Arguably, some elements of foreign internal defense and counterterrorism

Some tasks promote training and experience for conventional combat:

- Security assistance
- Security force assistance
- Humanitarian and civic assistance
- Some aspects of arms control[7]

Some tasks will require more specific training to prepare the forces for restrictive rules of engagement, the presence of civilians, the need for interagency cooperation, and the potential for strategic outcomes of apparently minor tactical decisions:

- Peacekeeping
- Peace enforcement
- Support to insurgencies
- Many elements of foreign internal defense, and aspects of counterterrorism

It is thus not surprising that stability operations are expected to accomplish quite a bit, including both development and coercion:

Stability operations promote and protect US national interests by influencing the threat, political, and information dimensions of the operational environment. They include developmental, cooperative activities during peacetime and coercive actions in response to crisis. Army forces accomplish stability goals through engagement and response. The military activities that support stability operations are diverse, continuous, and often long-term. Their purpose is to promote and sustain regional and global stability.[8]

But, in the context of changing views, it is important to note that different stability operations tasks and activities will have different requirements and, more importantly, different relationships with—and effects on readiness for—conventional warfighting.

THE HISTORY OF STABILITY OPERATIONS

Why . . . does our military history not examine the pattern of the wars against Native Americans from Colonial times to the final defeats of the Apache and Nez Pierce as one continuing and evolving conflict? Seen from a grand strategic perspective, a consistent pattern of military action directed towards armed nation building, and what we now call stability operations, extended for well over two centuries. It steadily and repetitively changed the face of America. We occupied our own country long before we occupied Germany, Japan, or Iraq.

—Anthony H. Cordesman, "Iraq, Grand Strategy, and the Lessons of Military History" (2004)

The preponderance of U.S. military operations have not been conventional; by some counts, American armed forces have been involved in hundreds of contingencies and only eleven conventional wars.[9] Even before the establishment of an American military, colonial troops used unconventional tactics in the French and Indian War.[10] Two decades later, during the Revolutionary War, Francis Marion became well known for his unconventional tactics against the British forces in the south. Efforts to use the military to promote stability, however, really began in the years preceding the Civil War, when the U.S. military engaged in numerous stability operations, not least of which were the wars against the Barbary pirates at the turn of the nineteenth century, the internal operations against Native Americans throughout the 1800s,[11] and the 1857–1858 suppression of the Mormons in Utah.

All of these operations, however, were undertaken as peripheral efforts by forces whose preparation was focused on conventional warfighting and a more aggressive, internationalist foreign policy in keeping with the concept of manifest destiny, which was reflected most concretely in the Spanish-American War. Indeed, the American Revolution was the birthplace not only of the nation but of a decidedly American, decidedly conventional style of war focused on set-piece offensive battles and continuous campaigns against the British (and underpinned by a great deal of assistance from the French).[12] Even during the Indian Wars, the U.S. military focused on conventional training:

> As far back as the Indian Wars Campaign of the 1860s–1890s the US Army concentrated most of its training time on conventional tactics, techniques and procedures, particularly officer training at the US Military Academy at West Point. Until the late 1870s or early 1880s, individual officer training on MOOTW at West Point was relegated to an occasional field training exercise or classroom lecture. The primary method of adapting traditional soldier skills to the "irregular battlefield" was relegated to unit training passed down by veterans as replacements were introduced to the isolated US Army posts of the West.[13]

The American "way of war," involving overwhelming mass, mobility, and technology, was again evident during the Civil War.[14] The experience in other kinds of contingencies was laid aside as the American armies faced off across battlefields. Yet immediately following the war, troops were again deployed for stability operations. Americans supported the coup against Queen Lili'uokalani in Hawaii in 1893; in precursors to today's nation-building efforts, they occupied the Philippines,[15] Nicaragua, and Haiti in the early 1900s; they successfully reduced Pancho Villa's troops in Mexico; they occupied Vera Cruz for six months in 1914; and they protected, in 1927, U.S. property in Shanghai during a civil war there.[16] These kinds of efforts dominated American troop deployments leading up to the world wars.

By the mid-twentieth century, World Wars I and II (and even Korea, to some extent) had again demonstrated the effectiveness of the mass + mobility + technology equation. Thus, as the bipolar international system emerged from the ashes of World War II, Americans prepared their forces to fight the Soviets across the Fulda Gap, bringing to bear the American "way of war" using a tremendous range of new technologies, impressive logistical capacity, and the ability to mass forces quickly and effectively throughout Europe. The advent of the atomic bomb and the rapid development of nuclear weapons in both the United States and the Soviet Union further challenged strategists to focus on what, at the time, was called "limited war"—conventional warfare short of an all-out nuclear exchange. The challenge was perceived as existential: preventing the spread of communist influence internationally ("godless communism" was antithetical to the American way of life)[17] while also avoiding a nuclear holocaust. Accomplishing this required not only nuclear deterrence but also conventional deterrence, to which end the Americans established a large conventional military presence in Europe as well as bases in Asia.

For fifty years, the Americans emphasized a Fulda Gap scenario in military doctrine, training, and organization, preparing for a conventional battlefield war with the USSR across the expanse of Europe. Military and civilian leaders continued to assume that preparation for war was adequate to ensure readiness for the contingencies short of war to which U.S. troops were frequently deployed.[18] The military's most immediate commitments following World War II were the massive nation-building efforts they performed throughout Europe and in Japan, involving more than one million American troops. Soon thereafter came the evacuation of Chinese Nationalist troops and civilians to Taiwan in 1955 and then a steady stream of contingency operations, including the 1958 U.S. intervention in Lebanon, the defense of the Laotian government in Thailand in 1962, and the Dominican crisis in 1965.[19] And, of course, there was the Vietnam War.

The Vietnam War demanded a taxing mix of COIN and stability operations: the Americans, armed and trained for battlefield warfare, found themselves in unconventional combat with both insurgents and conventional forces, in impassable jungles and populated terrain, trying to train and prepare their unsavory allies' often incompetent and untrustworthy troops while winning local hearts and minds, all under unclear and changing political guidance and with waning domestic support. Their efforts were further complicated by a big-war strategic approach that emphasized conventional maneuver tactics and body counts as measures of effectiveness. In the face of these competing imperatives, a range of stopgap and often ad hoc COIN and stability operations solutions were developed as American policy makers and military leaders attempted to navigate the challenges of Vietnam. These efforts are instructive. Among them were CORDS (initially, Civil Operations and Revolutionary Development Support, but changed in 1970 to Civil Operations and Rural Development Support), a groundbreaking program that brought civilians and the military together in a single organization in order to address the conflict's broad span of security, political, and economic requirements; the Phoenix program, a CIA-led operation that targeted the political and military leaders of the Viet Cong for assassination; and the early Strategic Hamlets program, with its roots in the British experiences in Malaya, wherein insurgents were cleared from a populated area, after which the South Vietnamese government, with U.S. assistance and support, would provide the local noncombatants with security, economic opportunities, and governance (readily summed up as "clear, hold, build"). COIN and all the elements of nation building were present: training local security forces, growing the economy, promoting good governance, and working effectively as interagency elements. All of these were conditions for success, but each entailed a steep learning curve and posed unique challenges. Although the U.S. forces' COIN capacity improved over the course of the war, in the end, the combination of American political ambiguity, competing strategic and practical imperatives, and the complexity of the conflict itself proved insuperable.

The Vietnam War has particular significance in the military's handling of COIN and stability operations. It soured American support for such operations, left a devastating rift within the military, and caused perhaps even greater damage to civil-military relations. It led to an abhorrence for "gradualism," the slow infusion of forces over time, and resulted in what has become commonly known as the "Vietnam Syndrome," a rejection of U.S. intervention abroad for fear that it could bog down American forces in a quagmire.[20] Vietnam gave the lie to the assumption that conventionally trained troops could conduct effective counterinsurgency and stability operations and demonstrated the limitations of the American "way of war." Though U.S. forces won battle after battle, they could not win overall.

More important perhaps was the formless yet lethal nature of warfare in Vietnam, a war without distinct battle lines or fixed objectives, where traditional concepts of victory and defeat were blurred. This type of war was particularly difficult for Americans schooled in the conventional warfare of World War II and Korea. And there was always the gnawing but fundamental question, first raised by John F. Kennedy: how can we tell if we are winning?[21]

The civilian and military leadership's response to Vietnam, perhaps understandable given the political atmosphere, was not to better prepare the force for such operations but to abjure foreign intervention and return with a vengeance to the mass + mobility + technology equation for military success. The few post-Vietnam Cold War contingency operations were therefore downplayed, conducted by proxy, or pitched as necessary exceptions or even as conventional operations. Thus, the 1975 Mayaguez incident, in which American Marines and naval forces saved a U.S. merchant ship from Cambodians, involved such a huge show of force (assault troops, bombing raids, warships) that a Tokyo newspaper asked, "Why did the [United States] have to use a cannon to shoot a chicken?"[22] The attempt to free American hostages from Iran in 1980 was kept top secret until the mission was underway and then failed tragically. The fiasco predictably was perceived in light of Vietnam and appeared to reinforce the message that U.S. armed forces should not undertake stability operations. *Time* ran an article that included an indictment of the American military: "A once dominant military machine, first humbled in its agonizing standoff in Viet Nam, now looked incapable of keeping its aircraft aloft even when no enemy knew they were there, and even incapable of keeping them from crashing into each other despite four months of practice for their mission."[23]

The first major post-Vietnam stability operation took place when American Marines and Navy SEALs deployed to Lebanon in 1982, alongside French, British, and Italian forces, as part of Multinational Force (MNF) Lebanon, a very brief escort operation intended to keep the peace as the Palestine Liberation Organization (PLO) evacuated from that country. In keeping with the post-Vietnam emphasis on controllable contingency operations, the MNF withdrew shortly after the PLO left the country. Days later, however, President Gemayel of Lebanon was assassinated, and a massacre took place at the Sabra and Shatila refugee camps, leaving hundreds of Palestinians dead at the hands of Lebanese Phalangists. President Reagan responded by sending Marines back into Lebanon as part of a larger and more heavily equipped MNF (MNF II), with the French and Italians. The objective this time was much broader: to help the new government maintain stability through peacekeeping. The decision to return to Lebanon was opposed by some in the U.S. military and a few members of Congress, who raised objections about sending American soldiers to fight someone else's war,[24] but, for the most part, stakeholders supported the redeployment. Sadly, the MNF became a textbook case of what not to do in peacekeeping. MNF II went into Lebanon in the absence of any peace agreement among the warring factions; there was, therefore, no "peace" to keep. It deployed without the acceptance of all the warring factions, putting MNF troops immediately at risk. And, by their actions—particularly in response to attacks—the Americans and the French very quickly lost their veneer of neutrality, thus increasing the likelihood of attacks against their forces. The result was, after a steady stream of lesser attacks, the deadly bombing of the U.S. Marine Corps barracks and the French paratroopers' base. Far from standing as an example of the legitimacy and value of stability operations, MNF II seemed to bear out the lessons of Vietnam, both that the Americans should not involve themselves in peripheral contingencies and that conventionally trained forces were not always ready for the more complex environment of stability operations.

In contrast to MNF II, 1983's Operation Urgent Fury was a reversion to what the American military does best. The invasion of Grenada was presented to the American public as a small conventional action, a "lovely little war," in the words of one media correspondent,[25] a stand against communism and its encroachment in America's backyard. It was performed using the basic tenets of American warfare: five thousand American and three hundred more coalition troops faced about two thousand Grenadians, Cubans, and others; the joint operation relied on speed, accuracy, mobility, and technology. By some accounts, it even served to palliate political calls for more joint warfare.[26] This, despite the fact that, when President Reagan ordered the invasion to evacuate American medical students following a coup on the island, the actual military mission was pure stability operations: "evacuate U.S. citizens, neutralize any resistance, stabilize the situation and maintain the peace."[27] The operation might have been a stability operation, but it was no Vietnam.

The post-Vietnam years of the Cold War thus included stability operations, but—with the exception of MNF II—when they involved the actual deployment of American troops, they were more conventional tasks, undertaken using the American way of war: speedy, joint, stand-off where possible, with a reliance on overwhelming force and technology. Opportunities for less conventional military deployments arose during this period, but rather than employing American forces in large numbers, the U.S. government used proxies. In Angola, the American government supported UNITA against the Soviet- and Cuban-backed MPLA. In Latin America, the Americans' involvement in both insurgencies and counterinsurgencies was intense but included very few U.S. military personnel. The Americans trained, armed, and materially supported Central Americans and sent private contractors and U.S. military instructors to the region, but they stopped short of direct military intervention.[28]

When in 1989 the Soviet Union shocked and confounded American civilian and military planners by collapsing, the time seemed ripe for reconsidering the military's role as an instrument of U.S. foreign policy. Interestingly, the constraints on less conventional operations were quickly relaxed, and the demand for stability operations increased. In the ten-year period following the Cold War's abrupt end, American policy makers turned again and again to the military, broadening the scope of operations for which U.S. troops were deployed—and deploying them much more frequently. A confluence of related factors led to this surprising intensification of the deployment of American troops for stability operations.

First, with the Cold War's end came the end of the Americans' clear strategic vision, which had been based on the superpower rivalry. This led to disquiet, but it also allowed a fresh look at the world, a look not through the Cold War lens that had focused the Americans' perceptions for a half-century. It was a "new world order," as President George H. W. Bush put it. Events in Kuwait, Somalia, Bosnia, and elsewhere had to be dealt with on their own merits, as individual cases, rather than as part of the U.S.-Soviet competition.

Second, the Americans suddenly found themselves the sole superpower. Even as some voices enjoined the government to trade guns for butter, others (not without their own agendas) were persuasive in pointing out the value of the unparalleled American military, an argument underpinned by the 1989 U.S. intervention in Panama and given punch by the need to respond to Saddam Hussein's 1990 invasion of Kuwait.

Third, events overcame deliberate planning. When the Kurds fled into the mountains in 1991 following the Gulf War, the American military worked with the international community to provide them assistance. There simply was no quicker or more effective response possible to the threats the Kurds faced from both Saddam Hussein and the elements. Meanwhile, the United Nations under the leadership of Secretary General Boutros Boutros-Ghali saw the end of the Cold War as an opportunity to be more aggressive in promoting peace. As the largest contributor to the United Nations and its most powerful member, the United States was under pressure to become more active. The famine in Somalia underscored both the United Nations' weakness and the U.S. potential to use its military to do good. Even as President George H. W. Bush's administration conducted an assessment of the need for peacekeeping, American forces were rushing the beaches of Mogadishu.

Finally, and perhaps most importantly, when the Clinton administration came to office, the president and many of his advisors not only approved of the United Nations' new approach but believed that the United States had a responsibility to be at the forefront of protecting human rights, promoting democracy, preventing war, and negotiating peace.[29] Furthermore, they believed that the military was an appropriate tool for achieving these goals. There was no other force in the world that could compete, and, more importantly, there was no other organization anywhere that could be so readily deployed and sustained, that was so organized and efficient, that had such flexibility, and that could undertake such a wide range of missions, simultaneously, when necessary. Although the president acknowledged that the military's primary mission was warfighting, he also saw for it a hugely expanded role, as he explained in remarks at the National Defense University in Washington, D.C.: "The military commanders who share this stage and the forces they lead know their first mission must be always to be ready to fight and win our nation's wars. But day in and day out around the world they are shaping an international environment, enhancing the security of America in the world so that peace can endure and prevail."[30]

Thus, between 1992 and 1998 alone, the U.S. Army conducted twenty-six operations other than war, whereas in the more than thirty years between 1960 and 1991, it had only undertaken ten such operations.[31] The Marine Corps, too, increased their operations tempo (OPTEMPO) after the Cold War, conducting sixty-two contingency operations between 1989 and 2000, in comparison with only fifteen in the previous six years.[32] These military operations encompassed, among other things, disaster relief, humanitarian assistance, peacekeeping, peace enforcement, noncombat evacuation operations, and counterterrorism and counternarcotics efforts, and they took place all over the globe, in Latin America, Africa, Europe, the Middle East, and Asia.

Many American politicians and military leaders at the time expressed concern about the increased employment of the military, arguing that the military's primary warfighting mission was being compromised. Chairman of the Joint Chiefs of Staff (CJCS) General John Shalikashvili held that view: "My fear is we're becoming mesmerized by operations other than war and we'll take our mind off what we're all about, to fight and win our nation's wars."[33] Army Chief of Staff General Eric Shinseki attributed the 10th Mountain and 1st Infantry divisions' low readiness ratings to "their commitments to ongoing peacekeeping operations in Bosnia and Kosovo."[34] Senator James M. Inhofe complained that

the U.S. military is facing readiness, modernization, and budget shortfalls which are seriously degrading its ability to meet the national military strategy—to be prepared to fight and win two major theater wars nearly simultaneously. At the same time, our smaller forces are being stretched thin by an unprecedented proliferation of noncombat contingency operations and missions.[35]

Other political and military leaders were less concerned, arguing that the operations provided some types of units with excellent training opportunities and citing studies that showed that readiness was not as threatened by OOTW as had been claimed.[36]

Whether they saw value in OOTW deployments or a hazard, however, most military leaders generally agreed on one thing, as they had always done, going back to the revolution: such contingency operations, very deliberately placed doctrinally as "other than war," were not the armed forces' primary mission. Although only the military could really do them well (Dag Hammarskjöld, the former UN secretary general, is credited with coining the now ubiquitous phrase: peacekeeping is "no job for a soldier, but only a soldier can do it"), and while they could be conducted as lesser-included cases on the margins of "real" war, they could not supersede the military's responsibility to fight and win the nation's wars. On this point, General Shalikashvili said in an interview on PBS's *Online Newshour*:

> I think we need to be very careful. It is very easy to fall in a trap of thinking that the world will call on us only in the peacekeeping, humanitarian kind of operation, and we need to remember and to remind ourselves all the time that first and foremost we must be able to fight and win our nation's wars, so the peacekeeping and humanitarian operations must be seen as tasks that we will have to do in addition to being prepared to fight and win our nation's wars, not instead of.[37]

General Colin Powell made the same argument in 1993:

> Notwithstanding all of the changes that have taken place in the world, notwithstanding the new emphasis on peacekeeping, peace enforcement, peace engagement, preventive diplomacy, we have a value system and a culture system within the armed forces of the United States. We have this mission: to fight and win the nation's wars . . .
>
> Because we are able to fight and win the nation's wars, because we are warriors, we are also uniquely able to do these other new missions that are coming along—peacekeeping, humanitarian relief, disaster relief—you

name it, we can do it. . . . But we never want to do it in such a way that we lose sight of the focus of why you have armed forces—to fight and win the nation's wars.[38]

It was completely in keeping with this belief, therefore, that—despite the many stability operations conducted in the 1990s—the Revolution in Military Affairs (RMA) continued to be the Department of Defense's top priority toward the end of that decade. Even as U.S. soldiers, sailors, marines, and airmen were still deployed to stability operations around the world, the civilian leadership in the DOD was embracing ultramodern conventional warfare and the technology that would give America the edge. Advocates called for retooling the military to allow for greater precision, lethality, speed, and stand-off capabilities, with an emphasis on missile strikes, fluid movement on the battlefield, and, above all else, information supremacy. The RMA depended heavily on technological developments that would allow for this perceived evolution in warfighting. Rather than the manpower-intensive, confusing, slogging efforts that, with the exception of the Gulf War, had typified U.S. deployments since the end of the Cold War, with civilians clogging the area of operations, mission creep, and ever-changing end states, the RMA offered a view of warfare as sleek, fast-paced, space-age combat between highly trained, tech-laden professional soldiers, sailors, marines, and airmen. The RMA did create its own divisions. Many senior military personnel were deeply skeptical of this "revolution." Although they were in agreement that the armed forces' role was to fight and win the nation's wars, they argued that there would need to be more boots on the ground, more heavy combat units, and more support than the advocates envisioned. U.S. Secretary of Defense Donald Rumsfeld emerged as a strong proponent of the RMA, and, under his leadership, the civilians—who tended to believe that the more skeptical military leaders' concerns were self-interested rather than substantive and, indeed, one of the causes of stagnation in the Pentagon—took the military further in his preferred direction, reorganizing around Stryker brigades to enhance deployability and sustainability and shifting budgets to promote research and development.[39]

When planning for the post-9/11 war in Iraq, therefore, Rumsfeld deliberately emphasized a force that would demonstrate the utility of the RMA. Leveraging advanced technologies, the operation would be speedy, effective, and efficient in terms of manpower and length of deployment. And, indeed, the initial combat operation was everything that Rumsfeld could have wished for. Iraqi forces crumbled, and American and coalition troops were able to take control of Iraq. Except they did not take control; there was no coherent plan in place for following up combat operations. Civilian and military planners had focused on combat operations to the exclusion of serious postwar planning.

Paul Wolfowitz reflected the prevailing blithe sentiment among defense planners in December 2002 when he said in an interview: "I think people are overly pessimistic about the aftermath."[40] The journalist and author Tom Ricks described in his book *Fiasco* how there was "no real plan for postwar Iraq that could be implemented by commanders and soldiers on the ground."[41] In fact, postwar planning was a hot potato, tossed first to Central Command, then back to the Pentagon, and then, two months before the invasion, to a newly established Pentagon office for postwar planning, the Office of Reconstruction and Humanitarian Assistance (ORHA).

Part of the problem was that, despite past experiences, military and civilian planners failed to account for potential outbreaks of violence following combat operations in Iraq and instead focused on potential humanitarian crises and refugee flows. This was true despite the fact that the likelihood of riots and looting was anticipated and had been raised in planning meetings.[42] The bigger problem was that Rumsfeld had a vision of a streamlined operation in which messy long-term commitments played no role; nation building was perceived as a tar pit to be avoided at all costs. In complete contrast to the kinds of manpower-intensive simultaneous stability operations new doctrine calls for, Rumsfeld demanded that a minimal force be deployed to Iraq to defeat Hussein's forces and then come home. American troops would not police Iraq; instead, the Iraqis would police themselves.[43] In his "Beyond Nation Building" speech in 2003, Rumsfeld laid out his ideal for a lean, high-tech force as embodied by U.S. operations in Afghanistan:

General Franks would not send a massive invasion and occupation force as . . . the Soviets had. Instead he keeps the coalition footprint modest. He adapted a strategy of teaming with local Afghan forces that opposed the Taliban. And the careful use of precision-guided weapons helped ensure that there were fewer civilian casualties in this war than perhaps in any war in modern history. As a result we did not alienate the Afghan people.[44]

He went on, in the same speech, to express his hopes for a similar effort in Iraq:

Some ask what lessons our experience in Afghanistan might offer for the possibility of a post-Saddam Iraq. It has a nice ring, doesn't it? A post-Saddam Iraq. As you know, the President has not made any decision with respect to the use of force in Iraq, but if he were to do so that principle would hold true. Iraq belongs to the Iraqis and we do not aspire to own it or run it. We hope to eliminate Iraq's weapons of mass destruction and to help liberate the Iraqi people from oppression. If the United States were to lead an international coalition in Iraq—and let there be no doubt it would be a very large one—it would be guided by two commitments. Stay as long as necessary, and to leave as soon as possible.[45]

Thus, in Rumsfeld's view, the U.S. military would be a precision fighting force and, once combat operations were over, would get out of the way for local authorities and American civilians to do their jobs. He thus took "fighting and winning the nation's wars" to the extreme, seeing it as incompatible with stability operations. Yet, even those within the military's upper echelons and among the civilian leadership who understood that the military would not be so quickly extricated from either war still accepted the long-standing paradigm that "the leadership, organization, equipment, discipline, and skills gained in training for war [would also be] of use to the government in operations other than war."[46] In 2002, with troops in Afghanistan and planning proceeding for Iraq, the armed forces were still being trained and organized for conventional war.

It became readily apparent in both Iraq and Afghanistan, however, that there would be no quick victory and withdrawal of American troops. In the absence of sustainable local institutions, legitimate police forces, or functioning militaries, and with the rise of violent local competition for power, American forces were required for protecting each country's civilian population, maintaining stability, combating terrorists and insurgents, and creating opportunities for political solutions and economic development. Until local institutions could be brought up to speed, the Americans would be stuck. As Colin Powell had warned President George W. Bush early on, when cautioning him about the challenge of governing a post-Saddam Iraq: "you know that you're going to be owning this place."[47] And as Bush came to acknowledge, the United States could not "stand down" its forces until the Iraqis "stood up" theirs.[48] Thus, both contingencies began to mirror the most enduring failure of conventionally trained troops, Vietnam, and evolved into the kinds of prolonged operations Rumsfeld had so strenuously tried to avoid.

As in Vietnam, the military's conventional training and organization proved inadequate to the types of conflict in Afghanistan and Iraq. Unlike in Vietnam, however—and marking a sea change in the treatment of stability operations more generally—the American military was open to adapting not only short-term organization and training for the contingencies but also doctrine. As will be detailed in the following chapter and explained in chapter 4, the Department of Defense mandated that stability operations be made equivalent to offense and defense as the military's primary mission; the Army followed up by producing both capstone and keystone doctrine that elevated stability operations; the Army and Marine Corps produced new counterinsurgency doctrine; and, as will be described in chapter 3, the services began to adapt their training to these new doctrinal requirements, which reflected the specific needs of the operations in Afghanistan and Iraq. After rejecting operations other than war for its entire existence—after making, for decades, the argument that a conventionally prepared force could not undertake such operations effectively—the U.S. military abruptly shifted gears and not only acknowledged a role for military forces across the full spectrum of conflict but adjusted its national security role entirely by adding stability operations to its primary missions of fighting and winning the nation's wars, thus accepting shared responsibility with civilians for promoting order and building host nation capacity.[49]

STABILITY OPERATIONS DEBATES

It used to be that if you defeated the enemy's forces in the field, what was left was just mopping up or restructuring, and the war was won on the battlefield. That hasn't happened [lately]. It hasn't happened in the time I served, for thirty-nine years. It probably hasn't happened since the end of the Second World War. There's a difference between winning battles, or defeating the enemy in battle, and winning the war. . . . And it's going to continue to be that way. . . . Right now the question that has to be answered is: does our military expand its role beyond the military aspect, or will we continue to stick it with this [peace building] mission without the resources, the training, the cooperation from others, or the lack of authority needed to get the job done?

—Anthony Zinni, in a speech to the U.S. Naval Institute
and the Marine Corps Association, 2003

To understand the significance of the elevation of stability operations to a primary mission, it is first necessary to understand the rationale that kept everything other than conventional war as secondary missions since the minting of the first American soldiers. Two debates have informed the role of stability operations in American military doctrine. The first is over the political use of the military; the second is over the requirements of stability operations in terms of training, organization, and equipment. The first is rooted in a disagreement that goes back as far as Clausewitz's assertion that war is simply politics by another means. The second is fundamentally about whether conventionally trained troops can effectively conduct any other kinds of operations, much less stability operations, as lesser-included cases.

THE POLITICAL USE OF THE MILITARY

Although Clausewitz saw force as simply one more element in the "admixture of means" available to statesmen protecting the national interest,[50] within the United States there has long been a distinction between the use of force for military and political purposes. Ostrom and Job explain that when used for stability operations,

> the armed forces may be said to have been engaged not for the achievement of a military objective per se, but for "political" purposes, and their actions said to constitute "political uses of the armed forces"—that is, overt policy acts directed by the U.S. president that fall somewhere between acts of diplomacy and intentional uses of military power such as in Korea and Vietnam.[51]

In their seminal book, Blechman and Kaplan discriminate between the military and political use of force, describing the latter as the use of military forces "without significant violence to underscore verbal and diplomatic expressions of American foreign policy."[52] In both of these definitions of the "political" use of the military, the distinction seems to be that the ultimate objective is something short of victory via offense or defense but something more than just diplomacy. In other words, it is the application of the military instrument to extend influence and power short of a full-fledged conventional confrontation.

The military can be used for "political" purposes in several ways: as part of a standalone effort in the absence of conflict, before or after combat operations as a means of shaping the environment favorably for war or peace, or, and this has only been recently acknowledged, as an inherent part of war, simultaneous with combat operations. American forces have long conducted stability operations under the first two conditions, but the last has been less common. Schadlow describes this last in light of the planning for Iraq: "the Iraq situation is only the most recent example of the reluctance of civilian and military leaders, as well as most outside experts, to consider the establishment of political and economic order as a part of war itself."[53]

Ironically, despite the frequency of stability operations deployments, there has been steady pushback against the use of the military for political purposes. That this is the case for the American public is a widely observed phenomenon.[54] Samuel Huntington attributed this tendency to an American political culture that resists government authority. He wrote that "this leads to efforts to minimize and restrict the resources of power (such as arms), to restrict the effectiveness of the specialized bureaucratic hierarchies, and to limit the authority of the executive in the conduct of foreign policy."[55] That is, limiting stability operations limits the president's foreign policy options and, therefore, his independent authority. Such reluctance has also been manifested by prominent military officers and civilians in the Pentagon, both in the aftermath of Vietnam and at Cold War's end, as American forces were more and more often deployed for stability operations. As will be discussed, both the Weinberger and the Powell doctrines are evidence of concern about the president's ability to deploy military forces capriciously, without adequate understanding of their limitations or of the opportunity—and real—costs of such efforts.

Concerns about the political use of the military are rooted not only in questions of presidential power, however, but also in questions of efficacy. President Eisenhower, for example, believed that deploying the military necessarily affected America's image abroad, and he was therefore wary of stability operations and their uncertain outcomes and potentially long timelines. He "felt that the use of military force irrevocably placed the prestige of the United States in jeopardy and that overwhelming power was necessary if force was to be used at all. Thus he believed that incremental uses of force were unlikely to be effective for both political and military reasons."[56] Eisenhower was also concerned about putting American forces into contingencies in areas in which America had few, if any, strategic concerns. The lessons Eisenhower drew from the war in Korea were that "U.S. forces should not become bogged down again on the periphery in ground warfare." He called on the Joint Chiefs of Staff to reduce "peripheral military commitments" in order to correct what he perceived as American "over-extension."[57] John Foster Dulles, Eisenhower's secretary of state, shared many of the same concerns. During Truman's presidency, Dulles had expressed fear that the Truman Doctrine "would involve the United States and its military in unwinnable wars that would taint U.S. prestige, making America appear both imperialistic and incompetent."[58]

After Vietnam accomplished precisely this, President Nixon established the policy of avoiding stability operations in peripheral areas with remarks he made to journalists in 1969 during a stop in Guam. Outlining what became known as the Nixon Doctrine, he said that the United States could not act without taking into account national and regional pride, that "Asia is for the Asians," that "we should assist but we should not dictate," and that "we must avoid that kind of policy that will make countries in Asia so dependent upon us that we are dragged into conflicts such as . . . Vietnam."[59] In other words, peripheral countries should fight their own wars and deal with their own internal conflicts, because the United States could not match local actors in will or motivation anywhere that its strategic interests were not directly engaged. Involvement in stability operations thus was perceived as risky and not cost effective.

Fifteen years later, Caspar Weinberger, then the secretary of defense under President Reagan, articulated a set of conditions that he felt should be met before policy makers deployed American troops abroad. Strongly influenced by his own military experiences, the failed dynamics of the Vietnam War, the 1983 debacle in Beirut, and his observations of policy makers' knee-jerk willingness to commit troops even in the absence of a clear political or military goal,[60] Weinberger's doctrine appears strangely prescient of what would become a trend in the deployment of U.S. military personnel for stability operations after the (at the time unimaginable) collapse of the Soviet Union. In brief, Weinberger cautioned that the military should only be employed when vital American or allied interests are at stake, in adequate numbers and with adequate support to ensure a win, with clearly articulated political and military objectives, with constant reassessment and adjustment, with the full support of the American public, and only after all other means of influence—political, economic, etc.—had been exhausted.[61] The Weinberger Doctrine was rooted in concerns about both presidential irresponsibility in the deployment of troops and the inefficacy of involvement in stability operations.

In presenting his doctrine, Weinberger said: "I believe that the tests I have enunciated here today can, if applied carefully, avoid the danger of this gradualist incremental approach which almost always means the use of insufficient force. These tests can help us to avoid being drawn inexorably into an endless morass, where it is not vital to our national interest to fight."[62] The defense secretary continued:

> employing our forces almost indiscriminately and as a regular and customary part of our diplomatic efforts would surely plunge us headlong into the sort of domestic turmoil we experienced during the Vietnam war, without accomplishing the goal for which we committed our forces. Such policies might very well tear at the fabric of our society, endangering the *single* most critical element of a successful democracy: *a strong consensus of support and agreement for our basic purposes.*[63]

Moreover, he argued:

> recent history has proven that we cannot assume unilaterally the role of the world's defender. We have learned that there are limits to how much of our spirit and blood and treasure we can afford to forfeit in meeting our responsibility to keep peace and freedom. So while we may and should offer substantial amounts of economic and military assistance to our allies in their time of need, and help them maintain forces to deter attacks against them—usually we cannot substitute our troops or our will for theirs. . . . We should only engage our troops if we must do so as a matter of our own vital national interest. We cannot assume for other sovereign nations the responsibility to defend their territory—without their strong invitation—when our freedom is not threatened.[64]

The proximate cause of Weinberger's articulation of these conditions was the tragedy in Lebanon, but his cautions were equally relevant less than a decade later in Somalia and, soon thereafter, in Haiti. Weinberger's doctrine was arguably aimed at civilian decision makers,[65] but many military officers adopted it readily, seeing its conditions as a defense against careless deployment of the military. Those officers and military leaders who balked at the use of the military as a first, best option in the 1990s and into the 2000s referred to Weinberger's doctrine when they saw that political leaders were unsure of their alternatives (or even objectives) but were facing a "do something" political environment demanding immediate foreign policy responses to international crises. Among these officers was General Colin L. Powell. In 1992, relatively early in the post–Cold War period, Powell offered his revised version of the Weinberger Doctrine in the form of a series of questions posed in a *Foreign Affairs* article:

> Is the political objective we seek to achieve important, clearly defined and understood? Have all other nonviolent policy means failed? Will military force achieve the objective? At what cost? Have the gains and risks been analyzed? How might the situation that we seek to alter, once it is altered by force, develop further and what might be the consequences?[66]

Powell's "doctrine" was a reiteration of concerns expressed by his predecessors about the political use of the military. Even more than the others it harkened back to just-war theory and its *jus ad bellum* ("right to wage war") admonitions that force should only be used as a last resort and when there is probability of success.[67] Powell's doctrine was in part a response to the rise of the Clinton administration and, in particular, to Madeleine Albright, who saw the use of the military as an important post–Cold War instrument of foreign policy. The tension between their two views was made obvious in a heated conversation that Powell later described in his memoirs:

> My constant unwelcome message at all meetings on Bosnia was simply that we should not commit military forces until we had a clear political objective. . . . The debate exploded at one session where Madeleine Albright, our ambassador to the UN, asked me in frustration, "What's the point of having this superb military that you're always talking about if we can't use it?" I thought I would have an aneurysm. American GIs were not toy soldiers to be moved around on some sort of global game board.[68]

Albright responded to the general's preferred conditions for military action with frustrated sarcasm: "You can use power when the earth is flat and you have six months to prepare and you're facing a crazy dictator with nuclear weapons and someone else is paying for it. But that is not always the situation."[69] Aggravated by the resistance she faced as she tried to convince the president to engage militarily to end the war in Bosnia, she described the Pentagon's opposition in terms of the Vietnam syndrome ("don't get involved in anything") and the Gulf War syndrome ("don't do it unless you can deploy 500,000 marines").[70]

The tension between Powell and Albright is a clear example of the debate between, respectively, traditionalists (those who believe the military must focus on fighting and winning the nation's wars in the traditional sense) and progressives—or "crusaders" or "counterinsurgents," in other parlance—who argue that stability operations are the proper use of the U.S. armed forces in a world where the hegemon faces no peer competitors but where failed states and nonstate actors can undermine its security.[71] While this debate has its foundation, in part, in concerns about presidential authority and the inefficacy (politically and practically) of using the military for political objectives, embedded within it is also an argument about security priorities and readiness. And this tension has never been more obvious than it is today, as it appears that the progressives have successfully influenced doctrine and everything that flows from it in a way that the traditionalists believe threatens America's security and draws attention away from existential threats to focus on transient and arguably minor international challenges.[72]

STABILITY OPERATIONS: UNIQUE REQUIREMENTS

There is a great deal of disagreement about whether and, if so, how the military can prepare for and effectively perform both stability operations and conventional operations. Traditionalists argue that the issue is less whether American troops should undertake stability operations and more whether they must consider such operations a priority coequal with offense and defense, one worth funding, organizing, and training for. They point to the military's long history of accomplishing stability operations even while preparing for war. They argue that the most obvious failed stability operations—in support of efforts in Vietnam, MNF II, and Somalia—were not failures of soldiers but rather of military planners and civilian policy makers who shackled the military with politically driven constraints and, in thus tying their hands, doomed them.[73] They refer to studies that have shown that troops trained for combat are effective in operations other than war.[74] And they warn of the costs of shifting attention, resources, and doctrine away from the military's primary mission, meanwhile asking why other instruments of foreign policy are not put to better use and why more resources, time, and effort are not put toward building up diplomatic and economic means of influence.[75] The military analyst Lawrence A. Yates described this point of view in his historical overview of military involvement in stability operations:

> Traditionally, the US military has not regarded stability operations as a "core" mission with a priority approaching that accorded to combat operations. The American military has traditionally focused on conventional warfighting as its most important mission, and while few officers have challenged the Clausewitzian axiom that wars are the "continuation of policy by other means," a pervasive belief maintains that, once an enemy's conventional forces have been defeated, the responsibility of the military for helping the policy makers achieve the broader objectives for which the hostilities were conducted has been largely fulfilled. While in many cases there may be a requirement for some specialized troops to participate in follow-on stability operations designed to solidify the war's accomplishments, the military traditionally has regarded most of those tasks as "someone else's job." In other words, it is the military's responsibility to win the war, not to win the peace.[76]

The progressives, on the other hand, make the argument that the U.S. military enjoys a surplus of conventional capabilities, has no peer competitor on the horizon, and, in this globalized world, is and will be challenged regularly in ways that demand stability operations. Progressives point to the contingencies in Afghanistan and Iraq and to the demand for peacekeeping, counterterrorism, support to counterdrug operations and nation building in both peacetime and war and argue that it is time for the U.S. military to prepare deliberately for these kinds of tasks. They note that when stability operations are a lesser-included case, personnel are not organized, trained, or equipped for action in complex contingencies and, moreover, have a steep and costly learning curve. Given that the U.S. military will be performing such operations, it should be better prepared to do them well from the outset.

Ultimately, although the debate seems (and is often presented as) immutable, the bulk of the differences in opinion between the traditionalists and the progressives are a function of how general the concept of stability operations is. The traditionalists and the progressives are both right, and they are both wrong. The traditionalists are correct that the U.S. military usually can conduct the "establish a secure environment" part of stability operations effectively without specialized training, equipment, or organization. Some stability operations tasks are akin to those undertaken in conventional war (shows of force), some are standard peacetime activities (security assistance and security force assistance), some are undertaken as part of exercises (humanitarian and civic assistance), and some use many of the same skills needed for conventional operations (strikes and raids against terrorists). As progressives will point out, however, the most challenging and demanding stability operations are in support of FID or COIN or are peace operations or elements of counterdrug operations. These require specialized skills, including language capabilities and cultural knowledge, development expertise, and diplomatic finesse. In fact, precisely because of this, most of the tasks associated with stability operations have long been the purview of the special operations forces (SOF).

The core SOF missions are direct action (DA; strikes and raids), special reconnaissance (SR; specialized information gathering), military information support operations (MISO; formerly psychological operations, or PSYOP, the use of information and media to influence a target population), foreign internal defense, civil affairs operations (CA; meeting the legal and moral obligations to people affected by military operations), information operations (IO; a broad category of information-control operations that includes MISO), and counterterrorism (CT).[77] The overlap between stability operations requirements and SOF core missions is obvious. Yet SOF remain relatively few in number. They are time consuming and expensive to train, hard to retain (since their special skills are in high demand in the private sector), heavily committed in counterterrorism efforts,[78] and many are in the reserves (especially the Army's Civil Affairs and MISO personnel) rather than the active military, further complicating stability operations planning and efforts.

Without adequate numbers of and access to SOF, many specialized stability operations tasks have been falling to conventionally trained troops. One article described this succinctly: "Today, all Soldiers, Sailors, Marines, and Airmen participate in what was formerly the domain of the specialist."[79] But the conventional forces tend to come at the same tasks differently. One Special Forces officer described the disparity in approach during Operation Uphold Democracy in Haiti:

> Uphold Democracy was a peace operation, yet ironically, before, during and after the operation, a combat mind-set existed in the principal US conventional unit in theater, the 10th Mountain Division (Light). . . . [Their] AAR quotation stated: "Every movement outside of a compound is a COMBAT OPERATION." . . . This type of 'warrior' sentiment during and after Uphold Democracy was not generally shared by SOF troops.[80]

Stability operations tasks traditionally undertaken by SOF tend to require the ability to coordinate with government officials and NGO personnel, to work in environments where civilians are present, to operate under restricted rules of engagement, and to consider the strategic effects of even the smallest tactical decisions. Vietnam, MNF II, and Somalia—the biggest stability operations failures—were these kinds of operations, as are the efforts in Iraq and Afghanistan. In all of these contingencies, it became apparent that conventional preparation was inadequate for putting the countries back together again. Yet, for such large stability efforts, conventional troops must be involved, given the limited number of special operators.

The traditionalists and progressives are also both right, because different elements of the armed forces will be affected differently by deployment for stability operations. One can compare across the branches. For the Air Force, stability operations required different technologies than conventional operations: fighter jets and bombers will be less valuable than tactical aircraft and drones. For the Navy, there needs to be shift from blue-water to littoral capabilities. The Marine Corps has a long history of small wars and has brought those skills to conventional warfighting and so operates well across the spectrum of operations. The Army, however, is most affected. It must behave very differently in stability operations than in conventional war. For the Army, whether the mission requires battlefield warfare or promoting local development will be hugely important, since entirely different skill sets must be brought to bear. Or one can compare across specialties. In the Army, armor, air defense, and field artillery probably will not get much use in stability operations, but SOF definitely will, infantry might, and intelligence and law enforcement will be crucial.[81] Clearly, stability operations will require different organization and planning than will conventional combat operations. If stability operations and conventional combat are simultaneous, that will require yet a different plan and organization.

CONCLUSION

When she hoped to convince civilian and military leaders that sending troops to Bosnia was necessary, Madeleine Albright—who fell unquestionably into the category of the progressives—received minimum support from Secretary of State Warren Christopher, who wanted to proceed cautiously, and National Security Advisor Anthony Lake, who deferred to Powell. Defense Secretary Les Aspin also expressed concern about U.S. operations and plans in first Somalia and then Haiti and called for clearer policy objectives and concrete efforts to reduce U.S. vulnerability both military and politically.[82] Yet, reflecting the difficulty in determining the appropriate use of the military, Aspin at a speaking engagement in 1992 accused the military of preferring, à la Powell, an "all or nothing" approach to deployment. He wondered aloud whether the American public would really stand for paying "$250 billion or even $200 billion a year for a military that is not very useful."[83] He called, instead, for an emphasis on "limited objectives."

The concept of limited objectives (clearly being adopted today in Afghanistan)[84] was intended to represent the practical and necessary fine line between relying too much on the military to achieve political purposes, on the one hand, and the military's preferred "all or nothing" approach, on the other. Aspin, much like Albright, criticized the latter as a waste of a fine military and tremendous resources, but he understood all too well the costs of too easily deploying the military to achieve broad and changeable objectives simply because no other solution presented itself as readily.[85]

A historical overview of the military's views of and experience with stability operations yields several key observations, but the most significant is that stability operations as a concept is simply too broad to allow for useful generalizations about effects on—or demands for—force structure, training, and equipment. Many stability operations can be undertaken with little effect on readiness, serve as training opportunities for combat operations, and support diplomacy. The most demanding stability operations, however—the ones most likely to affect combat readiness—are in support of COIN and FID. It is these types of stability operations that require special preparation, and it is these in which American forces have experienced the most memorable setbacks and the most challenging conditions. When stability operations in complex contingencies are conflated with more routine peacetime stability operations, efforts to measure their effect can become confused. It is also these more challenging stability operations—involving the extension of the military's purview to traditionally civilian roles under the least promising conditions—over which the debate between traditionalists and progressives continues. Whether or not the military is prepared to conduct routine civic action is not at issue. Whether the U.S. armed forces are able to shape successfully the environment and build local capacity in Iraq and Afghanistan is where the deeper question lies. And that question taps into the aforementioned debates over both the political use of the military and security priorities. Progressives argue that the world has changed and that the United States is facing a "complex era of persistent conflict,"[86] and thus

the military will be challenged time and again to undertake the most challenging stability operations, for which it must better prepare. Traditionalists
argue that the only thing that has changed is perceptions of the international
environment and the threats America faces. But the biggest real threats, they
argue, the truly existential ones, will need a conventional military prepared
for conventional operations, not overtaxed armed forces conducting high-
cost peripheral operations to achieve political objectives better accomplished
by civilians. This debate has not been merely academic; it has also played out
in doctrine, as will be examined in the following chapter.

TWO
DOCTRINE AND STABILITY OPERATIONS

Doctrine is the basic guidance for preparing and conducting military operations. It covers every aspect of such endeavors. The doctrinal hierarchy trickles down from each service's capstone manuals, which set the ground rules, to the keystone manuals focused on particular concepts, to doctrine on tactics, techniques, and procedures (TTPs). Doctrine is described as being both authoritative and subject to judgment in application.[1] Each branch of the military publishes its own doctrine; there are also joint and multiservice doctrinal manuals. Doctrine is constantly under review and is regularly reissued with revisions that take into account changing capabilities, lessons learned, and the evolving security environment. Doctrine at any given point in time is thus a snapshot of military priorities, abilities, fundamental principles, and concerns. As such, it is a valuable resource for determining, with respect to stability operations,[2] how significant a change has really occurred and, moreover, whether an evolution or a revolution has taken place in how the military perceives its role.

Doctrine is characterized by hierarchy: there are cascade effects among doctrines, within doctrines, and between doctrine and preparing the forces. First, since 1994, joint guidance has taken precedence over service doctrines. Because joint doctrine is usually produced and/or vetted by the services, however, it is unlikely to introduce surprising or incompatible guidelines. In fact, it is likely to reflect existing service doctrine on any given function. Second, joint doctrine and Army, Air Force, and Marines doctrine each are organized hierarchically, progressing from capstone (highest-order doctrine) to keystone (second-order doctrine) to TTPs (which have a very specific focus on practice). In each, a change in capstone doctrine requires adjustments at the subsequent levels. Changes made only at lower levels, however, may reflect shifts in technology or ability but not in a service's or the armed forces' fundamental roles and priorities. Third, there has long been an unstated hierarchy between special operations forces (SOF) and the conventional military, and this is reflected in SOF doctrine. In each service and within joint doctrine, special operations manuals are keystone doctrine, subsumed under capstone manuals. Though this is true for other military occupation specialties (MOSs), those forces are conventional, and their keystone manuals lay out their part in a broader conventional effort. SOF are unconventional. Their doctrine allows for independent operations across the spectrum of conflict as well as support for conventional efforts. While SOF help fight and win the nation's wars, they have also been consistently tasked with responsibilities "other than" war. SOF doctrine thus has focused more steadily on stability operations, but at the keystone level, without necessarily reflecting the various services' priorities. Finally, perhaps the most important doctrinal hierarchy is far broader: changes in doctrine often lead to adjustments in training, organization, education, and equipping. Doctrine drives force preparation, particularly for the Army. Because of this, doctrine is referred to as the military's "engine of change."[3]

This chapter explores how stability operations are handled within doctrine, at which levels they are addressed, the variations between services, the differences in special operations and conventional doctrine, and how all of this has evolved over time. Chapter 3 will explore the extent to which the doctrinal trends examined in this chapter are leading to concrete changes in the military's structure and abilities.

STABILITY OPERATIONS' DOCTRINAL DEVELOPMENT

Military doctrine over the course of its history has been overwhelmingly focused on warfighting. Yet of the three earliest U.S. military manuals, one—the 1935 Marine Corps manual *Small Wars Operations*—was dedicated to COIN and featured stability operations prominently. Five years later, the manual was revised and renamed the *Small Wars Manual*. The only other published American military doctrine at the time was the U.S. Army's *Field Service Regulations*, produced in the aftermath of World War I and updated in 1939 for World War II, and, later, the U.S. Army Air Force doctrine on strategic bombing, published during World War II. Thus, for a very brief time, stability operations were at the forefront of published doctrine. This did not reflect in any way a general military emphasis on stability operations. It was merely a historical quirk predating the military's development into a doctrine-based organization.

The *Small Wars Manual* was nonetheless an important milestone. The manual's authors acknowledged that their preferred term, "small wars," was "a vague name for any one of a great variety of military operations."[4] Such operations could be of any scope, intensity, duration, and cost and could involve "an infinite number of forms of friendly assistance or intervention." Despite their myriad differences, the operations were subsumed within a single category on the basis of their purpose and circumstances: they were "undertaken under executive authority wherein military force is combined with diplomatic pressure in the internal or external affairs of another state whose government is unstable, inadequate, or unsatisfactory for the preservation of life and of such interests as are determined by the foreign policy of our Nation."[5] The manual explained that the United States has a habit of interposing or intervening in the affairs of other states and could be expected to continue to do so. It stated, further, that small wars occur when such interventions or interpositions involve military operations conducted in support of, and under the controlling influence of, the State Department. The inception of such actions, the manual made clear, depended on official presidential instructions, usually in the absence of congressional input. The authors bemoaned the lack of authoritative texts on small wars, cautioning that lessons learned in "the World War" were not applicable in these very different situations. They called on the Marine Corps to leverage its extensive experience in small wars but cautioned that future opponents were likely to be better prepared than any irregular forces the Marine Corps had faced in the past. They concluded the introductory chapter with a reminder that the military does not make policy and must undertake these potentially sensitive operations with an appreciation for executive and legislative authority in terms of foreign relations.

This first doctrinal attention to stability operations proved to be a harbinger for how such operations would be treated when they resurfaced in military publications forty years later. For example, a vast array of diverse requirements and tasks was contained within a very general category. This remained true as doctrine in the post–Cold War period adjusted from *small wars* to *low-intensity conflict* (LIC) to *military operations short of war* (MOSW) to *military operations other than war* (MOOTW) to *operations other than war* (OOTW) to *irregular warfare* (IW). Today's doctrinal approach—recognizing the utility and variation of stability operations across the full spectrum of conflict—is a marked change. That these operations are something "other than" war but can coincide with battlefield action, however, remains as confounding today as when *Small Wars* was written, as does their political character, requiring civilian leadership and action as well as military-civilian cooperation. *Small Wars'* authors determined that such endeavors required special training and preparation by unique forces; whether or not this is the case and, if so, to what extent continues to be hotly debated. The final foreshadowing was that *Small Wars* was simply a sidenote in U.S. military doctrine, quickly overlooked with the onset of World War II and then the Cold War, irrelevant to the Air Force and the Navy, ignored for decades by the conventional Army, and appreciated only by the Marines, who always have seen their purview as encompassing such operations.[6] Stability operations—and operations other than war more generally—would remain on the doctrinal backburner until after 9/11.

In fact, the small wars manual represented stability operations' only appearance in conventional doctrine from 1940 to the mid-1960s. Such operations would receive no further attention until the U.S. Army, intent on capturing the initial lessons of Vietnam, introduced the 1964 keystone manual FM 100-20, *Counterinsurgency*. For the Army to publish a manual focused on something other than conventional warfighting was groundbreaking. Even so, the first version of 100-20 described COIN as involving large formations of U.S. troops, with some reliance on indigenous forces, and it paid relatively little attention to stability operations. This changed three years later, when the 1967 version of 100-20 was renamed *Internal Defense and Development* (IDAD), to reflect the emphasis on civilian agencies' involvement in counterinsurgency. The manual played down the role of military force and amplified host nation responsibilities but was clearly focused on capacity building and addressing underlying causes of conflict. This theme was picked up and expanded upon with each iteration of the publication. It reflected the Nixon Doctrine and policy makers' reluctance to deploy troops in large numbers for such operations and their preference for supporting local initiatives, but it also reflected the belief that addressing the roots of conflict was necessary for resolving conflict itself. Thus, in the 1972 and 1974 IDAD manuals, the U.S. Army was directed to provide logistical, training, and advisory assistance in support of broader and deeper civilian actions.[7]

Though stability operations got only minor treatment in Army keystone doctrine in the 1960s, implementing doctrine flourished. It was during this period that the term "stability operations" was coined. At the time, it was defined as "the full range of internal defense and development operations and assistance which we can employ to maintain, restore, or establish a climate of order within which the Government under law can function effectively."[8] Here, just as nearly fifty years later, doctrinal attention was being paid to the military's role in promoting stability by building host nations' capacity. The term quickly disappeared from doctrine, however, and was absent for nearly a half-century. Moreover, the new doctrine had only a limited impact. Even during Vietnam, stability operations were never addressed in Army capstone doctrine; they were relegated to limited keystone coverage in FM 100-20 and to TTPs. These manuals were nonetheless pioneering in their treatment of stability operations.

Like the Army, the U.S. Air Force produced implementing doctrine relevant to stability operations during the Vietnam War, in the form of a stream of tactical guidance on FID. The Air Force doctrine was developed as events unfolded in Vietnam. The service did not have time to put its new guidance into play in any significant way.[9] The Marine Corps, for its part, produced a keystone manual during Vietnam that remained focused entirely on COIN. Taking the *Small Wars* manual as its point of departure, the Fleet Marine Force Manual (FMFM)-21, *Operations Against Guerrilla Forces*, was published in 1962 and then reissued in 1964 as FMFM 8-2, *Operations Against Guerrilla Units*. The manual offered tactics and techniques for use by Marines combating insurgents or supporting friendly guerrillas. It spotlighted the security aspects of COIN and their relationship to complementary efforts to promote economic and political development.[10] In 1967, FMFM 8-2 was renamed *Counterinsurgency Operations*, but it was nearly identical to its predecessor.[11] The same year, the Marine Corps produced NAVMC 2614, *USMC Professional Knowledge: Gained from Operational Experience in Vietnam, 1965–1966*, which comprised 509 pages of lessons learned about specific tactics and techniques in guerrilla warfare, including booby traps and mine warfare.[12] In 1973, FMFM 8-2 was reissued without significant changes.

Thus, at the height of the Vietnam War, the little attention the services paid doctrinally to anything other than conventional war was dominated by stability operations—the requirement, in COIN and FID, for development and governance efforts to complement battles with insurgents. Such doctrine was limited to TTPs, however; stability operations were not dealt with in higher-order manuals.[13] And then, following Vietnam, even this doctrine was sidelined further. The Army shunted responsibility to the Special Warfare School at Fort Bragg, where proponency for such doctrine remained until 1984. Army SOF published and refreshed a number of TTPs, including guidance on noncombatant evacuation operations, foreign internal defense, and unconventional warfare, not to mention the relevant material in the higher-level Special Forces, Civil Affairs, and Psychological Operations doctrine, but the doctrine was intended specifically for special operators, not general-purpose forces. The Air Force, for its part, already had handed COIN to the special operators before the end of the Vietnam War. The tactical guidance the Air Force developed during the conflict was written in the Special Air Warfare Center (renamed the U.S. Air Force Special Operations Forces, USASOF). At war's end, the Air Force deactivated USASOF, sending a clear message about its conventional priorities.[14] Only the Marine Corps retained some post-Vietnam doctrinal focus on COIN, preserving FMFM 8-2 as keystone doctrine.

By relegating responsibility for COIN and FID to the special operations forces, the Army and Air Force made certain that stability operations were decisively out of the mainstream of military preparation, planning, training, education, and organization. They reoriented themselves, as did, to a large extent, the Marine Corps (the Navy was already thus focused), to the exigencies of full-scale warfare, the defense of Western Europe, and the development of high-tech weaponry. U.S. Army Historian Conrad Crane summed up the military's doctrinal response to Vietnam: "the American military in general said, 'We're not going to do this anymore.' Rather than learn from our mistakes or learn to do it better, the idea was, that's just too hard to do. We're going to figure out how to avoid that. And the focus went to beating the Soviets in Europe again."[15] By the late 1970s and early 1980s, the renewed emphasis on a Fulda Gap scenario had raised the Army's profile, which had diminished after the politically disastrous war in Vietnam, this time in terms of the new air-land battle concept, in which the Air Force and Army would work together cooperatively. The emphasis on joint battlefield operations, further enhanced by the Goldwater-Nichols reorganization in 1986, characterized the services' conventional doctrine, especially the Army's and the Air Force's, until the late 1980s.

Meanwhile, it was becoming clear that the armed forces' resistance to stability operations did not reduce policy makers' demand for military contributions to such efforts. The Americans' apparent shortcomings in their anticommunist operations in Latin America in the 1980s dragged the U.S. military's attention back to the challenges of insurgency. General Wallace Nutting, the commander of U.S. Southern Command, complained to the U.S. Army Training and Doctrine Command in 1982 that it was not adequately preparing U.S. forces for the low end of the spectrum of conflict, though, he argued, this was precisely where the Soviet Union and its supporters in Latin America were posing the most immediate threat.[16] Serious concerns about the U.S. ability to challenge effectively the rise of communism in Latin America sparked something of a COIN and UW renaissance. The Marine Corps had already, in 1980, released a new version of FMFM 8-2, *Counterinsurgency Operations*. The Army, far more reluctant than the Marine Corps to commit itself to such a role, nonetheless responded to the events in Latin America with the cobbled-together 1981 version of FM 100-20, *Low Intensity Conflict*. This iteration resuscitated some of the post-Vietnam implementing doctrine. It super-seded *Border Security/Anti-Infiltration Operations* (FM 31-73, 1967), *Advisor Handbook for Stability Operations* (FM 31-55, 1972), *Base Defense* (31-81 [Test], 1970, on security installations in Vietnam), *Military Police in Stability Operations* (FM 19-50, 1970), and *Stability Operations—Intelligence* (FM 30-31, 1970),[17] as well as the 1974 version of 100-20 itself, drawing from each to create a single manual. The manual referred to LIC, but it was little more than an amalgam of COIN lessons learned. The Army also published, in 1986, implementing doctrine for COIN, FM 90-8, *Counterguerrilla Operations*. At this point, only the Marine Corps and the Army were publishing any stability operations–related doctrine.

Although FM 100-20 was a half-hearted effort, the Army did take two major steps in the 1980s relevant to stability operations. First, it shifted proponency for LIC doctrine back from the Special Warfare School to the conventional Army, under the aegis of the Combined Arms Center. Second, and perhaps more importantly, the Army added LIC to its 1986 capstone manual for the first time. After Vietnam, the Army had struggled with its grounding concept. In 1976, it built its doctrine around the idea of Active Defense. A scant six years later, in 1982, it reversed itself, promoting offense as the key to victory while introducing the concept of AirLand Battle (ALB). Both of these manuals were heavily conventionally oriented, though the 1982 version made passing mention of the potential threat of Soviet-supported guerrilla and terrorist groups. The 1986 version changed that. While it still validated the logic of ALB for conventional operations, it reflected General Nutting's influence insofar as it acknowledged and discussed LIC. It did so within the context of ALB—and within the very limited scope of a single page—but the requirement for stability operations was nonetheless present for the first time in any service's capstone doctrine.

STABILITY OPERATIONS IN POST-COLD WAR DOCTRINE

The Cold War's end left American policy makers somewhat in the lurch. Whereas for fifty years U.S. strategic priorities had been clear, the Soviet Union's collapse meant that policy makers no longer had a clear set of priorities, no guiding imperatives, no obvious next steps, no established procedures to follow. The bipolar scales fell from their eyes, and they saw a world filled with both promise and amorphous, unfamiliar threats. Issues that would have been of little or no concern during the Cold War—a corrupt president in Panama or hungry babies in Somalia—suddenly loomed large. Issues that during the Cold War were imbued with huge potential consequences—the war in El Salvador—now seemed far less important. Indeed, the 1990s were defined by the fact that they were *post–Cold War*. The only thing that was really clear was that there was not going to be a Fulda Gap–type battlefield war with the Soviets. In light of this, military leaders and policy makers alike began to reconsider every assumption that had underpinned U.S. security strategy for the previous fifty years. It was during this period that the Commission on the Roles and Missions of the Armed Forces (CORM) was established to consider the new security environment as well as the increased political pressure to reduce defense budgets. In the same decade, the Base Force Review was undertaken, the Bottom-Up Review was introduced, and the first Quadrennial Defense Review was launched. All of these represented a serious effort to rethink the requirements of American security.

In the absence of any clear peer or even near competitors, the military seemed like a hammer in a world without nails. It also, however, was a functioning, tested, organized, resourced, deployable machine whose working parts—soldiers, airmen, sailors, and marines—were well-trained and dedicated instruments at the executive's disposal. The military would not be deploying to the Nicaraguas and El Salvadors of the world to help oppose or support insurgents as part of proxy wars with the Soviet Union. But it could potentially undertake a much broader range of operations to achieve a much broader range of policy objectives. In a new world order, one in which the United States was the undisputed hegemon, LIC represented not the fringe elements of an all-consuming existential conflict but, instead, the possibility of using power to achieve positive ends, whether making and keeping peace, securing humanitarian assistance, promoting democracy, or combating the criminals who were setting up deadly narcotics networks around the globe or the terrorists who already were demonstrating their reach, not least, at the time, from Libya. In this world, many people began to argue, the military could be reconfigured so that it was no longer a hammer but, instead, a far more delicate instrument.

This point of view, although it had many adherents, ran into a wall of opposition: leaders and analysts who believed it was the military's very heft that was valuable, who argued that U.S. power lay in the fact that it could not be challenged on the battlefield, and who, moreover, believed that the military had always done LIC and had always been able to do LIC precisely because of the armed forces' breadth and depth and preparation for war. Whittle down the military, they argued, retrain your soldiers and refocus them, and you lose the very power at the foundation of American hegemony. And once that conventional foundation was dismantled, drawn down, refocused, it would take years to build up again in the event such military power became necessary. The United States would be making itself vulnerable to a host of potential future peer competitors and reducing its capacity to respond to ongoing threats, from North Korea to Iraq.

Doctrine in the 1990s showed how torn the military establishment was regarding LIC. On the one hand, the topic received tremendous attention in conferences, think tanks, military publications, and other forums. The LIC doctrine of the 1980s was quickly adjusted to allow for a much broader range of actions, expanding beyond COIN and support for insurgency to include peacekeeping, the more aggressive peace*making*, support to humanitarian operations, support to counterdrug operations (as the War on Drugs took on a new life in the aftermath of the Cold War), and counterterrorism (terrorism being recognized as an evolving and more serious threat to U.S. interests after the 1983 marine barracks bombing in Lebanon and the 1988 bombing of Pan Am 103). LIC still remained, however, a secondary priority, after fighting and winning the nation's wars, and the discussion about whether the military should prepare for LIC specifically or focus on conventional capabilities while tapping into its resources and manpower for LIC when necessary—as it always had done, throughout its history—continued unabated.[18]

Every aspect of LIC was vigorously debated during this period—terminology, context, significance, nature, requirements, costs, and effects. Academics, policy makers, nongovernmental organizations, and military personnel were all deeply involved in the conversation. In 1995, in the introduction to Joint Publication 3-07, *Joint Doctrine for Military Operations Other Than War*,[19] Chairman of the Joint Chiefs of Staff General John M. Shalikashvili reflected that, while the military had historically focused on warfighting, it was "increasingly changing its focus to a complex array of military operations—other than war." Moreover, he advised military leaders that "Participation in MOOTW is critical in the changing international security environment. Although the goals and endstates may not be crystal clear, you should spare no effort in planning and executing MOOTW. Your support of national security interests in today's challenging environment is as crucial as it is in war."

Here, already, a scant six years following the fall of the Berlin Wall, military doctrine was guiding soldiers to not only conduct war but to shape the international security environment. Indeed, JP 3-07's first chapter began with a quote from retired U.S. Army General Fred F. Woerner Jr.: "Consolidating (the Cold War) victory requires a continuing US role and new strategies to strengthen democratic institutions. Military civic action can, in concert with other elements of US strategy, be an effective means of achieving US objectives around the globe." The doctrine then further reinforced this point by outlining the differences between MOOTW and conventional combat operations:

> **MOOTW focus on deterring war and promoting peace** while war encompasses large-scale, sustained combat operations to achieve national objectives or to protect national interests. MOOTW are more **sensitive to political considerations** and often the military may not be the primary player. More **restrictive rules of engagement** and a hierarchy of **national objectives** are followed. MOOTW are initiated by the National Command Authorities and are usually, but not always, conducted outside of the United States.[20]

JP 3-07 continued by explaining the range and types of MOOTW, under what circumstances DOD would be either the lead agency or in a supporting role, and how MOOTW can take place across the entire spectrum of conflict, from peace to war. Yet, even as LIC and then MOSW, MOOTW, and OOTW were lauded as new and valuable foreign policy means, the military insisted that they take a back seat to the armed forces' key role. Consider the adamant conclusion to JP 3-07's first chapter, which stated that although U.S. military forces would increasingly undertake MOOTW and had to prepare for them, "commanders must remember that their **primary mission will always be to prepare for, fight and win America's wars**. This is the US military's most rigorous task and requires nothing less than top priority when training and equipping our forces."[21]

Although in capstone doctrine LIC remained in the shadow of the military's primary offensive and defensive missions, the services expanded and deepened their coverage of LIC in keystone manuals. The Army's 1990 revision of FM 100-20, *Low Intensity Conflict*, predated the collapse of the Soviet Union but nonetheless proved to be an excellent early guide to the post–Cold War security environment. This version was jointly published as U.S. Air Force Pamphlet 3-20, as the Air Force took its first steps into LIC doctrine. The new FM 100-20 replaced the jury-rigged 1981 Army version of the manual, abandoning the reheated COIN lessons from Vietnam in favor of a more expansive understanding of LIC. Although it still referred to the negative effects of Soviet influence as well as to anti-Marxist guerrillas, the manual went well beyond guidance for insurgencies, devoting entire chapters to counterterrorism, peace operations, and peacetime contingency operations. Here were stability operations in all their variety, a broad and disparate category of operations that would, under different names, be maintained to this day. Perhaps most importantly, the manual described LIC as inevitable, necessary, and, crucially, an opportunity. LIC operations would, the manual explained, not only protect American interests abroad—access to resources, military basing and transit rights, friends' and allies' loyalty, and weakened enemies—but could advance U.S. goals, including "the growth of freedom, democratic institutions, and free market economies."[22] These were the first intimations of a legitimate peacetime use of the military to promote U.S. interests abroad.

FM 100-20/AFP 3-20 got the 1990s off to a head start in terms of LIC doctrine, and momentum picked up further as the full impact of the Cold War's end began to influence the perception and practice of U.S. foreign policy. Over the course of the 1990s, the Army published manuals on peace operations (FM 100-23, 1994) and noncombatant evacuation operations (FM 90-29, 1994) as well as jointly with the Marine Corps on domestic support operations (FM 100-19/FMFM 7-10, 1993). It also published relevant implementing doctrine, *Operations in Low Intensity Conflict*, FM 7-98 (1992).[23] It was 1993's version of FM 100-5, *Operations*, a capstone manual, however, that perhaps most clearly demonstrated how the Army conceived of LIC at the time. The terminology was updated from LIC to OOTW and, rather than taking up just a page, the new version of the doctrine included an entire chapter on such operations. Moreover, in the manual's introduction, the writers referred to "full-dimensional" operations (a precursor to full-spectrum operations) and stated the need for decisive Army capabilities "across the full range of possible operations in war and in operations other than war."[24] The manual covered many of the concerns still associated with stability operations today: that the operations would be joint, combined, and/or interagency; that they would take place in sensitive political environments wherein tactical decisions could have serious strategic effects; and that they could be required in peacetime as well as during or after combat operations. The manual's authors acknowledged that, though much of the doctrine and preparation for war would be applicable in OOTW, some would have to be adjusted to the different requirements. They warned of the rapidly changing circumstances that can typify OOTW and highlighted the need for flexibility, legitimacy, restraint, and perseverance, among other capabilities. Finally, the authors pointed out the increasingly frequent deployments for OOTW in the post–Cold War period. The manual thus created a solid foundation for the understanding of OOTW and emphasized the need to prepare for such operations. Nonetheless, in a fourteen-chapter volume, a single standalone chapter, the penultimate in the book, was devoted to OOTW, and the first sentence of that chapter was a warning shot across the bow of anyone too enthusiastic about stability operations: "The Army's primary focus is to fight and win the nation's wars."[25]

STABILITY OPERATIONS IN DOCTRINE TODAY

Although multiservice TTPs relevant to stability operations were produced in the beginning of the new millennium, including 2003's *Peace Operations* (FM 3-07.1/MCWP 3-33.8/AFTTP[I] 3-2.40), arguably more important was that Army capstone doctrine's treatment of such responsibilities kept shifting. TTPs had flourished in the past without significantly reflecting service priorities; the inclusion in capstone doctrine of tasks related to the promotion of stability, however, was a sign of real change. That this was taking place within the Army, which had so long resisted such efforts, was particularly telling. That is not to say there was not opposition. In the 2001 iteration of the Army capstone manual, published a few months before 9/11 and renumbered as FM 3-0, the authors introduced the concept of "full spectrum operations." Although the idea held a great deal of promise for integrated OOTW and conventional operations, the manual did not go that far. It maintained the basic structure of its predecessor. It did include a chapter on what were now being called stability operations in addition to another on support operations, and it referred explicitly to "the four types of Army operations: offensive, defensive, stability, and support." But, as in the past, the manual began with the familiar admonition about fighting and winning the nation's wars, though with a stability operations twist: "The doctrine holds warfighting as the Army's primary focus and recognizes that the ability of Army forces to dominate land warfare also provides the ability to dominate any situation in military operations other than war."[26] It was a decade after the Cold War's end, and OOTW were garnering serious doctrinal and service attention, but the Army still preferred to believe that they could be effectively conducted by a force prepared and resourced for conventional war. U.S. Army General William Wallace described it this way: "In FM 3-0 (2001) stability operations were 'other' joint missions stated in Army context."[27]

This notion held for only a few more years. It is no coincidence that, after 9/11 and the challenges of the insurgencies and nation building in Iraq and Afghanistan, the Army and the military more generally abandoned the dual assumptions that had typified their doctrinal approach to stability operations: first, that a conventionally trained force was adequate for all types of stability operations, and second, that stability operations should remain lesser priorities than full-scale war. The new doctrinal standards were laid out in the 2005 DOD Directive 3000.05, which itself was rooted in the (classified) Strategic Security Guidance FY 2006–2011 of March 2005. The directive specified that establishing and maintaining order (stability operations) and promoting sustainable peace compatible with U.S. interests (military support to stability, security, transition, and reconstruction) were now missions with "priority comparable to combat operations" and to be "explicitly addressed and integrated across all DOD activities, including doctrine, organizations, training, education, exercises, materiel, leadership, personnel, facilities, and planning."[28]

All of the services and the joint community made doctrinal adjustments in response to DOD's elevation of stability operations to a primary mission. The Air Force, anxious to demonstrate its utility in stability operations, has based its doctrine since the publication of DOD Directive 3000.05 on two clear assumptions: that it is inherently flexible and capable of contributing across the spectrum of operations and that the only stability operations that require specific doctrinal attention are COIN. Thus, rather than integrating stability operations across its capstone doctrine AFDD 2, the Air Force simply included a section on "smaller-scale contingencies" in its 2006 edition of AFDD 2, *Operations and Organization*. It did follow up a year later with an interim edition of AFDD 2 with additional attention to stability operations, though this comprised little more than a list of the relevant operations and a quick overview of the principles (unity, perseverance, and so forth) as outlined in doctrine.[29] The same year, however, the service released AFDD 2-3, *Irregular Warfare*, a manual focused on COIN and support to insurgencies, with some brief attention to counterterrorism.[30] This manual replaced the 2000 edition of AFDD 2-3, *Military Operations Other Than War*.[31] Interestingly, just as Army and joint doctrine were validating the importance of the broader range of stability operations, the Air Force was winnowing its doctrinal coverage to focus specifically on COIN. This approach was further amplified by the late 2007 publication of the tactical manual AFDD 2-3.1, *Foreign Internal Defense*. In making the decision to focus on COIN, the Air

Force reversed the short-lived trend in its doctrine—from AFP 3-20 and AFTTP(1) 3-2.40 to the 2000 version of AFDD 2-3—of embracing the full breadth of stability operations. A *Joint Force Quarterly* article in 2007 was critical of this approach, arguing that COIN is "an important element of stability operations but . . . just one mission set among many."[32] Yet this approach took into account what more general stability operations doctrine did not: COIN was where the real challenges lay in stability operations, and it was only for COIN and similar and related missions—FID, peace operations, support to nation building—that the military needed to make significant adjustments.

The Navy only began to introduce doctrine in the 1990s, but it has made great strides since it first introduced Naval Doctrine Publication (NDP) 1, *Naval Warfare*,[33] in 1994. That first piece of capstone doctrine was only seventy-two pages long, from introduction to glossary, and, of those, five pages were dedicated to naval OOTW, including an observation that the Navy would use many of the same skills in peacetime and in war. NDP 1 was thoroughly updated in 2010, yet the Navy's view of stability operations has not changed much, as is clear in this introductory observation:

> NDP 1 introduces who we are, what we do, and how we operate today. Use of the word "warfare" in the title of this publication is with a purpose. Though naval forces are increasingly involved in operations short of war and the prevent-and-prevail aspects of the maritime strategy, it is their usefulness in war that sets them apart from other agencies, public and private. Being able to defend the Nation and project combat power in war is our reason for being.[34]

It should not be a surprise, therefore, that the service's only stability operations–specific doctrine is two tactical manuals focusing on its crisis response role via humanitarian assistance and disaster relief. These are EXTAC 1011, *Naval Humanitarian Assistance Missions* (1996);[35] and the more recent NWDC TACMEMO 3-07.6-05, *Humanitarian Assistance/ Disaster Relief (HA/DR) Operations Planning*, published in 2005.[36] That is not to say that naval doctrine does not acknowledge a stability operations role, a responsibility, in less traditional missions, that comes with specific requirements. In fact, NDP 1 lays out six strategic missions. Three involve deterring or winning wars and depend on "regionally concentrated, credible combat power," but the other three (homeland defense, sustained cooperation, and conflict prevention) are basically stability operations and depend on "globally distributed, mission-tailored maritime forces."[37]

The Marine Corps' primary stability operations–related doctrine is still the keystone COIN manual, as will be discussed below. Their capstone doctrine, MDCP 1, *Warfighting*, has little to offer on stability operations. Keystone manual MCWP 3-1, *Ground Combat Operations* (1995),[38] has a brief chapter on OOTW, but there is no integration between such operations and more conventional efforts. The Marines' manual on civil-military operations is numbered MCWP 3-33.1, as supplementary to keystone stability operations doctrine, because it provides guidance on support to, and cooperation with, civilians.[39]

While the Air Force, Navy, and Marine Corps are affected by the elevation of stability operations, it is not surprising that their doctrinal adjustments have been relatively minor. The Navy can rely, for the most part, on its existing capabilities for whatever contributions it will make to stability operations. It will leverage its forward presence and its resources for crisis response—humanitarian assistance and disaster relief, as its doctrine illustrates, and noncombatant evacuation operations—and will play an equally conventional logistical role even in most of the least conventional stability operations missions, whether counterinsurgency, support to insurgency, peace operations, counterdrug operations, or counterterrorism. Even in purely peacetime efforts—consider the friendship voyage of the USS *Robert G. Bradley* down the coast of Africa in 2009—the specific tasks the Navy undertakes will be very similar to what it does in war or to train for war. The Air Force, too, can rely for the most part on its conventional capabilities for the kinds of stability operations in which it will become involved, with the stark exception of COIN, for which it has developed unique doctrine. The Marine Corps is the service of small wars. It will not be doing much extended peacekeeping (it is not sustainable in the same way the Army is), but it will be involved in COIN and support to insurgencies (though, again, with logistical assistance from the Army). It is no coincidence that the Marines cover stability operations in their keystone combat operations manual.

The Army is the service most affected by changing priorities. As the primary land service, the Army has found that although it can do most stability operations well with its conventional capabilities, the exceptions are stability operations coincident with COIN, FID, or the termination of war, which require retooling, retraining, and reorganizing for working among civilian populations in complex contingencies requiring human intelligence and flexible and adaptive responses to constantly shifting political and security environments. For the Army more than for the other services, elevating stability operations to a primary mission means trading off some conventional capabilities, reprioritizing the distribution of manpower and money, and planning differently than it has done in the past. In light of this, and given the organization's traditionally hoary resistance to such changes, the Army's doctrinal shift in response to the DOD directive has been remarkable. That is perhaps most obvious in the service's adoption of full-spectrum operations.

FULL-SPECTRUM OPERATIONS

General William S. Wallace, who was the U.S. Army Training and Doctrine Command commander in 2008, falls into the progressive camp.[40] In the foreword to FM 3-0 (2008), *Operations*, he wrote that America is at war and facing "an era of persistent conflict":

> This edition of FM 3-0, the first update since September 11, 2001, is a revolutionary departure from past doctrine. It describes an operational concept where commanders employ offensive, defensive, and stability or civil support operations simultaneously as part of an interdependent joint force to seize, retain, and exploit the initiative, accepting prudent risk to create opportunities to achieve decisive results. Just as the 1976 edition of FM 100-5 began to take the Army from the rice paddies of Vietnam to

the battlefield of Western Europe, this edition will take us into the 21st century urban battlefields among the people without losing our capabilities to dominate the higher conventional end of the spectrum of conflict.[41]

The distinguishing characteristic of the new *Operations*, which makes it a "revolutionary departure," is that, in it, full-spectrum operations have become the central tenet of U.S. Army doctrine. Whereas they appeared in 2005's FM 1 and were included in 2006's JP 3-0, FM 3-0 (2008) made them a centerpiece. This was a direct response to the view that the new security environment requires shaping as a primary and constant mission not only in addition to but in support of the Army's traditional responsibility for deterring and defeating enemies. As described in the manual:

Army forces must address the civil situation directly and continuously, combining tactical tasks directed at noncombatants with tactical tasks directed against the enemy. These tasks have evolved from specialized ancillary activities—civil military operations—into a central element of operations equal in importance to the offense and defense—stability and civil support.[42]

Overseas, full-spectrum operations therefore entail offensive, defensive, and stability efforts; at home, they include offensive and defensive operations as well as support to civil authorities.

FM 3-0 begins with a full chapter on the changing operational environment, with an emphasis on persistent conflict and new threats. The manual then reverts, in the second chapter, to a discussion of the more traditional spectrum of conflict (from peace to war), although it follows that with an introduction of the new idea of "operational themes." The assumption is that different themes will require different combinations of capabilities, including different force packages, task organization, and protection. Operational themes as described in this chapter tend to be coincident with the spectrum of conflict and are also designed as roughly consistent with operational phases. The themes include peacetime military engagement (shaping the peacetime environment), limited military intervention (such as strikes and raids), the full range of peace operations (which is quite interesting, since peace enforcement will require different force packages and task organization than will peacekeeping), and irregular warfare (including COIN and counterterrorism). All of the tasks in these four categories fall within the broader category of stability operations.

The doctrine acknowledges that there can be overlap between themes, that some tasks will fall into multiple themes, and that the phases, as represented by the themes, may not proceed linearly. The themes are therefore a very loose organizing principle. This has to be the case since, ultimately, the FM represents the Army's assumption of a hugely ambitious set of responsibilities requiring an extremely flexible force. Chapter 3 of the doctrine, "Full Spectrum Operations," makes this abundantly clear, with the following definition of the service's new operating concept:

> Army forces combine offensive, defensive, and stability or civil support operations simultaneously as part of an interdependent joint force to seize, retain, and exploit the initiative, accepting prudent risk to create opportunities to achieve decisive results. They employ synchronized action—lethal and nonlethal—proportional to the mission and informed by a thorough understanding of all variables of the operational environment. Mission command that conveys intent and an appreciation of all aspects of the situation guides the adaptive use of Army forces.[43]

Full-spectrum operations as a concept are intended to prepare the Army for any contingency—to make it ready not just to fight and win wars but to prevent them and to contribute, as they wind down and then in their aftermath, to the processes that will prevent their recurrence. The concept provides the basis for training, organizing, and equipping for what used to be called operations other than war, for those potential threats to international stability promulgated by criminals, terrorists, dictators, failing regimes, and revolutionaries. To this end, full-spectrum operations require tremendous amounts of information; accurate and timely analysis; constant reassessment; good judgment; flexibility in both mission and force employment (but avoidance of unintentional mission creep); and intraservice, interservice, and interagency communication and cooperation. The bulk of the manual offers practical guidance for wielding information, combat power, command and control, operational art, and so forth to address these challenging requirements.

The publication of 2008's *Operations* formed the basis of new joint doctrine, as well. The draft of a revised version of 1995's JP 3-07, *Joint Doctrine for Military Operations Other Than War*, entitled *Stability Operations*, was being circulated in 2010, as was an updated version of the 2006 joint capstone doctrine JP 3-0.[44] Also due for revision were joint publications on counterterrorism, counterinsurgency, foreign humanitarian assistance, foreign internal defense, and coordination with inter- and nongovernmental organizations. FM 3-0 also served, as capstone doctrine does, as the foundation for a new generation of keystone manuals and TTPs. Two of these—FM 3-24, *Counterinsurgency*; and FM 3-07, *Stability Operations*, hit the streets amid heightened public attention, applause from many quarters, and some real controversy. Deeply influenced by prominent stability operations progressives, the two new manuals reflected the elevation of stability operations, the continuing tensions and concerns surrounding U.S. involvement in Iraq and Afghanistan, and, perhaps more than anything, the post-9/11 narrative about the need to acknowledge and prepare for protracted conflict, emerging threats, and an increasingly menacing international security environment populated with terrorists, nonstate actors, insurgents, drug traffickers, and criminals.

FM 3-24, *COUNTERINSURGENCY*, AND FM 3-07, *STABILITY OPERATIONS*

FM 3-24 (jointly published as Marine Corps Warfighting Publication [MCWP] 3-33.5) was the Army's first COIN doctrine in twenty years and the Marine Corps' first in a quarter-century. It was written as a very deliberate response to the inadequacy of doctrine available for U.S. forces in Iraq and Afghanistan. FM 3-24 begins with a history of COIN and an overview of COIN theory, including the typical phases of a revolution and the nature of insurgent networks. A throwback to classic COIN conventional wisdom, the manual reminds soldiers repeatedly that they must win the civilian population, not just defeat the insurgents. It emphasizes the importance of good intelligence, and it focuses on flexibility and the need to adapt quickly. There is nothing surprising or new in the manual, but it is a comprehensive overview of COIN intended to reintroduce military personnel to valuable knowledge and hard-won lessons learned that the services deliberately buried following Vietnam.

Chapter 5 of FM 3-24, "Executing Counterinsurgency Operations," introduces "Clear, Hold, Build." It is this facet of the COIN doctrine that has developed legs beyond COIN. It underpins full-spectrum operations and reflects the military's extension of its role beyond traditional missions. The ideas are not new with respect to COIN, but in a security environment in which instability is considered threatening and wars do not end through victory but through nation building, such ideas have gained purchase in a new set of conditions, have traction in maintaining the peace, and can be applied as a means to resolve even conventional conflicts. The same ideas underpin FM 3-07, published in 2008. The stability operations manual was written, as General William Caldwell said in his foreword, "as a roadmap from conflict to peace." The general continued: "This manual postures our military forces for the challenges of an uncertain future, an era of persistent conflict where the unflagging bravery of our Soldiers will continue to carry the banner of freedom, hope, and opportunity to the people of the world."[45]

FM 3-07 is intended to complement FM 3-0. The manual's preface states that its six chapters "constitute the Army's approach to the conduct of full spectrum operations in any environment across the spectrum of conflict."[46] While this could be read as a usurpation of FM 3-0's function, given that FM 3-0 is the capstone doctrine in which the concept of full-spectrum operations is embedded, FM 3-07 is specifically meant to offer guidelines for integrating stability operations tasks into any kind of operation anywhere along the spectrum of conflict. In effect, having a separate stability operations doctrine indicates that the extremely varied tasks that fall under the stability operations rubric never truly integrate into traditional offensive and defensive operations but can run coincidentally with them, reinforce them, merge and break away again from them, and be undertaken independently of them. They are, ultimately, intended to promote stability—whether in peacetime, during a period of escalating conflict, in war, or after the bloodshed has ended. They run parallel to traditional missions, or they run on their own. Offense, defense, and stability operations are thus separate categories that can be used in concert with one another to achieve a political end.[47]

Unlike FM 3-24, FM 3-07 is truly revolutionary. Previous such doctrine offered awkward categories of operations other than conventional war and their subordinate forms: the familiar litany includes everything from peace enforcement and disaster relief to noncombatant evacuations and strikes. The doctrine made clear that these could be standalone or complementary operations but offered no unifying theme with which to think about them.[48] In fact, this problem plagued generations of stability operations doctrine; the catch-all category was a sign of such missions' subordination to the armed forces' primary responsibilities. The new FM 3-07, by contrast, is a clear reflection of the elevation of stability operations. It does not list them out; it does not offer up groupings of tasks. Instead, it is based on the mission: establishing, enhancing, supporting, and otherwise ensuring stability. And stability becomes very specific here: a smoothly functioning state across all sectors—security, justice and reconciliation, humanitarian assistance and social well-being, governance and participation, and economic stabilization and infrastructure.

This is not some messy amalgam of peacekeeping and arms control as was past doctrine: this is carving out a "shaping" niche for the military in the absence of, during, and following hostilities. It is an extension of the military's responsibility into capacity building. The tasks that seemed haphazardly pulled together in previous manuals make sense as a toolkit for contributing to stability simultaneously with efforts across the full spectrum of conflict. The doctrine does make clear that the military's role is, ideally, circumscribed and mostly involves assistance to civilian authorities. Armed forces can support governance, economic growth, and infrastructure development, though those tasks will predominantly fall to civilians; they can establish civil security and restore essential services;

and they can contribute to establishing civil control.⁴⁹ Chapter 3 explains how the military is adapting its skills, resources, and training to achieve these goals as part of a whole-of-government effort. Some of these tasks coincide with the familiar categories of stability operations (peace operations, support to humanitarian assistance, training foreign military forces, civic action, etc.), but this doctrine is far more precise and targeted than were past iterations. For example, as part of ensuring stability, the military may have to support monetary institutions and programs by facilitating an assessment of a central bank's capabilities or assisting in the distribution of currency to key banking outlets.⁵⁰ It should not be surprising that the manual devotes more than sixteen of its sixty-seven pages to explaining the new strategic context. FM 3-07 in its new form is a new approach to security, posits a new and increased role for the military, and is firmly rooted in the new security narrative and the elevation of these operations to a primary mission.

FMs 3-24 and 3-07 were released to tremendous hype and acclaim and were made available to the public via Amazon.com even as they were being distributed to U.S. troops. One report claimed that fifteen million copies of FM 3-24 had been downloaded.⁵¹ Yet the manuals have engendered criticism as well as applause. Colonel Gian Gentile, a traditionalist with regard to stability operations, wrote in an autumn 2009 article published in *Parameters* that "the principles and ideas that emerged out of the Army's counterinsurgency field manual (FM), FM 3-24, published in late 2006, have become transcendent. The field manual has moved beyond simple Army doctrine for countering insurgencies to become the defining characteristic of the Army's new way of war."⁵² A year earlier, the then–lieutenant colonel had expressed concern that "the centerpiece of the Army's operational doctrine is no longer FM 3-0, 'Operations,' it is FM 3–24, 'Counterinsurgency.'"⁵³ And, indeed, both manuals are the product of a clear agenda and are very natural doctrinal responses—as was the revised FM 3-0—to DODD 3000.05.

In fact, many of the same analysts and military officers responsible for the directive have been involved in writing or contributing to the subsequent doctrine. FM 3-24, for example, was co-written by the high-profile

Eating Soup with a Knife author John Nagl, U.S. Army General David Petraeus, and U.S. Marine Corps General James Amos. Nagl had been instrumental in promoting the elevation of stability operations to a primary mission. He saw such a change as a necessary step for saving the United States' foundering efforts in Iraq and Afghanistan and, more importantly, for preparing the U.S. armed forces for the security environment he foresaw well into the future. DODD 3000.05 and the doctrine that emerged from it were part of a larger battle between traditionalists and progressives—often referred to trenchantly as COINdinistas—for intellectual influence.[54] And the progressives, at least in the 2000s, were ascendant. FM 3-24 came out the same year that Praeger Security International re-released David Galula's classic book *Counterinsurgency Warfare: Theory and Practice*, with a foreword by Nagl. In 2008, FM 3-07, *Stability Operations*, was published. Its two forewords were written by Michele Flournoy and General William Caldwell; Janine Davidson wrote its introduction. One year later, David Ucko's book *The New Counterinsurgency Era: Transforming the U.S. Military for Modern Wars* came out, with a foreword by Nagl. That same year, David Kilcullen's well-received *The Accidental Guerrilla: Fighting Small Wars in the Midst of a Big One* was released, with thanks in the acknowledgments to Nagl, their mutual mentor David Petraeus, and Janine Davidson, Kilcullen's wife. In 2010, Janine Davidson's *Lifting the Fog of Peace: How Americans Learned to Fight Modern War* hit the bookstores, with a Nagl blurb on the back and an expression of gratitude to her husband, David Kilcullen, in the acknowledgments.

Nor was the battle fought only through books. In 2007, Michele Flournoy and Kurt Campbell established the Center for a New American Security, a think tank focused heavily on terrorism and insurgency with a who's who list of analysts with progressive views vis-à-vis stability operations, including Kilcullen, Tom Ricks, Andrew Exum, and, of course, Nagl, who took over the role of CNAS president when Flournoy was tapped for a post in the Obama administration. In fact, Obama recruited heavily from the CNAS ranks, further enhancing the organization's influence.

A very small group of like-minded policy analysts and military officers have thus been able to shape both U.S. COIN doctrine and policy and, perhaps more importantly, capstone U.S. military doctrine and security policy.[55] And they have shaped these in a distinctive direction rooted in the argument that the U.S. military's, and especially the U.S. Army's, standard assumption regarding LIC, OOTW, peace operations, stability operations, or whatever else they have been called throughout history has been completely wrong: U.S. forces trained and prepared for conventional war will *not* be ready for COIN or complex stability operations. Each of these analysts, each of these books, and the new COIN and stability operations doctrine all make the same point: the military must prepare, now, for what it will face in the future. Stability operations and COIN no longer can be undertaken as lesser-included cases. In his foreword to Ucko's book, Nagl summed up this position:

> When an insurgency erupted in Iraq in the hot summer of 2003, the U.S. military was unprepared to counter it. Since then, the Department of Defense has painfully relearned a number of old lessons about the nature and conduct of successful counterinsurgency campaigns. . . . Today America's wars are against insurgents, militias, and terrorists that leech off of disaffected indigenous populations for recruits and support for their extremist ideologies. Combating these enemies effectively requires U.S. forces that are thoroughly trained for counterinsurgency and nation building. While neither popular nor convenient, this focus is not a temporary excursion from preparing for a large-scale war; it must be an enduring priority for the U.S. military.[56]

Of course, the progressives could be wrong, and many argue, quite persuasively, that they are. The security environment may not have changed all that much. Nonstate actors arguably pose a negligible threat in real terms and reap benefits from exaggerations of their abilities. Failed and failing states do not seem to promise, in all cases, the kinds of safe havens the West has come to fear, nor do they seem to pose, in and of themselves, serious threats—not in the existential sense—beyond their borders or, at most, their regions. A military prepared for conventional operations is pretty good at most stability operations. Moreover, a military may better serve its own institutional interests—as well as the national interest—by resisting deeper and more extensive involvement in nation building and counterinsurgency rather than by embracing it. Indeed, all of the progressives' assumptions are debatable.

What is not debatable, however, is that these progressive analysts, policy makers, and military offices have helped—in a considerable way—to change the national conversation about security. They have leveraged the post-9/11 security narrative and contributed to it. They have helped to make a case for a modern form of warfare that is substantively different from wars of the past, and—by shifting doctrine—have helped shift the U.S. military itself in a new and uncharted direction. To what extent the military has shifted, in practical terms, will be explored in chapter 3.

A BRIEF OBSERVATION: SOF AND STABILITY OPERATIONS DOCTRINE

Perhaps more than any of the other manuals, the new FM 3-07 represents the shift to conventionally trained troops of some of the responsibilities that traditionally have fallen to special operations forces. That is not to say that SOF will not be involved in stability operations—indeed, demand for SOF has increased significantly, as will be discussed in chapter 3—but that some tasks that once were solely or primarily in their purview will now fall to conventional soldiers as well. Consider, for example, the SOF core activities:

> direct action, special reconnaissance, counterproliferation of weapons of mass destruction, counterterrorism, unconventional warfare, foreign internal defense, security force assistance, counterinsurgency, information operations (IO), military information support operations (MISO), and civil affairs operations.[57]

Although many of the methods that SOF will employ differ from those that conventional troops will rely on, and though SOF will be configured differently than will conventional troops (as will be discussed in chapter 3), there is tremendous overlap between these activities and stability operations' essential tasks. Civil Affairs, in particular, have found conventional troops being pushed into their lane. Civil Affairs has six general functional specialty areas: the rule of law, economic stability, governance, public health and welfare, infrastructure, and public education and information.[58] Yet, conventional troops today are directed by FM 3-07 to take on jobs such as providing essential civil services, supporting assistance to dislocated civilians, estimating food needs, assessing public health hazards, and so forth.[59] One response to this concurrence of responsibilities has been a subtle shift in Civil Affairs' responsibilities from primary providers to intermediaries between civilians and the military. This is represented not only in FM 3-07's third chapter, in which Civil Affairs' special capabilities and utility as interlocutors are highlighted in a brief subsection, but in Civil Affairs doctrine. Joint Publication 3-57, *Civil-Military Operations* (2008), for example, emphasizes Civil Affairs' role as liaisons between military forces and civilian governmental and nongovernmental agencies. JP 3-57 is itself a consolidation of two prior manuals: *Civil Affairs* and *Civil-Military Operations*. The consolidation illustrates the shift in Civil Affairs' roles from primary providers of services to experienced intermediaries.

FM 3-07 also shows that the special forces (SF) of all the services and MISO will find conventional troops sharing some of their traditional responsibilities, including providing support to law enforcement and police reform, training host nation security personnel and military forces, and establishing broad public information programs. The April 2011 Joint Publication 3-05, *Special Operations*, takes the new face of stability operations into account, replacing sections on MOOTW and the principles of war from prior iterations of the doctrine with a discussion of special operations across the full range of military operations. It also begins with a very direct clarification of the ways in which special operations forces are, in fact, special and distinguishable from conventional forces. It then goes on to emphasize the need for effective coordination between conventional and special operations forces, as well as integration of SOF, civilian agency, foreign military, and

NGO efforts. The manual's second chapter starts by pointing out SOF's unique relevance for stability operations, which they continue to refer to as irregular warfare. Of the SOF core activities, security force assistance, foreign internal defense, COIN, civil affairs, counterterrorism, and information operations will be most represented in stability operations, although the other core missions could come into play.

So what distinguishes what SOF bring from what conventional forces bring? In effect, in any of these core activities, SOF will bring greater maturity, training, language skills, cultural knowledge, insight, stealth, flexibility, and independence. The revised joint SOF doctrine is intended to reflect precisely this. Even as general military doctrine adopts the concept of full-spectrum operations, and as conventional forces therefore begin to assume responsibilities that, in the past, have fallen more frequently to SOF, it is important to remember what makes SOF valuable and how crucial it will be—perhaps more so than ever—to integrate them effectively into joint, combined, interagency efforts in complex environments with changeable missions. The doctrinal elevation of stability operations may ultimately be a boon for SOF, bringing them into the mainstream even as it brings the mainstream a few steps deeper into the more complex, nuanced world in which SOF have always operated.

CONCLUSION

The doctrinal record shows that it was only after 9/11—an attack on U.S. soil—and after the two wars in Afghanistan and Iraq had turned into confusing, difficult slogs that those who had been arguing for the ascendance of stability operations to a primary mission had the political capital to make the unprecedented change to U.S. military priorities. Their position was strong: there were no peer competitors on the horizon; the U.S. could win a conventional war with its proverbial hands tied behind its back; stability operations deployments were on a distinct upward trend because of U.S. interests in peace and stability; even conventional wars had prominent stability operations components, especially in the postcombat phase but even before then; and the conventionally trained military was falling short in the most challenging, least conventional stability operations, including COIN and stabilization efforts.

Within the military, this shift represented a dramatic realignment, reducing the near-total grip on military strategy and internal influence held by conventional leaders. The fact that this did not happen during the military's long history of deployments to stability operations, with big wars serving as painful punctuation among ongoing, smaller, less-heralded deployments; or during the proxy wars of the Cold War; or in the decade after the Berlin Wall fell as operational tempo for stability operations rapidly increased attests to the tenacity of the conventional concept and conventional leadership. It demonstrates the long-standing, almost immutable belief that a military prepared for war could also undertake stability operations. It reflects a conservative, realist view of the world as a battleground for power between great powers. The historian Lawrence Yates described it thus, with respect specifically to the U.S. Army:

> in the past, warfighting doctrine, supported by military education and training programs and reflecting the Army's institutional biases, has instilled the conviction in most officers that, despite war's diversity, "real" war is primarily a *conventional* undertaking—one in which the regular armed forces of a given state wage large-scale and sustained combat operations against the regular armed forces of an enemy state. In conventional warfare, the battlefield tends to be linear, the armies large, the combatants uniformed (and thus identifiable), and the technology highly sophisticated. The mission of the US military in such wars is to defeat the enemy's forces, or at least to inflict unacceptable damage on them, so that American policy makers can achieve the political objectives of a given conflict.[60]

The doctrinal shift thus legitimized, in new and concrete ways, the special operators, Pentagon personnel, and military officers who had long labored in relative obscurity on issues related to stability operations. It was both a product and a purveyor of a new view of security. And because doctrine changed, everything would have to change, even terminology. In the Army, for example, leaders were directed to substitute the term "operational environment" for "battlespace," which was no longer deemed acceptable.[61] Similarly, the term "human terrain" was replaced with "civilian considerations," "relevant information" replaced "relevant combat information," and "battle" was minimized in favor of the broader "operation." This was more than a rhetorical shift, however. As established at the chapter's outset, doctrine drives training, education, organization, and equipment. Chapter 3 will examine how changes in doctrine have affected the military in practical respects.

THREE
PRACTICAL ADJUSTMENTS TO ACHIEVE DOCTRINAL REQUIREMENTS

We have learned through painful experience that the wars we fight are seldom the wars we planned. As a result, the United States needs a broad portfolio of military capabilities, with maximum versatility across the widest possible spectrum of conflicts.

—Secretary of Defense Robert Gates (2010)

Adjustments to doctrine often contribute to changes in force structure, training, education, and equipping.[1] As doctrine is updated to reflect the military's decision to elevate stability operations to a primary mission, practical steps are being taken to prepare the force for this shift in priorities. It would be reasonable to expect that a dramatic change in doctrine, as outlined in the previous chapter, would be mirrored by equally dramatic modifications of the military. This both has and has not materialized. The military has grown tremendously in response to increased demands upon it since 9/11, there have been real changes in organization, spending has shifted in unprecedented ways, and the glimmers of a revised self-image have begun to appear. That said, the military is an enormous organization with millions of moving parts, deeply rooted mores and culture, co-dependence with the influential defense industry, the duty to defend America and its interests, and the weighty responsibility of training young men and women to sacrifice themselves and kill others if necessary in the name of national security. As a practical matter, there is a limit to the changes that such an institution can absorb; stability operations during COIN and FID require real tradeoffs in terms of preparedness for conventional war. As noted in the 2010 *Quadrennial Defense Review Report*,

> As described earlier, defense strategy requires making choices: accepting and managing risk is thus inherent in everything the Department does. Although difficult, risk management is central to effective decision-making and is vital to our success. For our nation, it can mean the difference between victory and defeat; for our men and women in uniform and their families, such decisions have life-and-death consequences. That is why the Department is focused so centrally on rebalancing our capabilities and reforming our institutions to better enable success in today's wars while preparing for a wide range of contingencies.[2]

Indeed, despite the military's enormity, it has already shown signs of wear as the operations in Iraq and Afghanistan continue: troops can only withstand so many deployments; health and psychological facilities have already exceeded capacity and been challenged with new forms of injuries; equipment must be adjusted and adapted to the requirements of different environments and new threats, such as improvised explosive devices (IEDs); and some parts of the force are overtaxed while others languish in relative disuse.

A force prepared for stability operations must be ready to put sizeable numbers of personnel on the ground; be able to rotate them in and out; have force protection capabilities for the most challenging environments (urban and populated); pay as much attention or more to human intelligence over satellite, electronic, or signal intelligence; be prepared to deal with local noncombatants, the U.S. interagency, and nongovernmental organizations; and ideally be prepared with cultural and language training to be as sensitive and attuned to civilian needs and interests as possible. This is not the force of the Revolution in Military Affairs. This is not a military designed for stand-off operations, and there is no question here of rapid, high-tech, antiseptic operations. The most challenging stability operations, ones promoting fundamental political, social, and economic changes in complex, rapidly changing, and often violent environments, do not leverage the Americans' comparative advantage in technology, nor do they allow for the United States' preferred small footprints and quick results.

The U.S. armed forces have begun to come to terms with these kinds of requirements, taking hard-won lessons learned from Iraq and Afghanistan, combined with the emerging doctrine, and making the necessary changes to the force. They have had to do so keeping their broader mandate in mind, in the face of both tradition and bureaucratic drag, under competing political pressures, and with an eye to the costs. They have done so under the avid leadership of Secretary of Defense Robert Gates (2006–2011), who saw such changes as both necessary responses to a new security environment and politically astute steps to protect the military as an institution. Such efforts take place within each of the military services, which are responsible for force generation for the combatant commands. The Army, as the primary land-force provider, has had to make the most significant and substantive adjustments, though the Air Force, Navy, and Marine Corps have all taken steps to improve readiness for stability operations as well. This chapter offers an overview of the extent and limitations of the services' adjustments to date.

FORCE STRUCTURE

The 2006 Quadrennial Defense Review (QDR) had several significant revisions from earlier planning documents. Among these was the new and improved force planning construct (FPC), which, in keeping with DODD 3000.05, emphasized the simultaneity of offense, defense, and stability operations and directed the services to prepare their forces in light of this. To this end, the Army, Air Force, Navy, and Marine Corps have made changes in the structure and organization of their forces to better support the broader requirements and persistent demands of the geographic combatant commands. The 2010 QDR outlined in detail the nature of the desired modifications (assuming unconstrained resources):

- U.S. ground forces will remain capable of full-spectrum operations, with continued focus on capabilities to conduct effective and sustained counterinsurgency, stability, and counterterrorist operations alone and in concert with partners.

- U.S. naval forces likewise will continue to be capable of robust forward presence and power projection operations, even as they add capabilities and capacity for working with a wide range of partner navies.

- We will also enhance our air forces' contributions to security force assistance operations by fielding within our broader inventory aircraft that are well-suited to training and advising partner air forces.

- The United States will continue to increase the capacity of its special operations forces and will enhance their capabilities through the growth of organic enablers and key support assets in the general purpose forces.[3]

By far the biggest change in any of the services in terms of force structure has been the Army's shift to a modular force. The 2009 Army Posture Statement boasted that "the Army has transformed 83 percent of our units to modular formations—the largest organizational change since World War II."[4] This modification was not driven by DODD 3000.05; rather, it was a product of experience in the post–Cold War combined with FM 3-0's introduction of the concept of full-spectrum operations. In effect, the peace operations and support to humanitarian assistance of the 1990s demonstrated the need for a more flexible force structure, especially in the Army. The Army's efforts in Somalia, Bosnia, and Haiti highlighted the shortcomings of a force organized into Cold War–style divisions. Too integrated and overly reliant on divisional bases, units that deployed individually were inadequately supported. Moreover, sending off divisional elements ultimately affected the readiness of the divisions as a whole, proving both inefficient and costly. In 2003, therefore, guided by 2001's FM 3-0, the Army reorganized around brigades. The focus on brigades gave the Army building blocks it could assemble for any kind of contingency. It meant that functional capabilities could be tailored to operational requirements, and it insulated the broader force from the effects of individual units' deployments.[5]

The foundational element of the new modular force is the brigade combat team (BCT), which comes in three forms: heavy, infantry, and Stryker (a mix of the first two). BCTs have an organic structure (maneuver, fires, sustainment, and reconnaissance units)[6] and can be augmented with other capabilities. As described in *Operations* (2008): "Augmentation might include lift or attack aviation, armor, cannon or rocket artillery, air defense, military police, civil affairs, psychological operations elements, combat engineers, or additional information systems assets. This organizational flexibility allows BCTs to function across the spectrum of conflict."[7]

For stability operations, this form of organization provides valuable adaptability. FM 3-90.6, *Brigade Combat Team* (2006), claims that "The BCT is designed for combined arms combat. However, as a versatile and flexible force, it also can conduct stability operations very effectively. The BCT will likely have to focus on simultaneous combat and stability operations."[8] Recognizing that BCTs are fundamentally combat units excellent at establishing initial security but less capable of reconstruction, stabilization, and peacetime capacity-building efforts, the Army introduced the BCT-S (Brigade Combat Team–Stability). The BCT-Ss are specially augmented with engineers, military police, and civil affairs personnel to provide security force assistance to host nations' conventional forces. Interestingly, these augmented BCTs have embodied in microcosm the debates about adjusting the force for stability operations. Trade-offs have had to be made in terms of pre-mission training (the initial focus tended to be on core combat skills rather than advisory capabilities, though the teams have been able to construct much more specialized preparation), and, once deployed, the BCT-Ss have had to balance their primary missions with their security force assistance mission.[9] With the flexibility for adaptation, as exemplified by the BCT-S, the modular force has proven to be a far more logical and efficient structure for stability operations than was the division-based force structure of the past. Even so, BCTs and BCT-Ss are not sufficient to meet all the needs of stability operations.[10] Because of this, smaller, more specialized, improvised entities have been developed, many of which work with or alongside the BCTs.

Among the extemporized organizations created to help meet the demands of stability operations are provincial reconstruction teams (PRTs), military transition teams (MTTs or MiTTs), border transition teams (BTTs), and police transition teams (PTTs). Of these, perhaps the best known are the PRTs. PRTs are made up of military personnel and civilians. The latter come variously from the State Department, USAID, the Department of Agriculture, academia, and even NGOs. PRTs are intended to create conditions under which U.S. civilian personnel, protected and supported by American troops, can help promote stabilization and reconstruction even in not entirely permissive environments. As is discussed at some length in chapter 5, although such teams have had some successes, they have been plagued by shortfalls in qualified civilians, inadequate continuity, and extremely broad and ambitious objectives. Military personnel have often had to assume positions intended for civilians and, even when civilians are present, the PRTs, as military organizations, tend to undertake primarily military tasks in support of military priorities. This ultimately undermines the units' effectiveness in promoting economic and political development.

MTTs are another type of ad hoc, specialized unit developed to leverage seasoned American military leadership to train foreign military and police forces, mostly in Iraq. Initially introduced by the Army, the Marine Corps now also runs MTTs, and the U.S. Navy and Air Force now have similar transition team–type units assisting the Iraqi Navy and Air Force. MTTs are deliberately top heavy, peopled with experienced officers and senior noncommissioned officers drawn from a variety of military occupational specialties (MOSs). Team members are brought together to train in the United States for three months before deploying. Such training is intended to help the MTT members understand their roles as advisors, trainers, and mentors, but soldiers sometimes come through the relatively brief training period with their combat mentality still firmly in place (one MTT member posting online about the units described such soldiers as "Rambo Ricky Recons" who couldn't shake the "Kill People, Break Stuff" mentality).[11] Also, MTTs remain relatively ad hoc entities, inconsistently organized, with steep learning curves. The teams are small (Army teams are usually eleven soldiers; the Marine Corps MTTs are typically fifteen) and, because of force protection concerns, often cannot patrol if a team member is unavailable. Furthermore, the MOSs in the teams do not always match team requirements (a congressional committee report described a mechanic being deployed as a communications specialist, for instance, and online posts by current and former MTT members observe similar problems). Also, the teams would often benefit from more interpreters, civil affairs personnel, and other experts (the congressional committee report specifically mentions a need for more detainee specialists).[12] Finally, MTTs work in challenging environments with foreign forces under conditions in which the language gap becomes the least of the problems, compared to host nation forces' different agendas, experiences, priorities, traditions, cultures, and skills. In this face of this, MTTs are more of a stopgap than a solution.

In 2000, the U.S. Air Force also responded to the lessons of the 1990s. USAF transformed its Cold War garrison force to a new structure: the Air and Space Expeditionary Force (AEF). Like the Army's modular force, the AEF is intended to enhance USAF's flexibility, responsiveness, and expeditionary capacity[13] while also relieving OPTEMPO problems and allowing airmen greater predictability regarding the possibility of deployment. As described in a 2010 overview of the service in *Air Force Magazine*, "USAF groups its power projection and support forces into 10 AEF 'buckets of capability' operating in five pairs."[14] Each AEF has over 17,000 airmen and over one hundred planes; each alone is "more formidable than the air forces of many nations."[15] Two AEFs are on call in any 120- or 180-day period; the rest are in the training and preparation phases of the twenty-month cycle. Organizing the force in this way allows the Air Force to be more adaptable and ready for multiple deployments. It also allows the Air Force to tailor its forces to meet combatant commanders' requirements with more modular, modifiable units. In Iraq, for example, "Expeditionary civil engineering, security forces, medical, and combat convoy units are heavily engaged outside the wire of air bases in Iraq and elsewhere to defend joint logistics nodes, build roads, conduct security patrols, and offer medical services in the joint effort to stabilize and reconstruct war-torn countries."[16]

The AEF structure is a deliberate response to the requirements across the full spectrum of conflict. As Brigadier General Henabray explained it in a 2006 briefing, there are "no more 'lesser included cases.'"[17] That said, the Air Force's responsibilities in stability operations tend to be far different from those of the ground forces. It is responsible, as in conventional operations, for mobility, eyes-in-the-sky intelligence, and strikes and interdiction. Ultimately, the AEF solution is less a response to the specific needs of stability operations and more a solution for service OPTEMPO and a rationalization for airmen's deployment schedules in an environment where multiple contingencies may be ongoing.

In addition to the AEF, the Air Force also introduced, beginning in 1999, Contingency Response Groups (CRGs) as first responders to humanitarian crises, the onset of combat operations, and other rapidly breaking contingencies. By teaming personnel from a range of specialties, the Air Force can theoretically tailor CRGs to the specific needs of any given operation. According to Air Mobility Command Instruction 10-403 (2007):

A Contingency Response Group (CRG) provides a light, lean and rapidly-deployable capability to open an airbase, regardless of the follow-on mission or aircraft type. It is composed of multi-skilled individuals, equipped with state-of-the-art equipment to facilitate airfield assessment, command and control, limited force protection, reach-back communications, timely intelligence, initial airfield operations, limited mobility operations, and rapid redeployment. It operates in austere, permissive, and uncertain threat environments, as well as in low light conditions. A CRG bridges the gap between seizure forces and the follow-on combat support forces. A CRG presents tiered forces, right-sized to meet operational requirements. Given that the CRG may be providing the initial deployment location leadership and be responsible for establishing preliminary operations tempo until arrival of the designated regional combatant commander or other designated sustainment force leadership, the CRG includes a senior field grade officer (O-6) to assume this critical role.[18]

As ground-operations elements that can rapidly open air bases under a variety of conditions for a variety of missions, CRGs streamline USAF's ability to deploy quickly and effectively. When North Africa erupted with uprisings in early 2011, for example, with the concomitant humanitarian crises as refugees fled Tunisia, Egypt, and Libya, the Air Force's 435th CRG's Air Mobility Squadron quickly set up the ground requirements to support and project humanitarian airlift missions into the affected areas.[19] With their small footprints, ability to function at low to medium threat levels, and preparedness for rapid, short-duration missions, these units are uniquely capable for a subset of stability operations: humanitarian assistance, noncombatant evacuation operations, and global strike missions.[20] They are not, however, particularly useful for the less conventional, longer-term stability operations such as COIN and nation building.

In terms of specific skills, USAF has increased its contingent of Battlefield Airmen, who deploy alongside ground forces. These elite specialists are always in high demand for, among other things, their ability to direct close air support from the ground (important in many stability operations and used extensively in the Afghanistan and Iraq wars).[21] They can conduct surveillance, direct strikes, mark airdrops, provide air traffic control, survey airfields, forecast the weather, conduct personnel recovery, and provide trauma care.[22] USAF has traditionally had difficulty recruiting and retaining Battlefield Airmen because of the rigor of the training requirements, as well as the tendency of men interested in such roles to enlist in the Marine Corps or the Army. Adding more Battlefield Airmen gives the Air Force more capabilities on the ground, allowing Air Force personnel to participate more effectively in stability operations.

For its part, the Navy has taken a number of steps to prepare for stability operations and, in particular, for the least conventional of them. In 2005, the Navy established the Navy Expeditionary Combat Command (NECC) as a warehouse for the various naval organizations it had in place and was planning for stability operations. Although the NECC forces represent only a small portion of the total naval force, they have already been in high demand. They are scalable, flexible, and adaptive, in keeping with the changes made by the Army and USAF. In addition to the Navy's special operations forces, the SEALs (Sea-Air-Land operators), the service has three active-component riverine (brown water) squadrons and, in 2011, proposed a fourth reserve riverine training unit.[23] The riverine squadrons, newly introduced after being scrapped after the Vietnam War, are responsible for maritime security on inland waterways, including denying the use of rivers and other interior channels as safe havens for insurgents, transportation routes for illicit goods or activities, or sites for attacks. NECC also has the maritime expeditionary security force, or MESF, a green-water hybrid created in 2007 by merging the mobile security squadrons and coastal warfare squadrons. The MESF's primary responsibility is force protection, a critical activity across the spectrum of conflict; the units are rapidly deployable, task organized, and sustainable. They can also undertake detention operations and law enforcement. Additionally, NECC's expeditionary training teams provide security assistance training in support of shaping the environment and establishing constructive military-to-military relations with foreign personnel. Also under NECC's command are explosive ordinance disposal (EOD) groups and active and reserve Seabee (naval engineers) battalions. The Global Fleet Stations, like the Africa Partnership Station, host information exchanges and training programs, and a new maritime Civil Affairs Group is intended to "provide civil-military operations capabilities in coastal and riverine environments . . . [in order to] augment but not duplicate existing civil affairs capabilities in the Army and Marine Corps."[24]

The establishment and growth of the NECC reflect the Navy's nascent commitment to contributing effectively to joint and combined stability operations. The change should not be exaggerated: approximately 8 percent (40,000) of the Navy's total military personnel operate out of the NECC at any given time. There is, currently, no career path in expeditionary tasks, and sailors usually train for expeditionary missions, deploy, and then return to the conventional force, as will be discussed in more detail later in the chapter. Nonetheless, the reintroduction of riverine units, the standing up of civil affairs units, and the growth of the MESF represent a shift from an almost entirely blue-water force to capabilities in green and brown water and indicate the Navy's responsiveness to DODD 3000.05.

For their part, the Marines were organized for flexible, responsive, scalable, and adaptive deployments well before the other services; their Marine Air-Ground Task Force (MAGTF) structure, based on integrated amphibious units, was established early in the last decade of the Cold War. MAGTFs come in three sizes, Marine Expeditionary Units (MEUs),

Marine Expeditionary Brigades (MEBs), and Marine Expeditionary Forces (MEFs), and have shown their utility time and again in stability operations deployments.[25] Nonetheless, the Marine Corps considers the security environment changed enough that it has identified several areas in which MAGTFs can be improved for conducting the full range of military missions, with special emphasis on enhanced sustainability and self-sufficiency without related losses of mobility.[26]

Finally, in light of the natural complementarity of stability operations and special operations forces, one would expect the relative numbers of special operators to have grown with the greater emphasis on this mission. And, in fact, even before the 2011 QDR directed increases in the SOF force structure, the numbers of SOF had expanded tremendously over the foregoing decade. Since 9/11, SOF manpower nearly doubled, and their budget nearly tripled.[27] Such growth pales in light of the insatiable demand for SOF, however, especially in Afghanistan. Even with twice as many SOF and three times the budget, with four times as many deployments, special operators have been spread thin.[28] Admiral Eric Olson, commander of the U.S. Special Operations Command (USSOCOM), speaking at the twenty-second annual Special Operations and Low-Intensity Conflict Symposium, said that SOF were "fraying around the edges":

> We grew a battalion in the 5th Special Forces Group in 2008, and it's deployed. We grew a battalion in 3rd Special Forces Group in 2009, and it's deployed. We grew a battalion in the 10th Special Forces Group, and it is preparing to deploy. Over the next two years, we'll grow battalions in 1st Group and 7th Group. We've been able to deploy 36 additional ODAs [operational detachment As, or A-teams]. And frankly, if you're on a 1-to-1 deployment ratio, which is the very most that you can sustain . . . as you grow 36 ODAs, you should deploy no more than 18. But the demand has gone up close to 50 in that time.[29]

SOF growth has taken place across all the service special operations commands. One interesting example is the Air Force Special Operations Command (AFSOC) expansion of the Sixth Special Operations Squadron for foreign internal defense and security assistance. The Sixth SOS is a combat aviation unit that advises, trains, and assists host nation air forces. The squadron was reactivated in 1994, at the height of post–Cold War peace operations, so that USAF could provide geographical commanders with advisory assistance across the full spectrum of conflict. Personnel are uniquely capable for the least conventional stability operations: they are language proficient, regionally knowledgeable, culturally aware, and politically savvy.[30] The history of the Sixth SOS is illustrative of the military's mixed feelings about stability operations. It was first an air commando unit in World War II, then deactivated. In the 1960s, it was reconstituted to provide capability for COIN and UW. Very active in Vietnam, the unit was briefly deactivated in 1969, only to be reactivated months later as a SOF training unit. In 1974, it was deactivated again. It would be another twenty years before the unit would come back to life, this time to conduct FID. Today, the squadron is expanding concomitant with demand.[31]

In addition to growing SOF, there have been significant changes to USSOCOM itself, which was tasked in 2004 with the responsibility for synchronizing and, when directed, conducting DOD's global counterterrorism operations. This was in addition to its established responsibility to organize, train, and equip SOF to support geographic combatant commanders and American ambassadors.[32] In 2006, reserve Civil Affairs and PSYOP (now MISO) units were transferred from USASOC to the Army to prepare them better to work with their conventional counterparts. Active CA and MISO units remained with Army Special Operations Command (USASOC) within USSOCOM. In 2008, USSOCOM was given proponency over security force assistance (SFA); it also became DOD's lead agency for countering threat financing.[33]

There have also been changes to the balance and structure of SOF forces. The 2006 QDR called for not only an increase in total SOF personnel but more specifically a 33 percent increase in PSYOP (MISO) and Civil Affairs units. It also directed the creation of a Marines Special Operations Command (MARSOC), higher SEAL team force levels, an SOF unmanned vehicle squadron, and an enhanced capability to insert and extract SOF forces into denied areas over strategic distances.[34] Progress on these goals was rapid. MARSOC celebrated its fifth birthday in February 2011. SEAL team force levels were slated to increase by 20 percent by 2012, although there have been some problems recruiting adequate numbers of SEAL candidates.[35] AFSOC added a dedicated special operations Predator squadron, as called for, and, meanwhile, the Army, Navy, and Marine Corps SOF are all using additional unmanned aerial vehicles (Marines are using hand-held drones; USASOC is preparing for two companies' worth of Gray Eagle unmanned aircraft, which they intend to deploy as platoons;[36] and the Navy is commissioning a new group just to focus on unmanned systems, including drones, robots, and underwater mechanisms).[37] Insertion and extraction capabilities are being improved, as demonstrated to tremendous effect by Operation Geronimo in 2011, when SEALs were able to fly stealth helicopters from Afghanistan into and then out of Osama bin Laden's compound in Pakistan, through a city bristling with Pakistani military. The specific systems SOF are putting in place are discussed below.

This brief overview demonstrates that some significant changes in force structure are being made in the U.S. military consistent with the requirements of stability operations. The Army's reorganization into a modular force is, itself, an enormous change, as is the augmentation of the Navy's green- and brown-water capabilities. The rapid growth of SOF across all the services and the expansion of USSOCOM's proponency to include SFA and counterterrorism are also indicators of a new set of military priorities. That said, changes are being made less as a response to changes in doctrine and big-picture priorities and more as a response to the immediate exigencies of ongoing wars. Even BCTs are basically combat oriented, so the Army and other services have tended to rely on ad hoc units like PRTs and MTTs to help meet the development needs of stability operations. The Air Force's adaptations for stability operations are intended to alleviate the negative effects of frequent deployments on airmen but do not maximize the service's potential for stability operations. SOF, meanwhile, are expanding force structure in response to demand generated in Iraq and, more substantially, in Afghanistan. In 2010, 86 percent of deployed SOF were in Afghanistan or its environs.[38] When that conflict eventually comes to an end, what will be done with the built-up SOF capability? Will stability operations be able to absorb the large SOF force being developed to meet current demand?

The changes in force structure taking place not only reflect current operational demands but are institutionally sound, given both interagency and interservice rivalries for resources and manpower under new conditions created by the emphasis on stability operations. Now the military must demonstrate its utility relative to civilian agencies, even as each service continues to tout its utility relative to the others. Growing force structure to guarantee flexibility, expeditionary capacity, and sustainability makes sense in the context of increased competition with civilians, as does extension of the military's capabilities for missions such as nation building, security assistance, and foreign internal defense. At the same time, each service will be staking out its own territory in stability operations, and jostling will inevitably be involved. The Navy's expansion into green- and, especially, brown-water missions, for example, is perceived as a threat and encroachment by some Marines and the service's supporters, who argue that the Navy is simply leveraging current operational requirements to expand its purview. In fact, the Marine Corps is also feeling pinched by the Army, with some Marines questioning its decision to sacrifice "big-army" capability to do instead what the Marines always have done.[39] Of course, as is the case with SOF, the Marine Corps is simply too small to meet the growing demands of stability operations, creating room for the other services to begin to adopt some traditional USMC responsibilities. And the Air Force has been lobbying hard, since the ascension of OOTW in the 1990s, to demonstrate its utility in stability operations.

In terms of organization, the structure set in place by Goldwater-Nichols—geographic combatant commands and a special operations command all supplied with forces trained and equipped by the military departments—is readily adaptable to the requirements of stability operations. As will be discussed in greater detail in chapter 5, both the newest command, Africa Command (AFRICOM), and Southern Command (SOUTHCOM) are organized specifically for conflict prevention via security assistance, military-to-military interactions, and other peacetime stability operations. The other combatant commands have also begun to adjust to accommodate the needs of stability operations. As reported to Congress in 2007, Northern Command is focusing increasingly on interagency coordination, for example, and European Command has a Stability Plans Branch within its Strategy, Policy, and Assessments Directorate.[40]

The services have also reorganized to be better able to deliver for stability operations. In 2006, for example, the Army established the Stability, Security, Transition, and Reconstruction Division (SSTR) in Headquarters G3/5/7, with responsibility for making sure stability operations are rationally integrated Army-wide.[41] The Marines created a similar SSTR section within their own headquarters, and the Air Force restructured its component headquarters within combatant commands to facilitate stability operations.[42] The Navy designated the deputy chief of naval operations to be the lead officer for SSTR as a prelude to the creation of the NECC.

The departments created additional institutions to support stability operations. The Army's Peacekeeping and Stability Operations Institute (PKSOI) at Carlisle Barracks, for instance, is charged with writing and contributing to doctrine and concept development, providing subject matter expertise, and is involved in the after-action review process. At the Army's Combined Arms Center, the Counterinsurgency Center, established as a joint Army/Marine Corps enterprise in 2006, provides analysis, research, and guidance on all issues related to COIN.[43] The Marine Corps' Center for Irregular Warfare's mission is very much the same (it provides subject matter expertise by researching best practices, coordinating and supporting integration of irregular warfare tenets into training and education, and conducting outreach with similarly oriented military and civilian entities). The Marines also have the USMC Center for Advanced Operational Culture Learning (CAOCL). The Air Force's Coalition Irregular Warfare Center of Excellence (CIWC) works with partner nations to improve all participants' air power capacity and coordination for stability operations. The Navy's Center for Irregular Warfare and Armed Groups (CIWAG) at the Naval War College also serves as a home for stability operations research, conferences, and contributions to training and education. There was also a Joint Irregular Warfare Center (JIW) at the Joint Warfare Command (JFCOM), but with JFCOM's closure, JIW is being drawn down. Each of these organizations is a means by which to develop and assemble experts, leverage experience, collect data and lessons learned, and conduct and disseminate analysis. They represent, in a fundamental way, the services' commitment to establishing a knowledge base for stability operations; they are comprehensive warehouses of information that help ensure that there is a learning curve in this realm of activities.

In sum, the changes in force structure are, for the most part, rational and cautious steps that allow for more efficient deployments across the spectrum of conflict. They are inadequate for the current wars (hence the requirement for PRTs, MTTs, and other ad hoc units), but they are vast improvements over the costly efforts to use the Cold War force structure in the peacekeeping operations of the 1990s. If, as progressives anticipate, the current OPTEMPO is maintained even after the wars in Iraq and Afghanistan end, the adjustments to force structure can be expanded upon. If, on the other hand, the United States scales back its involvement overseas and refocuses on big-war defense and deterrence, most of the changes will still work (the Air Force and Army building block structure, for example), though some may have to be reversed (the enormous SOF force and, perhaps, the Navy's extension into green- and brown-water environments). As of yet, no changes have been made that seriously reduce the military's capacity for its traditional missions. Although the armed forces' flexibility for multiple, smaller deployments has been enhanced, the capacity to undertake effectively the least conventional stability operations has not yet been formalized nor fully established.

TRAINING AND EDUCATION

The same kinds of cost-benefit calculations that lead to caution in changing force structure apply to training and education as well. Immediate needs are being balanced against future requirements, in an effort to maximize the force's ability to achieve both. Training and education both have inherent opportunity costs, though it is easier to adjust and modify training in the short and medium term than it is to revamp curricula or reeducate officers.

Troops learning battlefield techniques will need to be trained down for peacekeeping or for COIN, troops currently learning Arabic are foregoing learning Chinese, and troops going through the NTC when it is set up for stability operations are not experiencing the kind of battlefield exercises other units have gone through at the facility. Ultimately, whatever is being covered in exercises, the training grounds, or the schoolhouse represents a world of other topics and skills not being addressed. And there is an inevitable lag between identifying requirements and producing personnel prepared for them.

The necessity for tradeoffs was acknowledged in 2008's Army FM 7-0, *Training for Full Spectrum Operations*. In that manual, commanders developing training plans were directed to have a dialogue about, among other things, "the proportion of effort to be allocated among offensive, defensive, stability, and civil support tasks" and "the risks to readiness."[44] The doctrine further cautioned that "Army units must have the capability to train on stability tasks, such as 'Providing essential services' and 'Support to economic and infrastructure development,' while sustaining proficiency in offensive and defensive operations."[45] Three years later, in the Army's revised FM 7-0, *Training Units and Developing Leaders for Full Spectrum Operations* (2011), the Army's solution to this challenge appears to have become training and educating the troops for adaptability and independent decision making. Gone from the manual are discussions of opportunity costs and the potential for reduced readiness; in their place are affirmations of troops' flexibility and decisiveness. Consider the following, for example:

> The Army today must become far more flexible, built around units at every echelon with the training, competence, and ability to apply lethal and non-lethal combat power against a wide range of threats in complex situations. . . . Through training, Soldiers learn to act decisively while accepting prudent risks. Training assists Soldiers and leaders in developing mutual trust through a shared understanding of the unit's strengths and weaknesses. Training also reinforces the need for Soldiers and leaders to collaborate and dialog in order to achieve a greater understanding of the operational environment.[46]

Indeed, this appears to be DOD's solution to the tradeoffs question more broadly. In a 2010 speech, Undersecretary of Defense for Policy Michelle Flournoy stated: "Future conflicts and threats may take many shapes. Yet we can't prepare simultaneously and fully for every possible contingency—so we need to focus on flexibility and agility, on creating a force that is prepared for the most likely threats, and can adapt quickly to the unpredictable."[47]

Yet, no matter how adaptable the force is, no matter how much troops are trained in how to think rather than merely how to do, there is no way around the fact that big wars need big armies and that many stability operations—from training host nations' forces to supporting counterinsurgencies—are best undertaken by special operations forces (and, in fact, civilians). The tradeoff is obvious from the outset: as it has always done with regard to stability operations, the military will do its best, using conventional troops while maintaining its capabilities for offense and defense.

It is not that the requirements for stability operations are a mystery; it is that a military cannot be all things at all times. The Canadians have long known how to do stability operations: more than 125,000 Canadians have served as peacekeepers (they have trained and deployed more peacekeepers than any other country) since 1956;[48] they have been training military personnel in Africa, promoting stability and developing military-to-military relations on that continent, since the 1960s;[49] and they pride themselves on understanding the requirements for effective stability operations.[50] But Americans very deliberately have not pursued the Canadian approach, with the belief that doing so inevitably reduces readiness for war.[51] The American tradeoff has long been to give up readiness for stability operations while emphasizing offensive and defensive capabilities. The argument was that readiness for war translated into being mostly ready for stability operations; readiness for stability operations did not, however, translate into preparedness for warfighting.

The demands of post–Cold War peacekeeping operations, however, and concerns about the effects of such deployments on primary mission preparedness as well as concerns about effectiveness in such operations drove U.S. military and civilian analysts to begin to consider the training requirements for the least conventional stability operations. Howard Olsen and

John Davis, for example, made recommendations for training based on lessons learned in Bosnia,[52] and reams of other work on the subject were turned out in this period.[53] More recently, Leigh Caraher focused not on specific skills but on the preferred traits of a soldier engaging in stability operations, which traits included not only decision-making skills but also civil-military experience and an interest in history, culture, and politics.[54] Derek Reveron's list of important capabilities for effective security assistance is applicable to the most challenging stability operations: good intercultural skills, the ability to work with the interagency, ability to identify the needs of the host nation, regional experience, and language competency.[55] Hans Binnendijk and Stuart E. Johnson offer a similar rundown with specific reference to stabilization and reconstruction efforts.[56]

None of this is new. The requirements for effective stability operations are and have been known, even within the U.S. military. As mentioned in chapter 1, the Americans' CORDS program in Vietnam already had most of these elements fifty years ago:

> Prior to arriving in Saigon [CORDS Foreign Service Officers] attended a six-week course at the Foreign Service Institute's Vietnam training center. Each class received lectures on the history and economy of Vietnam, and the culture of the region. They learned some rudimentary Vietnamese, and talented linguists were singled out for further language instruction. Instructors also led classes on insurgency and guerrilla warfare that drew on the experience in Vietnam and other counterinsurgency campaigns, including the Hukbalahap Rebellion, a Communist guerrilla movement in the Philippines that was put down in the early 1950s with U.S. assistance. Finally, [they] received a week's training at Fort Gordon, Georgia.[57]

In fact, the question today is not whether or not the military understands what is required in terms of training and education but to what extent the services are willing to use the limited training and education opportunities they have to inculcate these particular skills in their fighting forces. The services' response appears to be intensified predeployment training to meet the specific requirements of the ongoing contingencies and some adjustments to lifelong learning, including greater emphasis on preparing troops for the requirements of joint and interagency operations. Among the changes to training and education are the reconfiguration of the joint training grounds to meet the needs of troops deploying to Iraq and Afghanistan; greater support and incentives for language training; and the collection and rapid translation into learning materials of the lessons learned about nation building, COIN, and stability operations more generally in Iraq and Afghanistan.

As early as 2007, the Department of Defense provided Congress with the following rundown of adjustments to training and education that were taking place in support of stability operations (per the requirements of DODD 3000.05):

- In 2006, the Chairman of the Joint Chiefs of Staff added stability operations to the CJCS Special Area of Emphasis List.
- "Every Air Force developmental education program and course from the Air and Space Basic Course through Senior Leader Development has added material addressing stability operations replacing some of the coverage of more traditional Air Force missions."
- The Naval Post-Graduate School and Naval War College added some courses and held some conferences related to stability operations.
- "The Marine Corps has undertaken to revise all individual, unit, and school programs of instruction to incorporate cultural awareness, language skills, and SSTR skills."
- "The Army integrates stability operations topics into leader education curricula as well as initial military training. Army Intermediate Level Education (ILE), for officers with 8 to 10 years of service, has reoriented from large-scale kinetic operations to full spectrum joint, interagency, multi-national operations that stress the culture and religious aspects of the operating environment."
- "The U.S. Army Peacekeeping and Stability Operations Institute in conjunction with the Dwight D. Eisenhower National Security Series, conducts workshops and conferences that support SSTR education and training. These events bring together the media, corporate and economic

policy representatives, academia and think tanks, all departments of the U.S. Government, nongovernmental and international organizations, the diplomatic community, members of Congress and their staffs, foreign officials and 16 specialists."

- "The Deputy Secretary of Defense's Strategic Plan for Transforming DoD Training identified SSTR training as a key task and directed additional emphasis in joint exercises at all levels. The Chairman of the Joint Chiefs of Staff exercise program has begun to re-orient training from primarily combat operations to a more balanced mix of full spectrum operations that includes stability operations."

- Additional language programs and cultural training.[58]

Even the Air Force, arguably the service least affected by a shift toward stability operations, has made some substantive adjustments:

The Air Force is changing the way it trains and educates Airmen. From basic military training and professional military education (PME) to large-scale exercises, the USAF is adapting to the demands of stability operations. New recruits now enter a longer basic military training course that includes the self-defense and small arms training needed to operate on a battlefield with fewer secure rear areas. A new Basic Combat Convoy Course [BC.sup.3] at Camp Bullis, Texas, prepares Airmen for *in lieu of* convoy duties in Iraq. For other selected career fields, the USAF is expanding common Battlefield Airmen training to better hone skill sets for both combat and stability operations, including counterinsurgency and CAS in an urban environment.[59]

These kinds of changes to training and education in each of the services are intended to address several things. First, stability operations may be simultaneous with offense and defense, but they require different skill sets and, perhaps more importantly, different mindsets. Second, stability operations require close interaction with locals—civilian and military—with the concomitant demand for language and cultural skills. Third, stability operations are usually combined, joint, interagency efforts that depend on systematic coordination and communication with civilian governmental and nongovernmental actors. And fourth, stability operations often require military personnel to undertake tasks and missions that would more ideally fall to civilian development experts and diplomats. The changes DOD enumerated before Congress in 2007 begin to address the need for simultaneity, a new mindset, familiarity with civilian environments, and interagency demands. There are practical constraints, however, on how fundamentally each of these challenges can be addressed through training and education.

Preparing troops to work with and among local civilians is perhaps the simplest training requirement on the list. Today, training exercises include many—sometimes hundreds—of host nation civilian "actors" and have been refined down to the most minute details in order to prepare forces for deployments abroad. Marine Corps advisor teams, for example, get intense training that includes "immersive rehearsal of common advisor situations supported by up to 800 host-nation role players" as well as training in rapport building, COIN, detainee handling, and the "whole of government" approach.[60] The joint exercises at the National Training Center (NTC) at Fort Irwin, California, are equally realistic.

> "I'm really pleased with what I'm seeing out here at NTC," said Command Sgt. Maj. Rick Megoloff, senior enlisted advisor for the Arkansas National Guard's 39th Infantry Brigade Combat Team. "The realism is outstanding. You have the civilians on the battlefield. You have the ability to use your interpreters. You have the ability to use all the systems our soldiers are using in Afghanistan. From that aspect you can't get any better when it comes to that."[61]

Of course, the presence of role players does not address the problems of different languages and cultures, but it does provide U.S. military personnel with a sense of what those problems will mean for them on a daily basis.

Interagency coordination, on the other hand, can be improved at the margins through military training and education, but the fundamental cultural and organizational obstacles between civilians and the military are more difficult to resolve. The year before the publication of DODD 3000.05, the U.S. Army Peacekeeping and Stability Operations Institute (PKSOI) held a symposium at Carlisle Barracks to bring together key stakeholders in stability operations. The report that emerged from that conference offered a broad, optimistic description of attention to training and education:

> The Department of Defense recognizes the importance of stability operations and is taking major steps to educate and train its personnel on all aspects of stabilization and reconstruction. These efforts include the addition of stability operations themes and actors at the combat training centers, mandatory and elective stability operations education at all levels of military education, and the refocusing of both operational and training doctrine to include a significant stability and reconstruction emphasis.[62]

What the report nonetheless highlighted, however, was where one of the most significant sticking points is in efforts to train and educate the force: the ongoing tensions between civilians—governmental and nongovernmental, host nation and American—and the military. From the lack of a shared vocabulary to concerns about NGOs' association with the armed forces in regions where humanitarian organizations' neutrality[63] is considered the base requirement for access to affected civilian populations, the concerns raised at the conference mirrored those that had been identified a decade earlier in the peace operations of the immediate post–Cold War period. The symposium's recommendations to include civilians in military training and exercises were also familiar and indicative of how little progress had been made in this regard. The implications for stability operations— and more specifically for civil-military operations—were clear. For missions (COIN, nation building, peacetime shaping of the environment, etc.) in which cooperation between civilian entities and military forces is crucial, the foundation was not yet laid. As a 2004 CSIS report explained: "Education that does not equip personnel to operate in a world of multinational and interagency operations . . . does not provide a useful service to its students or the nation."[64]

Some positive steps have been taken in this regard, at least in terms of developing common concepts for operations and cooperation:

A number of bottom-up efforts, including the recently published Army field manual for *Stability Operations* (FM 3-07), the State Department-sponsored *Counterinsurgency Handbook for Policy Makers*, and the United States Institute of Peace *Guiding Principles for Peace Operations* reflect good processes for developing more formal interagency whole of government frameworks. All were developed through rigorous inter-agency (and in some cases international) collaboration at the working level. These efforts, which have succeeded through the initiative of mid-level leadership among a network of practitioners, provide model processes for developing whole of government, versus agency-specific, perspectives.[65]

In terms of professional military education (PME), in their research in 2010 the House of Representatives' Committee on Armed Services' Sub-committee on Oversight and Investigations found that PME subject matter has adapted admirably to the elevation of stability operations to a primary mission. Their report noted: "PME curricula have adapted at differing, but generally appropriate, levels to new demands for instruction in language and culture; irregular warfare; and joint, interagency, intergovernmental, and multinational operations."[66]

Joint PME (JPME) has come to the fore over the past two decades; whereas JPME had once only been available in three joint schools, now all of the services' war colleges include it in their curricula. Interagency aspects of strategy are also being addressed. The National War College (NWC) pays particular attention to both of these:

The National War College's special focus on national security strategy, its highly developed curriculum, deep joint traditions, and interagency character set it apart. Over a quarter of the student body comes from the Departments of State, Homeland Security, and Treasury, the U.S. Agency for International Development, Federal Bureau of Investigation, and the Intelligence Community; the faculty reflects a joint, interagency, and academic mix. There is also a large representation of international military fellows.[67]

But even the process of bringing the stakeholders together in a systematic and comprehensive way remains difficult. The problems that plague civilians and military personnel at the tactical level can also reduce their ability to work together to develop cooperative training and education at the strategic and operational levels. These problems were as evident following the Gulf of Mexico crude oil spill in 2010 as they have been in establishing cooperation and communication for stability operations. The problem is ingrained enough that legislation was proposed in 2010 seeking the creation of an "Interagency Cooperation Commission" that could help ameliorate the challenges of coordination.[68] In the same year, the Command and General Staff College at Fort Leavenworth created the Col. Arthur D. Simons Center for the Study of Interagency Cooperation. An article in that center's inaugural journal publication explained:

> the problems inherent in the interagency process are not confined to just the policy coordination process, which the NSC facilitates quite well. The problem is the operational implementation of that policy. . . . There is no operational level executive agent or process to pull together the various elements of national power—diplomatic, intelligence, military, and economic. Further, even when an executive agency seems the likely and practical candidate as the lead agency, such as the State Department for stabilization and reconstruction efforts in pre or post conflict settings or the Department of Defense in conducting governance operations during low to medium conflict settings, it often lacks the capacity to effect proper execution of the policy.[69]

There is an additional and arguably more serious challenge for training and education with regard to civilians: inculcating the military with a more realistic understanding of what civilians can bring to the table in stability operations and, further, preparing for the eventuality that civilian development experts and diplomats will not be available or able to undertake the tasks and missions the military expects of them. In postconflict stabilization and reconstruction efforts, the armed forces have been repeatedly surprised and frustrated by civilian agencies' inability to contribute, but such disappointment is in large part rooted in the military's unrealistic perception of civilian agencies' capacity and objectives. Military leaders understand that for these operations, as well as for COIN, foreign internal defense, and other complex, unconventional stability operations, political and economic solutions must accompany military efforts, but they often expect more, along these lines, from U.S. civilian agencies than those organizations have been designed, equipped, or manned to undertake. The military thus builds into its operations expectations for civilian support and then must assume responsibility itself for those missions when civilians cannot contribute, whether because of nonpermissive security environments or because they simply are not available.

As long the military continues to undertake such operations, it will have to prepare to assume responsibility for many of the missions it has thus far expected civilians to take on. Yet these tend to fall far outside the military's customary purview. Because of this, Derek Reveron and Kathleen Mahoney-Norris explain, when describing the requirements of professional military education, that preparation cannot be limited to familiarization with other interagency entities: "Rather, [it] requires military officers to embrace their expanded roles in the geopolitical space as they increasingly serve as important political actors, fulfilling development, diplomatic, and educational roles."[70] It is in reference to these kinds of skills that the 2006 Army–Marine Corps COIN doctrine cautioned that "Soldiers and Marines are expected to be nation builders as well as warriors. They must be prepared to help reestablish institutions and local security forces and assist in rebuilding infrastructure and basic services."[71]

What do troops need in order to fulfill these broader responsibilities? At the very least, they need language skills and a sense of the local political structures, culture, and economic systems. RAND did a study in 2007 on Stryker brigades in Iraq, for example, in which the analysts found several areas of potential improvement in terms of stability operations training. The first was demand for language and cultural preparation: "SBCT soldiers frequently requested additional linguists (linguists who both spoke and wrote Arabic fluently and could be fully trusted were in short supply), even to provide simple open-source intelligence functions such as reading Iraqi media. There were also requests for more language and cultural training."[72]

PME efforts like those of the Marine Corps, which focus on promoting "cultural awareness and effective interaction with local populations and forces,"[73] are intended to help provide some of this, and all of the services have included cultural preparation in their revised training and education.[74] Oliver Fritz and Gregory Hermsmeyer laid out in some detail the Air Force's improvements in training in this regard:

> The Air Force is also expanding the language and cultural training Airmen need to succeed in a fluid, complex environment. In February 2006, General Michael Moseley, Air Force Chief of Staff, announced that Airmen would receive expanded language training. While the language requirement is still being developed, the initial program, already in place at the Air Command and Staff College, will stress cultural awareness and introductory language skills. . . . A broader PME program will eventually include basic language proficiency for new officers, a supplementary track for already serving officers, and similar courses at the Senior Noncommissioned Officer Academy. . . . Officers with requisite language and cultural skills will now be tracked as international affairs specialists and deliberately assigned to diffuse this expertise across a broad spectrum of billets and to enhance USAF effectiveness in population-focused operations.[75]

The Army is taking this equally seriously, as evidenced by the establishment of the Culture Center within the Army's Training and Doctrine Command. The center offers training materials and mobile training teams to prepare deploying units to operate successfully among foreign populations.[76] More generally, the military has plans for cadres of language-capable, culturally knowledgeable experts prepared for key strategic regions, even as hopes for improvements in the general-purpose forces' capabilities continue.[77] All of these steps are valuable, but none are adequate to meet the requirements of stability operations. Language skills and cultural knowledge take years of focused study to develop; it is important to inculcate troops with greater sensitivity and some language abilities, but fluency and cultural familiarity cannot be provided in predeployment training courses, and only a small portion of the total U.S. armed forces will ever spend time in intensive language programs for any given language.[78] Even specialists whose fields depend on language skills—notably military intelligence, civil affairs, special forces, and military information support operators—often have difficulty balancing the requirements of language proficiency with their other training demands.[79] Having cadres of language specialists can help, but even that cannot guarantee the right mix of language capabilities in adequate numbers for any given contingency.

As challenging as it is to ensure adequate language and cultural skills, the challenges of becoming a force of nation builders with the capacity to identify development and diplomacy requirements are even more daunting. Civil affairs clearly play a role; new organizations such as PRTs, which leverage civilians' knowledge and experience, can be incredibly valuable. Some argue that, despite the inherent difficulties involved, the regular military forces can (and must) take a lead in promoting economic growth and expansion in conflict-torn countries. Carl Schramm, for example, asserted in a *Foreign Affairs* article that the military is in fact in the best position to do this. He wrote:

> The U.S. military is well placed to play a leading role in bringing economic growth to devastated countries. It may have little resident economic expertise, but it has both an active presence and an active interest in places where economic growth is sorely needed. The U.S. armed forces usually are the most formidable and best-resourced entity in the troubled countries in which they operate; indeed, the Defense Department today controls one-fifth of U.S. foreign aid. In many cases, the U.S. military effectively serves as the legs of the other government agencies and of the NGOs offering assistance.[80]

Others, however, are less sanguine about the military's potential as an institution for economic development. Ann Marlowe, a participant in a panel with Schramm and Michael Meese of West Point, argued that the military should not take on economic development as yet another responsibility and should instead leave it to the experts. She observed that, no matter how brilliant he is, a "24-year-old recent West Point graduate is not going to be able to rewrite the tax code of whatever country we find ourselves in next."[81] Others point out that the military's objectives are fundamentally military and that any economic programming—or diplomacy, for that matter—that the military undertakes will be in the interests of achieving a military outcome. They also point out that military officers will more likely have a short-term rather than a long-term approach to economic development, a problem exacerbated by the tools (and funding options, like the Commander's Emergency Response Program, or CERP) at their disposal. More importantly, there is no clear, unified guidance on what kinds of economic development really must take place as part of stability operations nor how best to implement them, making it that much harder to prepare military personnel. The Center for Strategic and International Studies (CSIS) did a study on conflict-related economic development and found that neither government implementation plans nor military doctrine "contain sufficient detail to guide field actions or training. Conflicting ideas about whether, how, or to what degree to conduct development in a conflict zone further contribute to vague or incomplete doctrine. All of these conditions have an impact on mission success."[82]

Ultimately, the services' general approach to preparing the troops for stability operations—that is, provide them with the immediate tools required for deployments and adjust other training and education incrementally to incorporate some of the more practicable requirements—seems to reflect the realities of a far broader mission but the same amount of time for training and education. The approach accommodates the necessary tradeoffs by building greater flexibility and responsiveness into the force without seriously degrading its capacity for traditional missions. Thus, some troops deployed for stability operations will speak the local language; some will be familiar with the local culture; some will have interagency experience; some will understand and appreciate the interests, needs, costs, and benefits associated with NGOs; and some will be able to teach, train, support, advise, and assist host nation civilians and military personnel. Not every member of every unit will be culturally aware; not every member of every unit will know the language; and not every member of every unit will be an effective trainer. In fact, not every soldier, sailor, airman, or marine being asked to train a foreign counterpart will be asked to do so in his or her MOS. The conventional military cannot guarantee that the right set of capabilities will be embodied in the right individual at the right place and time. The services and DOD are therefore emphasizing independent thinking and decision making, shifting the general mindset to include stability operations as an acceptable mission and cooperation with civilians as an acknowledged and understood requirement and providing some of the most basic tools necessary to get the job done.

PROCUREMENT

Preparing the force includes equipping it. As demonstrated by the terrible lack of body armor and shortage of appropriate vehicles for the IED-pocked roads in the early days of COIN in Iraq, stability operations require different kinds of equipment than do conventional operations. Usually, just as with force structure, training, and education, tradeoffs will be required if the force is to be prepared appropriately for stability operations. Recently, however, the defense budget has merely grown to accommodate new requirements. Since 2001, the Pentagon's base budget has grown by 40 percent in real terms; if the costs of the wars in Iraq and Afghanistan are added in, the budget has grown by a whopping 70 percent in real terms over the same period.[83] Defense Secretary Gates's proposed DOD budget for fiscal year 2010 included $11 billion in increased defense spending; the proposed budget for fiscal year 2011 represented an increase of $18 billion over the $531 billion enacted for the previous year.[84] This has meant that the force can equip and modernize simultaneously for operations across the spectrum of conflict.

That is not to say there has not been a shift in priorities. This became clear when Defense Secretary Gates submitted his department's budget for fiscal year 2010, shaking up the defense establishment in unprecedented ways by challenging plans to acquire some extraordinarily expensive weapons systems—more F-22 Raptors and the Army's Future Combat System, for example—and opting, instead, for far less costly technologies with more utility in stability operations, like the Predator and Reaper drones. Gates did leave the Navy's pricier Littoral Combat Ships in the budget,[85] but that was because they help strengthen the service's ability to provide COIN support. Assessing the budget, the Atlantic Council's Magnus Nordenman wrote: "The focus here is clearly in not only supporting current operations in Iraq and Afghanistan, but also preparing the US military for putting boots on the ground in messy situations in bad parts of the world to fight insurgents and provide stability in the decades to come."[86]

Such a change in direction would likely have been impossible without growth in the defense budget and without the ongoing conflicts in Iraq and Afghanistan. Unlike force structure and training decisions, equipment decisions draw a great deal of attention from legislators. While there is legislative oversight for the other elements of force preparation, there is intense legislative stake in weapons systems, given the jobs they represent in lawmakers' districts. Thus, Gates' FY 2010 budget was received with anger and resistance by many legislators in whose districts and states the big-ticket items slated for cancellation are built. Indeed, though the Senate agreed in a very close vote in 2009 to cancel funding for some F-22s, the decision only eliminated the extra funding for planes that senators had added to the budget the previous month. Moreover, several senators and members of the House vowed to continue to fight for the program, despite Gates's assertions that the planes are not necessary to meet U.S. security requirements and deplete funds that would be better spent on other items.[87]

Undaunted by legislative dismay, Gates continued to refocus defense spending toward stability operations and COIN. For FY 2011, for example, Gates supported the purchase of more fixed-wing aircraft, helicopters, and special operations equipment but remained opposed to the congressionally supported plan to buy more C-17 transport planes and an alternative engine for the F-35 fixed-wing aircraft. He said of these, "I will strongly recommend that the president veto any legislation that sustains the unnecessary continuation of these two programs."[88] Among the items eliminated in Gates's FY 2012 proposed budget were the Marine Corps' Expeditionary Fighting Vehicle

(EFV), the Army's Surface Launched Advanced Medium Range Air-to-Air Missile (SLAMRAAM), and the Marine Corps' jet under the Joint Strike Fighter program (the Short Take Off Vertical Landing—STOVL—aka the F-35B).[89] Part of the decision to cut these systems was a function of anticipated cuts to the defense budget overall, but it also reflected a deliberate reorientation toward stability operations. Thus, as with the 2010 and 2011 Pentagon budget, the 2012 proposal includes more funding for unmanned aerial vehicles (UAVs) and other technologies that have clear utility across the full spectrum of operations.

STABILITY OPERATIONS' EQUIPMENT REQUIREMENTS

There is actually significant overlap between the objectives of the revolution in military affairs and the requirements of stability operations: flexibility, speed, accuracy, information dominance, and lethality all have roles to play even in the least conventional stability operations. The question, however, is how best to leverage technologies to achieve these under different conditions. When many personnel are on the ground, operating in small units, in complex and constantly changing environments, as will be the case in COIN, reconstruction, stabilization, and even some counternarcotics and disaster relief efforts, information dominance will be less a function of satellite intelligence, though that will have a role to play, and more a function of human intelligence. In such operations, accuracy will be more crucial than ever, since collateral damage works so immediately and devastatingly against political objectives. Speed is different, too, in this context: fast jets are less useful than agile helicopters and ground combat vehicles. And flexibility is key. The most valuable technologies for stability operations enhance networking, communications, intelligence, and mobility. They include helicopters, electronic warfare equipment, special operations equipment, fixed-wing tactical aircraft, and mine-resistant ambush-protected (MRAP) armored fighting vehicles. The 2010 QDR listed the kinds of equipment and capabilities needed for operations across the full spectrum:

The first is that U.S. forces would be able to perform their missions more effectively—both in the near-term and against future adversaries—if they had more and better key enabling capabilities at their disposal. These enablers include rotary-wing aircraft, unmanned aircraft systems, intelligence analysis and foreign language expertise, and tactical communications networks for ongoing operations, as well as more robust space-based assets, more effective electronic attack systems, more resilient base infrastructure, and other assets essential for effective operations against future adversaries.[90]

Consistent with this was DOD's harvesting of the Army's Future Combat System after Secretary Gates's decision to discontinue the incredibly ambitious (and well-over-cost) program in 2009. While the system as a whole was canceled, it yielded valuable COIN and stability operations–relevant technologies, such as drones, unattended ground sensors, and small ground robots.[91] The cancellation of the larger program and the concentration of effort on its "spin-out" technologies reflect a conscious shift in priorities.

All of the services and SOF have been improving their capabilities along these lines. SOF technologies received quite a few updates. In his 2010 Posture Statement, USSOCOM Commander Admiral Eric Olson emphasized the importance of SOF mobility, citing several improvements taking place on his watch. These include growing the helicopter fleet by eight MH-47 Chinooks by 2015, fielding upgraded MH-47G and new MH-60M helicopters, expanding the fleet of CV-22 Ospreys from twelve to fifty by 2016, recapitalizing the fleet of C-130s, and procuring additional light and medium aircraft with associated spare and replacement parts.[92] Among those aircraft are the Pilatus PC-12 (aka the U-28A) and the Sikorsky PZL Mielec M28 Skytruck. The advantages for SOF—and stability operations—of such "off-the-shelf" vehicles are clear in terms of the flexibility and accessibility they create:

The U-28A provides intra-theatre support for joint SOF by conducting night vision infiltration, exfiltration, resupply and other taskings. The PC-12 was selected for its ability to operate from short runways and operating costs are about a third less than a comparable multi-engine aircraft. . . . The rugged Skytruck can tactically insert and recover SOF teams and equipment in areas too demanding even for the U-28A.[93]

USAF has also adapted its technologies, especially intelligence and surveillance capabilities, to meet stability operations' requirements. Relevant upgrades include the Remotely Operated Video Enhanced Receiver (ROVER), which sends images to ground forces outfitted with receivers and wi-fi transmitters, providing eyes in the sky to units as small as platoons and squads. These can even help identify where IEDs have been emplaced.[94] USAF capabilities are crucial for postdisaster surveillance as well as for airdropping humanitarian assistance.

One of the Army's foci is the Ground Combat Vehicle (GCV), which should give soldiers "the tactical mobility of a Bradley, the operational mobility of a Stryker, and the protection of an MRAP."[95] The other emphasis has been on network technologies: the Warfighter Information Network (Tactical), or WIN-T. These two elements, combined with the spin-out technologies of the canceled FCS, are bundled into "capability packages" intended to streamline the provision of the right technology to the right forces at the right time. The service has also bought or upgraded helicopters key to operations in Iraq and Afghanistan, including the UH-60 Blackhawk, the CH-47 Chinook, and the AH-64 Apache.

The Marine Corps's modernization efforts are focused on finding technological means by which to reduce an individual Marine's weight while retaining adequate protection; improving weapons systems for more accurate fire support, to help prevent collateral damage; updating the service's air capabilities, including the continued addition of Ospreys to the fleet; and improved network technologies. Secretary Gates canceled the two most substantial of USMC's intended upgrades, however: the EFV and the STOVL. The first was supposed to give the service critical capabilities across the range of possible operational scenarios; the latter was intended to replace existing fixed-wing aircraft.[96]

Finally, the Navy's stability operations–related efforts revolve around its Littoral Combat Ships and the decision to augment the service's existing Maritime Prepositioning Squadrons with greater sea-basing capabilities in support of a broad range of operations, rather than developing a Maritime Prepositioning Force focused on high-end, forcible-entry operations.[97] The Joint High Speed Vessel (JHSV) is a joint Army-Navy program that provides support for security force assistance and theater security cooperation efforts, key elements of peacetime shaping of the environment. The Navy's amphibious warfare ships "represent the Navy and Marine Corps commitment to an expeditionary Fleet capable of power projection, security force assistance, and theater security cooperation in diverse operating environments."[98] Additional relevant upgrades include a range of information dominance programs, including improved networking and satellite capabilities and the E-2D Advanced Hawkeye aircraft, which are useful for tactical operations and offer both overland and littoral surveillance capabilities.[99]

Overall, in terms of equipping the force, there is a notable (and oft-noted) shift in emphasis toward enhancing capabilities at the lower end of the spectrum, though the preponderance of procurement remains oriented toward conventional combat capabilities. Many observers have taken the trends in equipment purchases to mean that the military as a whole has truly embraced stability operations and a long-term view of the changed security environment. Yet a good deal of the change—arguably the bulk of it—has been driven not by considerations of the future but by immediate needs in Afghanistan and Iraq. MRAPs, body armor, helicopters, ground sensors, drones—all of these have utility in stability operations in general, but they have been developed, purchased, and distributed because of the pressing demands of ongoing COIN and counterterrorism efforts. Moreover, the technological requirements of stability operations tend not to exert too much budgetary pressure; such operations benefit from advances in technology intended for conventional warfare (networking capabilities, intelligence equipment, and so forth), and their specific needs are for much less expensive equipment (ground combat vehicles can be bought by the dozens for the price of a single fighter jet or missile system).[100] Meanwhile, although some higher-profile weapons programs have been canceled, hard decisions about priorities—and the related unavoidable battles with the legislature—have been limited by the defense budget's growth since 2001. Until there is real pressure on the military's budget—and until U.S. troops are out of Iraq and Afghanistan—it will be difficult to determine how serious DOD and the services are with regards to prioritizing future stability operations requirements.

CONCLUSION

Examining recent adjustments to force structure, procurement, and education and training is instructive. It would be tempting to draw conclusions from the fact that, ultimately, not much has changed. The Army's force structure did shift dramatically after repeated deployments in the 1990s demonstrated the inflexibility of the division-based organization, but the modular force is not a direct response to DODD 3000.05. SOF has grown disproportionately, but this is more attributable to the demands of Afghanistan and Iraq than to any doctrinal or perceptual shift. Adjustments to training, too, can be seen as short-term efforts to meet the requirements of COIN and nation-building deployments; turning the NTC into Afghanistan was not reflective of new doctrine but of the need to prepare forces for the treacherous environment into which they were being sent. As for procurement, the defense secretary's rejection of some of the pricier weapons systems can be explained as a preemptive effort to control, in an economic recession, the inevitable demand to scale back military spending after a decade of rapid growth. In other words, one could argue that an overview of military preparation shows not much more than reactions to current events and imperatives and in no way strongly indicates the military's embrace of stability operations in any practical sense.

Yet such an assessment would be mistaken, in that it would fail to take into account the one really significant change that has occurred: the military has, in fact, begun to take stability operations seriously. Training may reflect short-term considerations, but the 2003 establishment of the Army's

Peacekeeping and Stability Operations Institute, the 2007 creation of the Marine Corps' Center for Irregular Warfare, and the founding of the other service research organizations dedicated to stability operations reflects a serious effort to develop in-house expertise, institutional memory, and analytical understanding of the new security environment. Likewise, though the Army's and Air Force's more modular forces may not have been developed with stability operations specifically in mind, the same cannot be said of the Navy's riverine squadrons or of the Air Force's emphasis on expanding the number of Battlefield Airmen. The services' procurement choices may be partially a reflection of current needs, but it is how they are being justified in congressional hearings and in the services' annual posture statements that are most revealing, with references to stability operations' requirements, the changing security environment, and the military's need for flexibility across the full spectrum of operations.

In other words, the U.S. military's embrace of stability operations appears, this time, to be more lasting than ephemeral. It is not merely a response to Iraq and Afghanistan; it is an entirely new perspective on the military's role and missions. After Vietnam, the American armed forces could not abandon COIN and stability operations fast enough; they became *über*-conventional, big war–oriented battle forces. Even the minimal doctrine created to support efforts in Indochina was discarded; the procurement practices during the war were already focused on a postwar conventional military.[101] Today, in contrast, Iraq and Afghanistan are largely seen as precursors to future operations. DOD and the services are revising force preparation to be consistent with this new outlook. This is well represented by a presentation the U.S. Army Combined Arms Center for Training distributed with the publication of FM 7-0, *Training for Full Spectrum Operations*. The presentation included the following directives: "Train as You Will Fight," including developing lethal and nonlethal capabilities; relying on agility and fostering leaders' ability to deal with ambiguity; and "Change the Army Mindset," including an admonition against returning to a strict focus on major combat operations and an emphasis on preparing an expeditionary army with agile leaders for full-spectrum operations.[102]

What explains the remarkable difference between the U.S. military's attitude toward COIN and stability operations after Vietnam and its views on stability operations today? Why have the armed forces so thoroughly embraced this mission, elevating it and formalizing it, building institutions around it, creating new leadership positions to integrate it, training and educating the troops for it, and changing the entire way in which the military sets its priorities? Why is the military's mindset so completely different, regarding stability operations, than it has ever been in the past? This is the question examined in chapter 4.

FOUR
EXPLAINING THE MILITARY'S MISSION REVOLUTION

T he foregoing chapters discuss how DODD 3000.05 represents a dramatic change in the military's raison d'être and show that it has resulted in new doctrine and some considerable adjustments to the U.S. armed forces. This chapter seeks to explain in more detail why this took place. Before addressing that question, it is necessary to concede that some highly qualified observers see the shift as far from revolutionary and, indeed, long in the making. Army Major General David Fastabend, for example, the one-time director of concept development and experimentation at the Army Futures Center at the Army's Training and Doctrine Command, was deeply involved in the formulation, writing, and presentation of the Army's post–Cold War capstone doctrine, FM 3-0. From his standpoint, the embrace of stability operations as a primary mission developed over time, and the DOD directive in 2005 was little more than a post hoc official acknowledgement of what already, in all practical terms, had taken place.[1] This is consistent with the general's view of doctrine as a constant, deliberate process. He wrote, "This view of doctrine as an endless evolution reflects reality rather than an institutional preference."[2] Likewise, U.S. Coast Guard Lieutenant Commander Vasilios Tasikas rejected the characterization of DODD 3000.05 as a drastic change. He wrote that the

> U.S. military has spent the last two decades trying to ignore or curtail the
> reality of lengthy and costly post-conflict operations. This neglect stems
> from a long-standing, but inaccurate, perception of the proper role of the

military as an instrument of national power. . . . The truth is that the United States has always engaged in protracted military endeavors short of full-scale wars.[3]

Yet, though the military has long undertaken stability operations and though its thinking about such missions may be depicted as evolving linearly since the end of the Cold War, such an interpretation does not capture either the real significance or the substance of the change. Although stability operations received increasing doctrinal space and military attention over the post–Cold War period, that does not necessarily equate to evolution. During that period, both civilian policy makers and military leaders struggled with identifying American security interests in the absence of the omnipresent Soviet threat. Concerns about narcotics trafficking rose briefly to the fore but were soon eclipsed by what, at the time, seemed to be a rash of collapsing states: Bosnia, Somalia, Haiti, Kosovo. Peace operations became the foreign policy focus and were foisted on an often unwilling U.S. military, along with new terminology, justifications for the use of force, and debates over rules of engagement and the nexus of political and military instruments. Humanitarian intervention was also briefly toyed with, though the experience in Somalia effectively dampened interest in such operations. Counternarcotics, peace operations, and humanitarian intervention all fall within the broad category of stability operations, but each has different requirements in terms of doctrine, training, force structure, education, and equipping. Indeed, far from presenting a coherent evolution, the post–Cold War period shows American troops being deployed for a range of different kinds of operations under a variety of security assumptions. Moreover, during most of this period, a significant preoccupation was to ensure that each kind of operation could be undertaken without impinging on readiness for major contingencies, that is, conventional warfare. The decision in 2005 to embrace stability operations as a primary mission represented the abandonment of those assumptions, which had underpinned military involvement in such operations for the duration of the U.S. armed forces' existence: that a military prepared for war can undertake such operations on the margins and, more importantly, that it should do so only to the extent that primary mission readiness is not compromised. Elevating to a core responsibility the kinds of operations that had been defined specifically in terms of being "other than war" was a stark transformation, one representing an unprecedented conceptual adjustment[4]—a deliberate change in priorities as well as an expansion of the military's purview beyond deterrence, defense, and offense to include addressing the causes of conflict, which had been more traditionally the realm of civilian development specialists and diplomats.

So what explains this change? Most attribute it to the demands of the post–Cold War—and especially post-9/11—security environment, a direct response to a new breed of threats facing the United States as the result of the end of the superpower competition. The argument, roughly, is that the U.S. military has an unassailable conventional superiority, but its military capabilities are less suited to responding to the chaos unleashed by the collapse of the bipolar balance of power. This is the story that progressives tell. U.S. Army General William S. Wallace coined the now ubiquitous phrase "a complex era of persistent conflict," which is used to justify and explain changes in the U.S. military's focus. Marine General Charles Krulak described the security environment as less the "Son of Desert Storm" and more "the Stepchild of Chechnya."[5] In this new environment, described starkly by Robert Kaplan in his 1994 *Atlantic Magazine* article "The Coming Anarchy"[6] and by Martin van Creveld in his book *The Transformation of War*,[7] some forms of stability operations (counterinsurgency, support for insurgency, counterterrorism, etc.) are "fast becoming the dominant form of war in our age." Van Creveld argues that under such circumstances, "there are solid military reasons why modern regular forces are all but useless."[8] As early as 1991, Robert Pfaltzgraff was stating that "in an unfolding security environment characterized by dramatic change and instability," the "United States will face a continuing need to develop [appropriate] doctrines, technologies, and force structures."[9] Nathan Freier, who has written prolifically on what he calls the "new status quo," explained in one of his books that "DOD will be the nation's most useful, adaptable, and broadly employable national security instrument for the foreseeable future. This shift requires arming defense leaders, strategists, and operators with a different intellectual toolkit than that appropriate to or valued and developed in the pre-9/11 era."[10]

Yet, though shifts in threats—or perceived shifts in threats—certainly have contributed to the military's adjusted attitude with regard to stability operations, they are not sufficient for explaining it. The "systemic level" environmental argument is intuitively appealing but insufficient as an explanatory variable. Among other things, it cannot account for the over fifteen-year lag between the end of the Cold War and the timing of DOD 3000.05. Such a significant lag potentially could be explained at least in part by a (very) gradual learning curve or by a generational delay, but there would be need of such a secondary variable to account for it. Furthermore, there have been many changes in the security environment since the establishment of the American military, and they have led to dramatic changes in strategy (flexible response, massive retaliation, deterrence, containment) and to reconfigurations of the force. Yet they never before led the military to change its entire raison d'être, as it did by elevating stability operations to a primary mission. Again, a secondary variable would be necessary to explain why this time a real or perceived shift in the threat has led to a wholesale revision of the military's role. One could argue that the difference between now and previous changes in the strategic environment lies in the shift's nature, arguably from the security concerns inherent in state-based balance-of-power politics to those emerging from a less state-centric system characterized by the rise of transnational nonstate actors. To accept this, however, one would have to accept that there has been a fundamental transfer of power and influence in the international realm from states to nonstate actors. This is in fact asserted in the Army's capstone field manual, FM 3-0, *Operations* (2008): "States, nations, transnational actors, and nonstate entities will continue to challenge and redefine the global distribution of power, the concept of sovereignty, and the nature of warfare."[11] But in reality, this does not seem to have taken place. States remain the premier entities in international relations; nonstate actors can annoy, sting, embarrass, and manipulate, but they pose no existential threat, rely on states for haven, and are remarkably susceptible to policing and other security measures intended to curb their influence. In fact, the security environment simply has not changed enough to account for the adjustment to U.S. military priorities. The possibility of a battlefield conflict still exists. The Soviet Union collapsed, but the Gulf War of 1991 did much to validate the need for a powerful conventional American military. The major regional conflicts for which the United States prepared during the 1990s could still take place (including a renewal of warfare in Iraq, eventual war with China, an Israel-Iran conflagration, or the onset of a hot war on the unstable Korean peninsula). Although the United States today is heavily involved in counterinsurgency and nation building, it also has a long history of such undertakings, none of which led to a change in the American armed forces' mission. Indeed, the nation building conducted by U.S. forces in Europe and Japan after World War II was on a far greater scale than anything in which American troops are involved today, but the U.S. armed forces' mission at the time was nonetheless to fight and win the nation's wars. As for the rise of al Qaeda, it unquestionably has posed a new challenge to the United States, insofar as the organization has global reach and can threaten U.S. and friends' and allies' interests worldwide. As with all terrorists, however, al Qaeda's reliance on a handful of dramatic attacks is rooted in the group's limitations, not in its strengths. As an institution, it does not have enough heft to merit reorienting the U.S. military. Although the 9/11 attacks have been cited as the proximate cause for the U.S. invasions of Afghanistan and Iraq, they are not sufficient for explaining the U.S. actions in either case. The Americans' decision to undertake regime change in two states, with the concomitant commitment to nation building and involvement in COIN, rather than focusing entirely on a targeted counterterrorism campaign against Osama bin Laden is better explained by broader U.S. regional interests and the political culture of the American administration than it is by the actual threat posed by al Qaeda. Ultimately, although changes in the security environment are contributing factors to DOD's decision to elevate stability operations to a primary mission, they are not sufficient to explain it.

Other explanations have also been offered for the military's decision to embrace stability operations. One links the new threats to new responsibilities: Max Boot, for example, argues that only the United States is in a position to be the world's policeman, what Madeleine Albright called "the indispensible nation." He goes on to cite deployments of the U.S. military for peacekeeping and other stability operations. Hearkening back to Teddy Roosevelt, Boot says that the United States has an obligation to stop "chronic wrongdoing" for "the simple reason that no one else can do the job."[12] Another commentator links it to an international agenda rather than to security imperatives: Andrew Bacevich states that militarization of U.S. foreign policy is a function of defending global openness or, in other words, of protecting trade and therefore is not explicitly tied to the end of the Cold War or a changed security environment.[13] In contrast to these big-picture arguments, Derek Reveron sees the military's actions as practical responses to the reality of U.S. policy makers who, without sufficient tools at their disposal, nonetheless demand the promotion of stability. Under such circumstances, he explains, the military has adjusted, even demilitarized, to be able to meet the nation's needs.[14] Janine Davidson agrees that the military is responding to such demands but focuses on the organizational conditions that allow such adjustments. She posits that post-Vietnam institutional changes allowed the military to incorporate more effectively its experiences into its learning processes. The organization has become far more adaptable. Given their many and often prolonged military deployments for stability operations, the armed forces responded with changes to doctrine, training, education, and organization to allow for improved performance in such missions.[15] Davidson's work is part of a much larger literature on the roots of military change, one in which analysts and academics examine how systemic pressures (changing threats), new technology, domestic politics, and military culture interact to lead to innovation. This ground is covered at length in Theo Farrell's and Terry Terriff's edited volume *The Sources of Military Change*.[16] It is also at the heart of the well-known debate inherent in the works of Barry Posen and Stephen Rosen: the former sees strategic imperatives filtered through civilian leaders who exert pressure on the armed forces, and the latter sees innovation springing from within the military itself.[17]

These analyses all offer useful insights into the factors contributing to the military's elevation of stability operations to a primary mission. The post-Soviet international security environment serves as a systemic variable.

American exceptionalism, a domestic variable, plays a role as well in determining both the U.S. agenda and the means by which it is pursued. Frequent deployments for stability operations have led the military to adapt to new requirements. Yet these variables remain somewhat freely floating in the literature, without coming together to explain the timing of the armed forces' decision to publish DODD 3000.05. A focus on instability is not an inevitable outcome of the collapse of the Soviet Union, nor is the military's adoption of stability operations the only means of promoting U.S. interests or of responding to recurrent deployments, as resistance to such a move has taken place despite a history of involvement in similar contingencies. DODD 3000.05 was, in short, neither the only possible response to a systemic imperative nor a direct outcome of the rash of post–Cold War complex operations.

There are two additional and related variables that must be taken into account to explain adequately the military's new approach: threat narrative and American political dynamics.

SECURITIZED INSTABILITY

Often used by constructivists, the concept of a threat narrative refers not to actual threat but to a combination of the perception and portrayal of threat. Because of limited knowledge, analytical shortcomings, and human bias, the threat itself is both unknowable and prone to deliberate misrepresentation; the narrative that emerges therefore fails to depict accurately the actual threat. Janice Gross Stein describes threat narratives as a function of both cognitive and motivated misperceptions, with cognitive distortions rooted in failures of attribution, estimation, and judgment and motivated errors driven by leaders' fears, needs, and interests.[18] This idea of a threat narrative distinct from actual threat underpins "wag-the-dog" scenarios and has even been applied to U.S. perceptions of the extent of the Soviet threat.[19] The concept of the threat narrative does not imply that there are no actual threats; instead it suggests that interpretation serves as a filter to how threats are perceived and represented and can lead, variously, to threats being overlooked, underappreciated, exaggerated, or otherwise misunderstood.

The threat narrative unfolding today around instability is not unlike what happened in the years after the Cold War's end. At the time, the end of the Cold War led to a huge rethinking of international relations and security concerns. In the absence of an obvious big-war threat, in light of the humanitarian crises engendered by state failures in Europe and Africa, given the window of opportunity for a UN Security Council no longer hamstrung by the bipolar competition, and because of the preponderance of military resources held by the United States and its allies, intense debates arose about the extent of sovereignty and the conditions under which states or international organizations could or should intervene on behalf of belea-guered populations.[20] Then, as now, there was talk about a new security environment. The new terminology that sprang up—humanitarian intervention, peace engagement, peace enforcement –emphasized a role for the armed forces in the "new world order." Yet, as the impulse to become involved in such contingencies quickly waned (with a series of fairly devastating failures), recognition dawned that although the environment had changed, that in itself was not responsible for the sudden rash of peace operations. Rather, the temporary dominance of one contingent in the multilateral debate over states' appropriate roles and responsibilities in the post–Cold War world explained the initial rush to intervene.

The post–Cold War threat narrative has been fluid, changeable, and argu-ably far more mutable than the security environment. The peace operations of the 1990s were simply one face of the United States' broad redefinition of its national priorities after the Soviet Union's collapse. No longer fearing an existential threat from a peer competitor, American policy makers could focus on protecting broader U.S. interests, including facilitating free trade, reducing nuclear proliferation, and promoting democracy. As these priorities became elevated, security concerns were revised to include threats against this more expansive American agenda. Initially, the threats were defined individually and as they arose: new attention to drug trafficking led the United States into Panama and revived the war on drugs, attacks in the mid-1990s on the World Trade Center and the federal building in Oklahoma engendered concerns about terrorism, and the humanitarian crises in Somalia, then Bosnia, and then Rwanda raised new questions about America's motivating interests, priorities, and responsibilities. Each contingency was treated as a one-off, but each contributed to the emerging U.S. security concept. This was evident in the 1996 U.S. National Security Strategy, in which President Clinton explicitly stated the shift in U.S. security priorities:

> America's security imperatives, however, have fundamentally changed. The central security challenge of the past half century—the threat of communist expansion—is gone. The dangers we face today are more diverse. Ethnic conflict is spreading and rogue states pose a serious danger to regional stability in many corners of the globe. The proliferation of weapons of mass destruction represents a major challenge to our security. Large-scale environmental degradation, exacerbated by rapid population growth, threatens to undermine political stability in many countries and regions. And the threat to our open and free society from the organized forces of terrorism, international crime and drug trafficking is greater as the technological revolution, which holds such promise, also empowers these destructive forces with novel means to challenge our security. These threats to our security have no respect for boundaries and it is clear that American security in the 21st Century will be determined by the success of our response to forces that operate within as well as beyond our borders.[21]

More recently, the dangers have come to be perceived more generically, as instability and its root causes, that is, conditions antithetical to trade, development, and democracy. Whether it is postcombat anarchy in Afghanistan and Iraq, the rise of cartels in Mexico, or the entrenchment of al Qaeda and other Islamic extremists in Yemen and Somalia, Americans now see it in their own security interests to address both the problems and their sources. Once again, but without the benefit of the domino theory or the context of a superpower foe, Americans perceive their own security as inextricably linked to the stability of small states scattered across the globe and, in a new development, to the containment of nonstate actors. Though the rise of potential peer competitors remains a concern (with particular focus on a resurgent China), more immediate attention is now being paid to instability. This has led to an expansive security agenda that basically requires the United States to solve quality-of-life issues worldwide in order to reduce the threats to its interests:

> In the 21st century, defined as it is thus far by an unprecedented and increasing interdependence, human development is both a moral end in itself and also a central pillar of our national security. For as long as civil conflicts can beget global crises, as long as preventable diseases destroy the social fabric of entire countries and entire continents, as long as half the human race lives on less than two dollars a day, the developing world will neither be just nor will it be stable.[22]

The shifting threat narrative has resulted in the securitization of instability. The concept of securitization was developed by Barry Buzan and Ole Wæver, among others, whose work on this has come to be known as a form of constructivism called the "Copenhagen School," which posits that security is not an objective condition but, rather, the product of a political process; it is a social construction. Wæver writes: "we can regard security as a *speech act*. In this usage, security is not of interest as a sign that refers to something more real; the utterance *itself* is the act. . . . By uttering 'security' a state-representative moves a particular development into a specific area, and thereby claims a special right to use whatever means are necessary to block it."[23] An issue thus becomes a security concern when it is named as such; the naming elevates the problem to the highest priority, an existential threat, and thereby gives the government the authority to deal with it by extraordinary means. Wæver calls this "panic politics," and Buzan says it allows for a departure from normal rules and legitimizes the use of force.[24] Securitization theory does not deny or assert the objective importance of any given issue; it merely posits that, in political terms, the issue only is important when it is *named* as important.

Michael C. Williams explains that, using the concept of securitization, the Copenhagen School can "argue simultaneously for both an expansion and a limitation of the security agenda and its analysis." The expansion takes place with reference to the range of threats and in terms of who or what is threatened. The constriction is in terms of who can legitimately and effectively name something a threat and under what conditions.[25] Immediately after World War II, President Truman justified the establishment of NATO by securitizing European underdevelopment. There were other ways to balance a rising Soviet Union, a prime motivator for the United States, but, as John Ruggie explains, a collective security arrangement addressed both that concern and the perceived need for a transformed, unified, economically modern Europe that would not be prone to further warfare.[26] The Marshall Plan also was justified in terms of American interest in a fiscally healthy Europe, as were the Bretton Woods institutions and even the United Nations. Such a securitization of European instability—this perception that the health of Europe's economy and the continent's stability were U.S. security interests demanding proactive American financial and military responses—was made possible by changing international conditions. In the interwar period, President Wilson had made a similar effort to securitize European instability, that is, to impress upon the American public the security implications for the United States of an unstable Europe, but he lacked adequate support in Congress. Indeed, even after World War II broke out, Americans resisted for years before engaging and might never have done so absent the attack on Pearl Harbor. By the time World War II ended, however, there was a new international context: a more global economy and a clearly dominant America. These conditions helped Truman make a more successful argument regarding the postwar security implications of an unstable, underdeveloped Europe.

More than half a century later, there has been an even broader redefinition of American security interests. It now includes not only instability worldwide but the conditions—poor governance, economic disparities, ideological extremists, and so forth—that contribute to it. The perceived threat, furthermore, is defined not only in terms of the United States itself (border incursions and terrorist attacks on the homeland) but in terms of more ideational U.S. interests, including free trade, democracy, and liberty. As with the securitization of European underdevelopment, the securitization of instability could only take place under certain conditions. These did not exist during the Cold War, when insurgencies, terrorism, and the like were seen through the prism of the U.S.-Soviet standoff. Arguing that they were threats to the United States in their own right would not have been taken seriously. Absent the Cold War, however, each act of terrorism, each failed or collapsing state, and each expansion of transnational organized crime had to be dealt with on its own terms.

Initially, without an overriding strategy or security agenda, addressing each contingency as it arose proved to be challenging; it was not clear when and under what conditions the United States should engage. Ruggie described this as an "enduring American dilemma: how to be politically not only *in* the world but *of it* when no overarching external threat exists," and he celebrated post–World War II presidents for building the "conceptual bridge" between Americans' sense of exceptionalism and the international order that kept the United States actively involved in the world.[27] The same bridge is evident today, rebuilt over twenty years by American leaders navigating the post–Cold War atmosphere of uncertainty. Perceiving themselves to be in "a new world order," enjoying a new hegemony, and sharing a global "agenda for peace," it is little wonder that many American political leaders began to consider global instability the security problem. Doing so was all the more reasonable in light of the dominant American belief that economic interdependence and democratization not only underpin U.S. interests but are contributors to a more peaceful international realm. Anything that could threaten trade or that undermined democracy was therefore antithetical both to peace and to the U.S. national interest.

Although some policy makers conceived of instability itself as a threat fairly early on, they were challenged by prominent leaders who actively promoted the traditional view of security. A speech-act only works if it is performed by credible people and if it is not countered by equally credible opposition. When Madeleine Albright publicly called for the use of the U.S. military to combat instability worldwide, she met strong resistance from General Colin Powell, who released an article warning against impulsive deployments of the armed forces in support of unclear, undefined, and unrealistic political objectives. The United States swung back and forth for nearly twenty years on this internal debate over the extent and dimensions of American security interests, responsibilities, and the appropriate means of addressing them. As Kenneth Waltz explains, "constancy of threat produces constancy of policy; absence of threat permits policy to become capricious. When few if any vital interests are endangered, a country's policy becomes sporadic and self-willed."[28] It took the events of 9/11 to create the conditions for those advocating direct U.S. engagement in reducing worldwide insecurity to assert real influence.

After 9/11, American civilian leaders responded with the war on terror, the war in Afghanistan, and the war in Iraq. Mary Kaldor points out the significance of the terminology:

> The moment that Bush chose to describe what happened on 11 September as an attack on the United States rather than a "crime against humanity," he firmly placed the event in a traditional war paradigm. By using the term "war," Bush constructed a language of polarization, accentuated by his famous sentence, "you are either with us or against us."[29]

Terrorism was thus escalated to an act of war in a speech-act.[30] This was part of a remarkably swift redefinition of threats against the United States to include anything that could contribute to terrorism. Countering terrorism, the logic ran, required not only combating terrorist organizations and their active supporters wherever terrorism might take root, including the vacuums created by failed or failing states from Pakistan and Yemen to Somalia and Uganda, but also addressing general conditions like anarchy, poverty, and social disaffection, i.e., instability.[31] This view was reinforced by distressing trends worldwide: the rise of piracy, the deluge of opium and heroin out of Afghanistan, rebels in Africa cutting off or controlling access to oil and crucial mineral deposits, violent drug wars threatening Latin American governments' authority, and the extended reach of Central American gangs throughout the Western hemisphere. Suddenly the world seemed to be under siege, the great powers held hostage by angry, poor, and often radicalized hordes posing "asymmetric threats" and desperate to undermine the existing system.

Failed states are the anarchic epitome of instability. The 2005 *U.S. National Intelligence Strategy* called failed states "breeding grounds of international instability, violence, and misery";[32] the 2006 *U.S. National Security Strategy* also cited the dangers of failed states as breeding grounds for terrorism.[33] Unsurprisingly, the Commission on Weak States and U.S. National Security found, in 2004, what its name would suggest:

> Weak and failed governments generate instability, which harms their citizens, drags down their neighbors and ultimately threatens US interests in building an effective international system, providing the foundation for continued prosperity, and, not least, protecting Americans from external threats to our security.[34]

Harry Verhoeven describes this tendency to see failed states as a threat as "securitization of the Global South."[35] He explains that "Since 11 September 2001, this phenomenon has been particularly associated with terrorism, trans-border criminality and global instability. The international community presents this 'Orthodox Failed States Narrative' as an objective, apolitical analysis of a 'new' problem."[36] Such a narrative is clear in countless statements by U.S. civilian and military officials in the aftermath of 9/11, as exemplified by Marine General Anthony Zinni's book *The Battle for Peace*, in which the general states: "The real threats do not come from military forces or violent attacks; they do not come from a nation-state or hostile non-state entity; they do not derive from an ideology (not even from a radical, West-hating, violent brand of Islam). The *real* new threats come from instability."[37]

Clearly, the securitization of instability has taken place. Yet, although the process of elevating instability to a national security threat made it possible to turn to the military, doing so was not the obvious option. In fact, the earliest assumptions were the opposite. Several prominent authors, writing in the immediate aftermath of the Cold War (though, admittedly, before 9/11), agreed that there was need for a broader view of national security (including "treating nonmilitary external security threats to national well-being as security issues"),[38] but they also agreed that use of the military would, in fact, decline, both because of changes in threats and because of the armed forces' reduced relative utility as a tool of foreign policy. Richard N. Haass published his influential book *The Reluctant Sheriff* at that time and assumed that the United States would take on a greater policing role internationally. He also argued, however, that the United States should not "rely exclusively on the military to implement a doctrine of regulation," because such an approach would be "expensive by any measure, and there is only so much of it to go around. It is not appropriate for many tasks or certainly not as appropriate as other instruments."[39]

Indeed, civilian agencies have long been tasked with addressing the causes of instability, promoting development and good governance, protecting U.S. interests through diplomacy and growth, and otherwise implementing, over the long term, the kinds of programs and policies intended to reduce the causes of instability. The State Department mission statement reads, for example, that the agency should "advance freedom for the benefit of the American people and the international community by helping to build and sustain a more democratic, secure, and prosperous world composed of well-governed states that respond to the needs of their people, reduce widespread poverty, and act responsibly within the international system."[40] USAID's mission also focuses on addressing the foundations of instability:

> USAID plays a vital role in promoting U.S. national security, foreign policy, and the War on Terrorism. It does so by addressing poverty fueled by lack of economic opportunity, one of the root causes of violence today. As stated in the President's National Security Strategy, USAID's work in development joins diplomacy and defense as one of three key pieces of the nation's foreign policy apparatus. USAID promotes peace and stability by fostering economic growth, protecting human health, providing emergency humanitarian assistance, and enhancing democracy in developing countries. These efforts to improve the lives of millions of people worldwide represent U.S. values and advance U.S. interests for peace and prosperity.[41]

Securitized instability might, therefore, have led to greater State Department and USAID roles, a refurbishing and bolstering of the institutions.

Instead, the civilian agencies have struggled all the harder as their traditional functions are handed to the military. This is the case because of institutional privileging.

INSTITUTIONAL PRIVILEGING

Many observers will explain that the military has been tasked with responsibility for promoting stability internationally simply because the other government agencies—especially the State Department and USAID—have dropped the ball. And there is some truth to this perspective. Indeed, with particular reference to postconflict stabilization and reconstruction efforts, the armed forces officially are supposed to do no more than provide support to civilian agencies, rather than assume leadership themselves. National Security Presidential Directive 44 (NSPD-44), published in December 2005, a few days after DODD 3000.05, specifically directs the secretary of state to "coordinate and lead integrated United States Government efforts to stabilize and reconstruct" postconflict countries and tasks all the other agencies to assist the State Department in its efforts.[42] Yet this formulation of responsibilities is unrealistic, hinging on the mistaken assumption that civilian agencies are equipped—in terms of funding, staffing, and even structure—to take on such missions. This is simply not the case. Even in peacetime, such projects are beyond the scope of the civilian agencies' abilities; in postconflict situations, which are often fraught with residual violence, civilians' mobility and utility will be undercut by security concerns. Moreover, the idea of a postconflict period is itself a false construct: stabilization and reconstruction efforts are often part of the solution to conflict rather than something to be undertaken in its aftermath. Such efforts may be necessary even while systematic violence is ongoing. Unlike soldiers, civilians cannot be expected to operate in such an environment. If they are present, they can be more a liability than a help, given their protection requirements. Furthermore, NSPD-44 refers very specifically to stabilization and reconstruction efforts. However, the promotion of stability internationally, in defense of U.S. interests, has been understood much more broadly, and it includes counterterrorism efforts, counterinsurgency operations, military support to failed or failing states, and even foreign military exchanges and training in the interests of professionalism and respect for civilian authority. None of these responsibilities fall within civilians' purview, and many are likely to overlap with or characterize conflict or postconflict situations. It thus could appear that there is no alternative to a deployment of the military for stability operations where there is a potential for violence and that civilian agencies have little, if any, role to play in promoting international stability under such conditions.

Yet although civilian agencies' shortcomings are widely observed and blamed for the military being tasked with traditionally civilian diplomatic and development duties, less attention is paid to why the civilian agencies are so weak and unsuitable for combating instability relative to the military. Some of the answer lies in policy makers' selection of missions. The missions listed above—counterterrorism, counterinsurgency, counternarcotics, and so forth—are reactive. They are responses to emergencies, crises, or crime. They are the last resort, after the system has broken. They are highly visible and dramatic. These kinds of operations—and the concomitant military deployment—are appealing if the desire is to look responsive, create the appearance of decisive action, respond to crises, or operate in areas engulfed in violence. Longer-term programming that promotes preventive economic and democratic development or the establishment of transparent, consistent, constructive relationships is less showy and garners less attention. And these latter projects are the realm of civilian institutions. For many reasons, including election cycles, concerns about the U.S. image abroad, and competition for influence with other countries, American and, more generally, Western policy makers increasingly opt for the short-term approach. Henry Kissinger sees this preference for immediate gratification as a widespread trend: "as western democracies are ever more driven internally by short-term considerations, the constituencies for the long term shrink; the political rewards are for actions either which demonstrate immediate benefits or reward short-term passions."[43] Such an approach privileges the military over civilian agencies.

C. Wright Mills explained this kind of behavior less in terms of political expediency and more in terms of perception, positing that policy makers and legislators simply believe the military is more likely to provide a successful solution to international problems. This has led civilian agencies to be systematically weakened in the budgetary process.[44] Congressional decisions regarding the funding of the Department of State and USAID relative to DOD are characterized by a counterproductive cycle in which underfunded and undermanned civilian institutions cannot bear their share of the foreign policy demands and therefore receive even less budget support relative to the well-resourced military. In effect, policy makers prioritize those foreign policy courses of action in which the military has a comparative advantage and then find the civilian institutions (predictably) lacking; the civilian institutions are then punished in the next round of budgeting because they have been deemed ineffectual. This means that the civilian agencies, over time, in the absence of funding, become truly deficient, undermined in their ability to conduct even their core competencies. Under such circumstances, it is not surprising that even as the armed forces' responsibilities have expanded, civilians' capabilities have contracted.

A specific and significant example of the effects of legislators' and policy makers' differing perceptions of the civilian agencies' and the military's relative utility came at the Cold War's end. At that time, decision makers were giddy about the untapped potential of the huge, powerful, deployable U.S. military but expressed concerns that the civilian agencies—the State Department, USAID, the U.S. Information Agency (USIA), and the Arms Control and Disarmament Agency (ACDA)—were not running efficiently. Studies were undertaken in both branches of government. Under the influence of Senator Jesse Helms, a particularly vocal opponent of foreign aid, USAID was subordinated to the State Department, and USIA and ACDA were eliminated entirely.[45] Along with the consolidation came severe budget cuts. In the period from 1992 to 1998, Congress made annual cuts to the International Affairs Budget, resulting in "a 38% decrease in our foreign affairs programs (as a percentage of the United States GDP)."[46]

This is in part a function of the same dynamic in Congress that afflicts civilian agencies' reception with policy makers; the military simply has more appeal. As Reveron and Mahoney-Norris note:

in spite of calls for budgetary reform to increase social and economic assistance provided through the State Department, Congress simply finds defense issues more compelling. Politicians have an interest in associating themselves with patriotism and strength, so it is much easier to find advocates for counterterrorism training than for women's empowerment programs. The conventional wisdom on Capitol Hill is that while defense spending is understood by American voters to be a matter of national security, international assistance sounds unnecessary.[47]

Civilian agencies are further disadvantaged in the legislative process, relative to the military, by their lack of a constituency. State and USAID have no natural constituencies to provide them with congressional clout, whereas DOD has not only forces in uniform (nearly 1.5 million active personnel, in addition to over 800,000 reserves) but also a far greater number of civilian employees than State or USAID (643,000 as of September 2008)[48]—not to mention contractors, retirees, veterans (23.2 million in 2008),[49] and all of these people's family members. Defense contractors represent another extraordinarily influential constituency for DOD, bringing money and jobs into congressional districts across the country. Defense contractors are also steady donors to political campaigns and parties; in the 2004 presidential race, defense company workers donated more than a million dollars to the Bush and Kerry campaigns.[50] And, lest lawmakers should forget how weapons systems production enhances security while creating jobs, the defense industry hires lobbyists:

> In 2008, [reporter August Cole of the *Wall Street Journal*] found [that] Northrop Grumman almost doubled its lobbying budget to $20.6 million (from $10.9 million the previous year); Boeing upped its budget from $10.6 million to $16.6 million in the same period; and Lockheed-Martin, the company that received the most contracts from the Pentagon [in 2007], hiked its lobbying efforts by a whopping 54 percent in 2008.[51]

Most defense contractors have unionized workforces; this, too, resonates with lawmakers. Moreover, all of these constituents have been distributed very deliberately across the nation, with representation in key congressional districts, in a practice known as "political engineering."[52] Secretary Gates illustrated the breadth and depth of DOD's domestic constituency when he observed that the "F-22 aircraft is produced by companies in 44 states; that's 88 senators." These constituents also tend to form politically powerful groups, including, to name just a few, the Veterans Association of America, Disabled American Veterans, Vietnam Veterans of America, the National Defense Industrial Association, Servicemembers United, and the National Military Family Association. Ultimately, this enormous military constituency translates into greater congressional willingness to fund defense budget requests in their entirety. The foreign affairs budget, in comparison, is often allocated below administrations' requests.[53] Secretary Gates remarked on this as well, during a May 2010 speech at the Command and General Staff College in Fort Leavenworth, Kansas: "I went to the Hill and asked for a budget for FY '11 of $549 billion in the base budget. I got $549 billion, at least out of the Budget Committee. The State Department went with a budget of less than one-tenth that size and got cut $4 billion."[54]

The congressional appropriations process also gives DOD advantages over its civilian counterparts in procuring resources. Gordon Adams explained, in a Stanley Foundation report, how the congressional armed services committees involve themselves directly in the budgetary process, while the Foreign Affairs committees focus instead on policy hearings.[55] This structure, so debilitating to the civilian institutions, has nonetheless been reinforced by the agencies themselves. DOD's planning process is intended to justify budgetary requests and demonstrate programmatic requirements in a compelling way. State, on the other hand, has proven far less capable in this regard. One MIT study found that the "Department of State lacks a disciplined, multi-year process to review the costs, risks, and consequences of broad alternatives, align programs and budgets with leadership priorities, and foster coherence."[56] The Quadrennial Diplomacy and Development Review (QDDR)[57] instituted by Secretary Clinton for inaugural publication in 2010 was intended in part to address this lacuna by mimicking the Department of Defense's Quadrennial Defense Review (QDR). The benefits, theoretically, are multifold; not only will the civilian agencies have a better sense, themselves, of what their capabilities and requirements are (thus creating greater efficiencies, cooperation, and more effective programming within and among them), but they will also be able to communicate those more convincingly to Congress, making more specific and defendable budget requests in the service of clear U.S. interests. Even the process of undertaking the QDDR eventually should yield, hypothetically, more compliant lawmakers, since their input will be part of the effort every four years, thus enhancing communication between the civilian agencies and legislators and giving Congress a stake in the process's success.[58]

In part because of their handicaps in the legislative budgetary process, the civilian agencies have faced severe funding and resource shortfalls. Even today, when one USAID official describes the institution as flush with funds, new hires, and strong congressional support, he also points out the enormous disparity between funding for development and funding for security, citing the fact that the military has 230 times the number of personnel that USAID does.[59] A 2009 House Foreign Affairs Committee Report described the stark situation: USAID has only five engineers and twenty-nine education specialists for all of its worldwide projects. State has a 12 percent vacancy rate in overseas foreign service positions and a higher vacancy rate in the United States. The report concluded that this hollowing out of the civilian capability "cripples" these agencies' "ability to aggressively pursue and protect American interests abroad."[60]

Other contemporary numbers bear out the discrepancy between civilian and military funding: President Obama's 2011 fiscal year international affairs budget request represented only 1.4 percent of the entire federal budget and less than 7 percent of funding for national security.[61] The Department of Defense's budget is over $700 billion a year; the State Department's is just over $50 billion. And State has to fight to retain even that. In April 2010, the Senate Budget Committee proposed $10 billion worth of cuts in State Department and other international program funds.[62] The outcome of the consolidation and cuts in budget and manpower has been a weakened civilian capability. Representative Howard Berman described the outcome: "DOD is filling the vacuum left by the State Department and USAID, which lack the capacity to carry out their diplomatic and development functions. There is no doubt that these agencies have been weakened by a severe shortage of resources."[63]

One observer of this trend admonished that, unless checked, "The military will own every practical tool of foreign policy. . . . State will be an also-ran who holds the door while the DOD does its thing."[64] A 2006 Senate Foreign Affairs Committee Report validated such concerns about a civil-military imbalance. It explained that underfunding of the State Department and USAID meant that "U.S. defense agencies are increasingly being granted authority and funding to fill perceived gaps. Such bleeding of civilian responsibilities overseas from civilian to military agencies risks weakening the Secretary of State's primacy in setting the agenda for U.S. relations with foreign countries and the Secretary of Defense's focus on war fighting."[65]

Institutional privileging is a long-standing, self-reinforcing phenomenon. Yet, when the U.S. security concept revolved around conventional warfare, such institutional privileging did not result in militarization. The armed forces may have received a preponderance of resources relative to the civilian agencies, but, far from trying to compete for traditionally civilian roles, they strongly resisted being tasked with them. This has now changed.

THE MILITARY'S EMBRACE OF STABILITY OPERATIONS

These domestic variables—the securitization of instability and institutional privileging—explain why the military has become policy makers' instrument of choice, but they do not directly explain the military's revolutionary decision to elevate stability operations to a primary mission. In fact, the military has a history of strongly resisting policy makers' efforts to expand its purview into what it considers the civilian domain, and it has often done so on the basis of arguments about maintaining primary mission readiness. This was the aforementioned case when Colin Powell spoke out against Madeleine Albright's call to deploy the military for new missions. Colonel Harry Summers made the same point around the same time, somewhat more colorfully: "The military needs to stick to its knitting. And the American people ought to insist that it stick to its knitting because the dangers of it not doing so can be profound."[66] Admiral Gene Laroque said of using the military for stability operations:

> There's another perhaps even more significant drawback. That when the military begins performing functions that are really not military in the normal sense of the word, they degrade their military capability. They become less combat-ready. And the primary purpose of the military ought never to be forgotten; and, that is, the military is to wage war and win wars and defend the United States. And we never want to take that skill away from the military or in any way diminish that capability.[67]

To understand the armed forces' uncharacteristic embrace of stability operations in the face of this kind of resistance, one must take into account both the changed strategic environment (and perceptions thereof) and the ongoing competition for domestic resources. Regarding the former, although the institutional privileging that has long helped to nurture DOD is powerfully rooted, the resources DOD can justify requesting diminish in a world without peer competitors. The need to prepare for conventional warfare no longer ensures the military the resources, manpower, and funding it once garnered almost without question. Furthermore, as technology creates efficiencies and allows for strategies that reduce manpower requirements even in conventional war, the implications for DOD include reduced force structure. In other words, the military's traditional mission cannot guarantee against scaling back. At the same time, the securitization of instability created opportunities for resources and influence, but the military was not the most obvious instrument for addressing either instability or its causes. As Haass made clear in *The Reluctant Sheriff*, the logical contenders for such jobs were civilian agencies. For the military, the potential scaling up of civilian agencies represented a double blow in the domestic competition with State and USAID. A strategy relying primarily on diplomacy and development to address instability and its roots would have allowed growth in the civilian agencies and, meanwhile, represented a lost opportunity for the armed forces at a time when their primary mission was likely to yield less support than in the past. In other words, institutional privileging would not have disappeared overnight, but the first minor inroads against it would have been laid.

DODD 3000.05 can be seen as a response to precisely such concerns. With a single directive, the Department of Defense staked out a claim in combating instability—both its causes and its effects. It clarified the U.S. armed forces' preparedness to operate alongside civilians to prevent, respond to, or clean up after violence, defining stability operations as "Military and civilian activities conducted across the spectrum from peace to conflict to establish or maintain order in States and regions."[68] It set the stage for the military assuming responsibility when civilians could not: "Many stability operations tasks are best performed by indigenous, foreign, or U.S. civilian professionals. Nonetheless, U.S. military forces shall be prepared to perform all tasks necessary to establish or maintain order when civilians cannot do so."[69] And it demonstrated the military's commitment to such operations:

> Stability operations are a core U.S. military mission that the Department of Defense shall be prepared to conduct and support. They shall be given priority comparable to combat operations and be explicitly addressed and integrated across all DoD activities including doctrine, organizations, training, education, exercises, materiel, leadership, personnel, facilities, and planning.[70]

DODD 3000.05 arguably helped the military assert itself in the bureaucratic competition: less than a year after the directive was released, a new program was created under the National Defense Authorization Act, giving DOD the authority to spend up to $200 million of defense appropriations for training and equipping foreign military personnel for stability operations and COIN.[71] The following year, the amount authorized under this program, Section 1206, was increased to $300 million, and, by 2010, the combined allocations since 2006 totaled approximately $1.2 billion.[72] For 2011, the House increased the authorized funding limit to $500 million, and the president indicated that he would request nearly that.[73] Section 1206 came to be perceived by many as symbolic of institutional privileging, with some concern that the funds were not included in the foreign affairs budget under State's control, where the secretary could ensure a coincidence between their use and broader U.S. policy goals and efforts.[74] The authority represented the effectiveness of DOD's approach.

Section 1206 was established, moreover, even as other DOD authorities and funding accounts were being increased. Both the Regional Defense Combating Terrorism Fellowship Program (CTFP) and the Commander's Emergency Response Program (CERP) predated DODD 3000.05, and they continued to grow after its release. The former was established as a permanent authorization in 2002 and directed funds through DOD to support international security personnel's training in combating terrorism. Initially, the program was capped at $20 million annually. After 2007, the cap was raised to $25 million and then, later, to $35 million. The latter authority, CERP, evolved into a formal authority from an ad hoc solution to the problem—in post-Saddam Iraq—of rationally dispersing the dictator's ill-gotten cash. The decision was made in 1993 to allow U.S. military division and brigade commanders to allocate those found monies for development projects in response to immediate needs in their respective areas of responsibility. The following year, finding the commanders' involvement in development to be valuable, Congress allocated $140 million from the U.S. budget for CERP. A representative of the U.S. Office of the Inspector General for Iraq Reconstruction said, "CERP was meant to be walking-around money for commanders to achieve a desired effect in their battle space. Slowly, it has become a de facto reconstruction pot of money."[75] The program since has grown to be a sizeable funding authority in both Iraq and Afghanistan. Between 2004 and 2010, Congress authorized approximately $3.99 billion for CERP in Iraq and well over $1.6 billion in Afghanistan.[76]

The increased importance of both of these authorities raised questions similar to those asked about Section 1206: Would the military promote development in ways that were consistent with the programs and efforts being undertaken by State and USAID? Did it make sense to have DOD administering programs that seemed more consistent with responsibilities that traditionally fell to civilians? Did DOD have the necessary expertise for using such funds in the most productive and efficient ways? Such questions were raised precisely because DOD's entry into the field of stability operations was unexpected, strategic, and represented lost opportunities for State and USAID.

CTFP and CERP were each successes in DOD's effort to show its continued relevance. They indicated that perhaps the military would be able to hold its own even with a new American security paradigm focused on instability. Nonetheless, recognizing the budget pressures created by the worldwide economic recession and reading the writing on the wall following the November 2010 U.S. midterm elections, on January 7, 2011, Secretary Gates announced preemptively that an internal review had identified over $154 billion in defense savings.[77] The next day he stated that the long-term (five-year) defense budget would be reduced by $78 billion.[78] Both of these steps were defensive, driven in part by pressure from the White House and influenced by the understanding that several of the new Republican congressional representatives, particularly those identifying with the Tea Party, did not believe that military spending should be sacrosanct in a time of huge deficits and a slow economy. Tellingly, both the new Speaker of the House and the new majority leader made public statements that they would not oppose trimming military spending.[79] Gates's proposed cuts would include 47,000 troops from the Army and the Marine Corps, approximately 6 percent of their total forces,[80] as well as several weapons systems. And these self-inflicted cutbacks were deemed necessary even with American troops deployed in Iraq and Afghanistan, even with deliberate retooling of the military for counterinsurgency, counterterrorism, and support for reconstruction and stabilization.

The armed forces were obliged to plan these reductions despite the role they have assumed in stability operations. Had they not been able to point to the requirements of the surges in both recent wars or to the need for military support to postconflict nation building, their ability to protect force structure and budgets would likely have been diminished even more. And, indeed, their involvement in these activities meant that any reductions that passed Congress would be from a larger force than otherwise and from a larger budget. Even with the proposed troop reductions, the Army has forty thousand more soldiers than it did when Secretary Gates took office, and the Marine Corps has seven to twelve thousand more troops. As for the defense budget, it doubled between 2000 and 2010, according to Chairman of the Joint Chiefs of Staff Admiral Mike Mullen,[81] so the reductions that pass are out of an already enormous budget (one-fifth of the federal budget, totaling approximately $536 billion in 2009, not including the nearly $200 billion additional annual spending on the two wars).[82] What's more, the reductions really only represent a decline in planned growth to a little less than 1 percent rather than an absolute decrease in available funds.[83]

Tellingly, Secretary Gates's budget decisions over his tenure also reflected the military's strong commitment to stability operations. As discussed in chapter 3, big-ticket weapons systems programs, such as the Army's Future Combat System and the Marine Corps' Expeditionary Fighting Vehicle, perceived as untouchable until Gates's audacious move, were reduced or eliminated in favor of reallocating funds for the manpower and equipment required in stability operations, specifically in counterinsurgency. Gates emphasized "health care, intelligence, reconnaissance, Special Forces, theater missile defenses, helicopters and UAVs." And although he estimated "that only about 10 percent of the budget [was] devoted exclusively to irregular warfare," he believed it reflected a growing and necessary trend,[84] and he argued that his proposed budget represented the "minimum level of defense spending necessary given the complex and unpredictable array of security challenges the United States faces around the globe."[85]

The military could have continued to reject stability operations—and continued to argue, as it did historically, that though it can carry out such operations successfully, undertaking specific preparations for them or over-deploying for them reduces its readiness for war. But instead, in the face of changing perceptions of threat, the military's civilian leadership formally adopted stability operations as a primary mission. The military saw the prevailing winds and adjusted course. In this way, it leveraged the combined effects of securitized instability and institutional privileging to make up for declining public attention to the possibility of a truly challenging conventional war. No longer facing a superpower opponent, lulled into a sense of security by overwhelming success in America's two conventional conflicts with Iraq (the 1991 Gulf War and the 2003 Iraq War), and convinced that the spread of capitalism and democracy are both reducing the likelihood of grand-scale wars, Americans have refocused their attention. They fear cyberthreats and terrorists more than bombing raids; they worry more about transnational gangs and pirates than national war machines.[86] They are more concerned about the aftermaths of war than about the wars themselves. In a sense, the U.S. military has succeeded itself out of its old job. It has proved itself insuperable in conventional combat. The widespread belief has emerged that asymmetric threats have arisen precisely because no one can expect to beat the American military on the battlefield or in the air. Under such circumstances, justifying continued military enlargement is difficult, as is justifying the tremendous expense of next-generation technologies or of expanded force structure. But institutions understand that their survival is in adaptation and growth.[87] No longer able to rationalize their budget and resource requirements with ever greater offensive and defensive power, the military needed a new mission. This is what the securitization of instability provided. Institutional privileging, in turn, created an opportunity. The military just needed to capitalize on both. DODD 3000.05 is the result of that conjunction of interests. The military expanded its purview and, in doing so, found renewed validation for its manpower, funding, and voice.

Lieutenant Colonel Charles Dunlap was already making a similar argument in the early 1990s. Dunlap, the author of *The Origins of the American Military Coup of 2012*, contended nearly twenty years ago, when the military was first being tasked with what were being called nontraditional missions, that many people in the military saw in such a role an opportunity to preserve force structure.[88] Yet, though some within the military undoubtedly believed at the time that the armed forces' future lay in stability operations, the majority of military leaders remained wedded to the more established view that they should emphasize fighting and winning the nation's wars. Indeed, the relaxation of the military's views on stability operations did not come easily, nor has it been universally accepted. In fact, though DOD 3000.05 set in motion a real transformation of the U.S. armed forces, as previous chapters have shown, there are still prominent military thinkers who believe such efforts can and should be reversed and others who suggest that the changes are insubstantial and far from revolutionary. The internal battle over the future of the U.S. armed forces thus is not over. It is raging between the traditionalists who believe that the military should focus its energy and resources to maximize its effectiveness as a fighting force and those who believe the military has a greater role to play in molding the broader strategic environment. The disagreement is focused in part on the nature of transformation itself—to a high-tech war machine or to a counterinsurgent organization skilled in policing, training, and providing assistance. But the debate is also more general, dealing with the nature of warfare, with those who see a blending of stability operations and warfighting as the hallmarks of the present and the future going toe to toe with those who believe that there needs to be a deliberate separation and distribution of such responsibilities between civilian and military institutions.

This battle for the future of the military is playing out in the Department of Defense, especially in the Office of the Secretary of Defense (OSD) and among military and civilian analysts, acting and retired officers, and within each of the branches of the armed forces. Secretary of Defense Robert Gates was in the forefront of those justifying changes in the U.S. military's priorities, adhering, as he has, to the presumption that instability is a new and significant security challenge. He wrote, in a 2010 *Foreign Affairs* article, that

> the recent past vividly demonstrates the consequences of failing to address adequately the dangers posed by insurgencies and failing states. . . . The kinds of capabilities needed to deal with these scenarios cannot be considered exotic distractions or temporary diversions. The United States does not have the luxury of opting out because these scenarios do not conform to preferred notions of the American way of war.[89]

In his view, the U.S. military has no choice but to adjust to an evolving strategic environment, and, in doing so, it will fulfill its responsibilities, reduce its long-term costs, create efficiencies, ensure adequate preparation, avoid surprises, and emerge as a stronger and more relevant tool of foreign policy. This perspective is gaining traction within the military. Indeed, DOD officials and military officers are increasingly turning Clausewitz's well-known maxim on its head, arguing that politics have become an extension of war. At the 2010 Army War College conference, U.S. Army Historian Colin Crane cited Chairman Mao's claim that "politics is war without violence; war is politics with violence." Retired Major General Nash stated that the "purpose of the military is to advance and secure America's interests, not just war." Retired Lieutenant Colonel Nathan Freier claimed that the U.S. Department of Defense now sees war as a "lesser-included case," reflecting "really fundamental changes in the security environment."[90] He went on to state that the military is now responsible for combat, security, engagement, relief, and reconstruction and that because only the U.S. Department of Defense can accomplish these things, it therefore should undertake them. Perhaps most tellingly, another participant invoked Abraham Lincoln, stating that we must "have faith that right makes might,"[91] insinuating that the United States is powerful precisely because it has the moral high ground and, with that, responsibility. There were some presenters who were leery of the near-universal assumption among panelists at the conference that the military was facing a far more expansive range of responsibilities because of the evolving security environment. The civilian analyst Paul Kan, for example, said during a question-and-answer session that the U.S. military "needs an appetite suppressant for what we call a security issue."[92] Nonetheless, the gist of the discussion throughout the event was that the military can, and therefore should, involve itself in a much broader array of missions, including assuming tasks that have traditionally fallen to civilians.

DODD 3000.05 indicates that the progressives, who in the 1990s could not quite sell their leadership on a new raison d'être for the military, have since been able to capitalize on the securitization of instability, have positioned themselves to create change, and have begun the process of moving the military in a very new direction. Their efforts have resulted in a marginally changed force with substantially changed doctrine and a rapidly changing mindset. The U.S. military is not short of war fighters, high-tech machinery, fast-flying planes, enormous ships, or tanks and artillery. It remains, for the most part, a conventionally oriented organization prepared for the battlefield. But the changes are there, from the unprecedented sacrificing of weapons systems in order to bolster COIN and stability operations in Secretary Gates's budgets to, as will be discussed in the following chapter, the restructuring of the U.S. military's Southern Command (SOUTHCOM) and the creation of the Africa Command (AFRICOM) as organizations intended to emphasize peacetime "shaping" operations. These and other changes related to DODD 3000.05 have implications for U.S. foreign policy, for policy makers, for civilian agencies, and for the military itself.

FIVE
IMPLICATIONS OF MISSION REVOLUTION

The military's adoption of stability operations as a primary mission, including adjusting doctrine and preparation in order to better incorporate stability operations across the spectrum of conflict, has implications for the military itself, for civilian agencies, and for U.S. foreign policy more generally. This is the case even though the military has always undertaken stability operations, it is the case even though the bulk of the military remains dedicated to conventional combat operations, and it is the case despite efforts to ensure a "whole of government" approach to global instability. The effects of the military's elevation of stability operations are a function of the securitization of traditionally civilian concerns and both a consequence of and a contributor to civilian agencies' lack of preparedness for nation building. They are a product of institutional privileging even as they reinforce it. They encourage rather than dissuade foreign policy decisions to deploy military forces to achieve starkly political ends, building foreign governments' capacity in peacetime, during insurgencies, and following wars. They represent the abandonment of the cautious Weinberger and Powell doctrines and guarantee that U.S. forces will be faced with the most challenging, least conventional, and messiest of stability tasks, those that, in the past, have had the lowest success rates and the highest costs. Ultimately, these implications boil down to one dynamic: militarization.

The term militarization is often employed as a pejorative, used to criticize efforts as disparate as the U.S. response to the earthquake in Haiti and its development projects in Afghanistan.[1] It is used as a warning, too, such as when Defense Secretary Gates highlighted the threat, in the summer of 2008, of "creeping militarization."[2] It is a reference to the military's assumption of civilian tasks but also to securitization, to policy makers' changing views of what constitutes threats to national security.[3] Militarization can be deliberate or a form of mission creep; it can be the product of the military's decision to expand its purview or the unintended outcome of overreliance on the military in lieu of other options.

These last two variations are embodied by what will be referred to here as, respectively, "peacetime extension" and "fill-the-gap" operations. The military's embrace of stability operations has contributed to both, with very different consequences stemming from each. Peacetime duties—or Phase Zero operations—represent a burgeoning arena for military action and new opportunities for the armed forces, and they create both opportunities and costs for civilian agencies and policy makers. Phase Zero is "essentially a conflict prevention strategy—the military engages its counterparts to build capacity, good governance, and infrastructure, thereby providing countries with the necessary tools to address their own problems."[4] In a 2006 *Joint Force Quarterly* article, U.S. Air Force General (Ret.) Charles Wald wrote that Phase Zero takes place "prior to the beginning of Phase I." By placing Phase Zero before the planning phase, thereby including it in the conflict continuum, Wald suggested that Phase Zero is typified by imminent violent conflict. In truth, however, Phase Zero simply describes the absence of violent conflict—peace—and posits a sustained peacetime role for the military. Postconflict stabilization operations are Phase Five efforts (though the numbering and number of phases varies by doctrine).[5] Phase Five ostensibly falls at the other end of the conflict spectrum and involves the U.S. military's provision of postconflict security (anything from policing street corners to active counterinsurgency efforts) as well as assistance to civilian-led nation-building efforts. In practice, Phase Five stability operations can begin long before Phase Three (employment) is complete and even can forestall Phase Four (redeployment). In fact, Phase Five stability operations often will not take place in a permissive environment and may even be required for bringing active conflict to an end. It is in this phase that militarization is often an unintentional, "fill-the-gap" enterprise resulting from mission requirements that only the military can fulfill but for which it is an imperfect instrument. This form of militarization, unlike "peacetime extension," can create serious problems for the military, if U.S. forces find themselves involved in the unfamiliar realms of economic development, promoting good governance, infrastructural development, and democratization as a function of their efforts to promote stability and in the absence of civilian agencies capable of assuming such roles. It is this form of militarization against which military leaders are showing some resistance, given the potentially debilitating effects of such responsibilities on the armed forces. In a sense, Phase Five operations both reflect and reinforce civilian shortfalls while challenging the military in serious and potentially harmful ways.

Thus two very different forms of militarization—"peacetime extension" and "fill-the-gap" operations—bookend traditional combat missions, and each will have very different repercussions. In each case, the armed forces will find themselves attempting, in the name of stability, to prevent conflict and build local economic and political capacity. The important distinction is that the former are operations the military chooses to undertake; they reflect a deliberate expansion of the armed forces' purview into conflict prevention through diplomacy and development, albeit with an emphasis on foreign militaries. They are best reflected in the establishment of the U.S. African Command (AFRICOM) and the reorganization of the U.S. Southern Command (SOUTHCOM), as will be discussed further on. The latter is a function of changing strategic priorities and the related shift from involvement in big wars with defined ends to messier, ongoing conflicts where "victory" may involve long-term nation-building efforts. In stability operations like peace operations, COIN, and support for nation building, traditionally civilian tasks become, to some extent, instruments of military ends. This not only changes the nature of civilians' work but means that if they cannot do it, the military must pick up the slack.

Both kinds of militarization have serious—but very different—implications not only for the civilian agencies to whom many such tasks, under different circumstances, fell in the past but also for the armed forces, who have made significant adjustments in preparation for them. Indeed, if peacetime extension persists, and if the military continues to be tasked with Phase Five jobs—which is all the more likely given its preparation for them, as described in the preceding chapters—then the ultimate outcome could be the simple shifting of responsibility for certain missions from civilians to the armed forces. Militarization would no longer be a concern but an established fact.

Spinning this out to its extreme, Thomas P. M. Barnett offers a radical but not entirely unrealistic vision of future military involvement in traditionally civilian spheres. In his book *The Pentagon's New Map: War and Peace in the Twenty-First Century* and subsequent work, Barnett advocates splitting the U.S. military into two forces: the Leviathan, for fighting big wars, and the System Administrator (SA), for taking care of unconventional contingencies, including lingering conflicts and the aftermath of regime change. Barnett writes, "I do wish to change this military dramatically, but I likewise believe the time has come to admit that we need two militaries: one to fight wars and one to wage peace."[6] He continues: "In short, we need a force for *might* and a force for *right*."[7] Barnett does not rule out a civilian role in peacemaking. He writes that the SA will be "network-centric," "designed for outward connectivity," emphasizing not just jointness but "interagency cooperation." The SA "will not need to join the civilian world outside the Pentagon, it will largely live in that world."[8] Barnett's plan offers a "you-can-have-your-cake-and-eat-it-too" scenario in which the military is split to allow for both the Rumsfeld-era Revolution in Military Affairs (RMA) and the ongoing reworking of the military to adapt to the requirements of COIN and other unconventional operations.

Barnett's vision may be drastic, but it is consistent with the concepts of Phase Zero and Phase Five operations insofar as he describes the continuous employment of military forces both to prevent conflict and to help clean up after—and prevent further—violence. Phases Zero and Five are a significant part of U.S. foreign policy efforts worldwide, and they both reflect a serious shift toward greater military influence and control. Whereas civilians have long been responsible for peacetime attempts to avert conflict with diplomacy, aid, trade, and development, the military is becoming involved in such efforts in places considered of high strategic value (especially the Horn of Africa). Whereas civilians have long been in charge of taking the reins, postconflict, to begin the process of rebuilding, in the absence of a clear line to define the end of conflict, the military will remain. Although there have always been roles for the military when environments were not entirely permissive—shows of force to deter violence, when war was looming, or the provision of postcombat security in the aftermath of violence—today, the military's role is often at the forefront.

Perhaps the best examples of Phase Zero peacetime extension are AFRI-COM and SOUTHCOM, the geographic combatant commands (GCCs) designed and refurbished, respectively, specifically to prevent conflict. As for Phase Five, one need look no further than Iraq and Afghanistan to see how experiences in each war inform, legitimize, and reflect the effects of the military's embrace of stability operations.

PEACETIME EXTENSION: GCCS

The military has an important role in engagement—helping to shape the international environment in appropriate ways to bring about a more peaceful and stable world.
—General John Shalikashvili, 1997 *U.S. National Military Strategy*

As 2008 drew to a close, the U.S. Defense Department's newest regional command, AFRICOM, went fully operational. Preexisting American regional commands' mission statements emphasize military security and defense, with head nods to cooperation and promoting peace and development:

The U.S. European Command conducts military operations and builds partner capacity to enhance transatlantic security and defend the homeland forward.[9]

and

U.S. Pacific Command protects and defends, in concert with other U.S. Government agencies, the territory of the United States, its people, and its interests. With allies and partners, U.S. Pacific Command is commit-ted to enhancing stability in the Asia-Pacific region by promoting secu-rity cooperation, encouraging peaceful development, responding to con-tingencies, deterring aggression, and, when necessary, fighting to win.[10]

Note that these focus on protecting and defending (traditional military missions) and, in support of that or secondarily, working to partner with locals to enhance security. AFRICOM's mission statement, however, repre-sents a new and different focus:

> United States Africa Command, in concert with other U.S. government agencies and international partners, conducts sustained security engage-ment through military-to-military programs, military-sponsored activi-ties, and other military operations as directed to promote a stable and secure African environment in support of U.S. foreign policy.[11]

There is nothing here about protecting and defending the U.S. homeland, people, or interests. The emphasis is on promoting stability and local secu-rity in support of U.S. foreign policy through military engagement and in concert with U.S. civilian agencies and international partners.

At nearly the same time that AFRICOM came on line, the U.S. South-ern Command (SOUTHCOM) completed an enormous overhaul that also emphasized joint, interagency, and public- and private-sector cooperation.[12] Although SOUTHCOM's mission sounds more traditional ("to conduct military operations and promote security cooperation to achieve U.S. strate-gic objectives"),[13] its reorganization reflects a reconceptualization of its role. As SOUTHCOM Commander Navy Admiral James Stavridis explained, "If I would put one word on it, it's partnership. That is our motto—Partner-ship for the Americas—and our objective is to become the best possible international, interagency partner we can be."[14]

AFRICOM and SOUTHCOM are the embodiment of the military's embrace of a new, broader mission. The emphasis on nonkinetic operations in permissive environments represents a dramatic shift in how the military perceives its value and role. Now, rather than just fighting and winning the nation's wars, U.S. armed forces are being deployed to address violent conflicts' underlying causes, a responsibility that, until recently, has been left to civilian agencies. SOUTHCOM's transformation and AFRICOM's creation as deliberately interagency organizations were among Defense Secretary Robert Gates's top priorities during the Bush administration.[15] They are the product of a top-down initiative to create what some DOD officials described as a "combatant command 'plus'": a command that retains "the roles and responsibilities of a traditional geographic combatant command, including the ability to facilitate or lead military operations, but also includes a broader soft power mandate aimed at building a stable security environment."[16]

Defense policy makers thus redefined the proper role for the military in geographic areas where it is not conducting kinetic operations and took deliberate steps for active peacetime extension aimed at "shaping" security environments. This actually began in the post–Cold War period, with the 1997 QDR, which called on the military to "shape-respond-prepare." The QDR was itself a response to President Clinton's 1996 National Security Strategy, which focused on enlargement and engagement. Although the bulk of shaping involves military-to-military relations, it can extend dramatically into development and diplomacy. Thus, in stark contrast to the other GCC's missions, AFRICOM's is to "promote a stable and secure African environment in support of U.S. foreign and national security policy."[17] In her opening statement for one of the preliminary congressional hearings about AFRICOM, Deputy Assistant Secretary for African Affairs at DOD Theresa Whelan described AFRICOM's focus on "war prevention, rather than warfighting."[18] AFRICOM's 2008 Posture Statement explained that the command will "deny terrorists freedom of action and access to resources, while *diminishing the conditions that foster violent extremism.*"[19] In its 2009 Posture Statement, the command identified these conditions as "corruption, endemic and pandemic health problems, historical ethnic animosities, natural disasters, and widespread poverty."[20] As one analyst explained it:

> Africa command . . . drew on a revolutionary new military doctrine that added steps to the traditionally defined four-phase process of U.S.

military engagement: deter/engage, seize initiative, dominate, and transition. Africom falls into a new "phase zero," before any of these other four: conflict prevention. According to a participant at a recent Africom conference, that means doing everything possible to avoid having to get involved in "another 25-year Plan Colombia" to clean up a long-term, well-entrenched mess—a reference to the $5-billion plus involvement of the United States in that country's drug and insurgency problems.[21]

Like AFRICOM, SOUTHCOM's primary goals, as expressed in *Command Strategy 2016*, are to ensure security and enhance stability, including addressing root causes. The strategy notes that "in many cases . . . [poverty and inequality] create the conditions from which security challenges arise to threaten democracies throughout Latin America and the Caribbean."[22] With the iteration of the third goal ("enable prosperity"), SOUTHCOM tips socioeconomic and political development into the armed forces' mission.[23] Although these issues are being perceived in a security context rather than from a broader foreign policy perspective and therefore are military objectives, they effectively require SOUTHCOM to involve itself in the traditionally civilian roles of promoting development and democracy. In its formulation of these goals, SOUTHCOM justifies its involvement in a wide range of humanitarian activities and other projects that lie outside the purview of a traditional combatant command.

Joint Publication 1 (2007) formalizes Phase Zero peacetime extension by requiring that all GCC commanders help stabilize failing or failed states by "employing all instruments of national power—diplomatic, informational, military, and economic."[24] Thus although AFRICOM and SOUTHCOM are the only GCCs designed specifically for such efforts, the remaining GCCs are required to work in concert with civilian agencies to prevent, reduce, or address instability. The armed forces' specific responsibilities in this realm, per JP 1, are shaping the operational environment through military engagement (military-to-military diplomacy, in effect),[25] security cooperation (especially training), and deterrence. These efforts, according to the doctrine, help "keep the day-to-day tensions between nations or groups below the threshold of armed conflict while maintaining US global influence."[26] It is the first of these, military engagement, to which peacetime extension refers; it is in this particular realm that the military has expanded its purview beyond its traditional role.

IMPLICATIONS FOR THE ARMED FORCES, CIVILIAN AGENCIES, AND U.S. FOREIGN RELATIONS

The U.S. military accrues real benefits from involving itself in permissive environments in strategically significant places like Latin America and the Horn of Africa, where the threats facing American interests are at the low end of the conflict spectrum. In addition to the obvious benefit of an expanded mission—and thus expanded justification for resources and manpower—peacetime extension provides U.S. troops with opportunities for real-world training and experience (especially in civic action, medical assistance, and veterinary assistance), familiarizes local leaders with U.S. armed forces under constructive conditions, and enhances partnerships with local militaries through exchanges and interactions. Meanwhile, the costs to the military of such efforts are relatively low compared to other military missions. In effect, peacetime extension is the equivalent of local fire stations driving their trucks out to town fairs. There is a cost involved, but the activity is a no-risk, benign form of community outreach.

Perhaps most importantly in terms of foreign policy, Phase Zero operations allow American military personnel to gain a foothold—through the development of local knowledge and contacts—that could help in the event of a crisis. This was demonstrated to tremendous effect during the events in Egypt in early 2011. U.S. military leaders have thirty years' worth of close ties with their Egyptian counterparts, many of whom were trained in the United States. Moreover, the Egyptian military has become accustomed, since the Camp David Accord, to U.S. security assistance (funds, weapons, and training). When the public protests began, following the collapse of Tunisia's government under similar circumstances, the United States had real insight into the Egyptian military's leadership and priorities, had open lines of communication, and held some potential leverage.[27] While there were undoubtedly many contributing factors influencing the

Egyptian military's decision not to fire on the protesters and to allow the fall of Mubarak's government, the extensive and deep U.S.-Egyptian military-to-military relationship certainly contributed to leaders' calculations. Admittedly, that relationship is unusually close and is replicated in only a few other countries, but peacetime extension is intended to help build that kind of relationship with states in strategic regions.

Although some civilians have come to praise peacetime extension as a valuable policy tool,[28] many expressed serious initial concerns during the SOUTHCOM/AFRICOM planning stages. In Section 942 of the 2009 National Defense Authorization Act (NDAA), Congress laid out a series of reporting requirements for SOUTHCOM, indicating apprehension that its new mission would both diminish its military capacity and unnecessarily duplicate or impinge on civilian activities.[29] That same year, the House of Representatives expressed similar doubts about AFRICOM, with the Committee on Armed Services worrying that

> the committee finds that within the command's mission statement, it has listed a variety of tasks that appear to depart from traditional Department of Defense (DOD) missions, including medical HIV/AIDS assistance, humanitarian assistance, and disaster relief . . . the committee is concerned that AFRICOM might become the primary agent of U.S. efforts in those areas where they might be better served by other agencies or departments taking the lead.[30]

To mitigate these potential problems, AFRICOM emphasized in its 2009 and 2010 posture statements that it does not aim to assume traditional civilian activities in the areas of diplomacy and development. It included interagency personnel from outside the command's headquarters in the planning and coordination stages of its programs,[31] incorporating not just DOD employees, as other GCCs do, but also personnel from civilian foreign affairs agencies such as the State Department and USAID. To reduce confusion among civilians, AFRICOM replaced the traditional military J-code divisions with functional directorates.[32] Whelan describes the command as having an "integrated civilian/military architecture."[33] SOUTHCOM's restructuring was intended to achieve this same architecture. It transformed itself into a more interagency-oriented organization along the same lines as AFRICOM, increasing the number of civilian agency personnel assigned to the command and organizing around the same kind of functional director-ates.[34] Each command also has two deputies reporting to the commander: an ambassador, who advises the commander on foreign policy issues and civil-military activities, and a military officer in charge of military operations.

The commands' more holistic vision represents a positive development, as does their emphasis on interagency and public-private collaboration. However, in the course of implementing a Phase Zero approach to security, the commands not only subsume to some extent the broad foreign policy missions that formerly fell under the primary purview of civilian foreign affairs agencies, but they coordinate interagency efforts as well. Their efforts to integrate civilians will not necessarily enable them to better support civilian agencies. The commands are military organizations that serve their own prerogatives before incorporating interagency perspectives. Ambassa-dor Edward Marks, who was U.S. ambassador to Guinea-Bissau and Cape Verde, explains that including civilian personnel within the command does not change its military nature. He argues that because the command is led by a senior military officer, it will "inevitably encourage an emphasis on military perspectives and programs in internal government deliberations and processes."[35] A February 2009 report on AFRICOM published by the Government Accountability Office (GAO) echoes his reservations in its discussion of the possible barriers to communication between the State Department and DOD in the context of AFRICOM. The GAO posits that different institutional goals would lead to varying conceptions of the problems that the command addresses.[36] Even though the command incor-porates other agencies in the strategic planning process, the end result will always be a DOD product.[37]

Moreover, despite improvements in integration, the GCCs still are defining an appropriate role for themselves vis-à-vis civilian foreign affairs agencies. This is a difficult task. In a February 2009 article in *Armed Forces Journal*, Charles Ray, a former ambassador and retired Army officer, explains how this delineation of roles has been "open to interpretation" and warns that the "lack of clarification and specificity in defining jurisdiction is a catastrophe waiting to happen."[38] This catastrophe would be rooted, in part, according to Ray, in the differences between civilian and military capabilities and cultures and the problems incurred when military leaders become responsible for civilian tasks. He writes that "military organizations are mission oriented and tend toward linear thinking," yet entities that specialize in international relations "require nuanced thinking and nonlinear approaches."[39]

Even if civilians were integrated fully into the GCCs, the model still has some troubling implications for foreign policy. Foreign governments in the SOUTHCOM and AFRICOM areas of responsibility will be confused as to who has the lead in U.S. policy in their regions, especially if State Department and USAID personnel are co-located at the combatant commands. This could—through inadvertent example—undermine civilian control of the military in Africa and Latin America, two of the world's regions most susceptible to military abuses of power. A Congressional Research Service report published in December 2008 offers precisely this critique, arguing that the U.S. military's increased involvement in state building and development activities may actually undermine these activities' goals, by strengthening the stereotype in underdeveloped countries of the military as more competent than its civilian counterparts, thus justifying the military's assumption of civilian entities' responsibilities.[40]

Another problem is in terms of military assistance, specifically security force assistance (SFA). As the armed forces expand SFA, which is perceived as a growth area, they are crowding the State Department. SFA, unlike the State Department's security assistance (SA), is driven more by operational requirements than by broader U.S. foreign policy concerns. The problems can be multifold: the training provided to foreign forces may meet immediate U.S. operational needs, but the militaries receiving such training may fail to meet necessary standards in terms of human rights, professionalism, and respect for civilian authority. Moreover, the militaries' capacity may be strengthened out of all proportion with civilian governmental institutions, leading to a disparity of influence. An April 2011 Stimson Center report recommended decreasing the much expanded military role in this arena, returning responsibility for military assistance to the State Department.[41]

Relatedly, the Phase Zero operations embodied in the AFRICOM/SOUTHCOM structure send a problematic foreign policy message: that first and foremost, the U.S. values its security relationship with foreign countries and that concerns about diplomacy and development are secondary to security issues. Representative John Tierney, chairman of the National Security and Foreign Affairs Subcommittee of the Oversight and Government Reform Committee, argued, with particular respect to AFRICOM, that conducting interagency coordination in the context of a military command "presents a tension between the importance of representing U.S. activities in Africa as peaceful and respectful of African national sovereignty, and the perception that DOD is the lead agency for U.S. relationships with Africa."[42] In fact, a 2006 report commissioned by the Senate Foreign Relations Committee noted some host nations' worries about America's increasingly military overseas profile and potential U.S. motives for expanding the military's international reach.[43]

FILL-THE-GAP OPERATIONS: IRAQ AND AFGHANISTAN

Though postconflict reconstruction ideally should be a civilian responsibility, there is a legitimate and often necessary role for the military when such efforts take place in nonpermissive environments, that is, when violence is ongoing. Where there is no clear military victory or political resolution in a conflict, the nature of violence is likely to shift and change with continued local competition for political and military control. Under such circumstances, if the United States wishes to help normalize the situation to the point that political and economic solutions can be found, American troops will be required to help establish secure conditions and will likely help train local military and police forces as well. Also, reconstruction, nation building, and development are often themselves necessary to bring violence to an end. They can even be—as in counterinsurgency—components of warfare, crucial elements in a struggle for "hearts and minds." When such operations are deemed to be in the U.S. national interest, the challenge is to have adequate civilian involvement without compromising security operations or jeopardizing noncombatants. On a sliding scale of the possible distribution of such responsibilities, the military could assume full responsibility, on one end, and civilians could assume full responsibility, on the other. When a conflict is hot and violence is ongoing, the latter option will be neither possible nor practical. Civilians will simply become targets, vulnerabilities, and their efforts will be undermined by instability. Furthermore, civilians may choose not to enter nonpermissive environments. Unlike soldiers, diplomats and government aid workers have made no commitment to risk their lives. Though they are contractually obligated to work wherever they are posted, they do not, unlike soldiers, face jail time if they refuse to deploy.[44] And civilians are not trained for big projects like nation building; their training, whether in diplomacy or development, is for sustained maintenance of U.S. interests, working with local governmental and nongovernmental partners. Thus it can prove difficult to find an adequate number of appropriately experienced and trained civilian personnel to fill development and diplomacy roles in conflict zones. Yet the other end of the spectrum is equally problematic. Troops will assume more traditionally civilian responsibilities—i.e., the promotion of governmental and economic development—when ongoing violence does not allow for the secure deployment of civilian diplomats and aid providers or when the demand for governance promotion and development assistance exceeds what civilian agencies can fulfill. To date, when troops have been tasked with such responsibilities, their approach (as shown in Iraq, Afghanistan, and countless other engagements) has been ad hoc, with some successes and many failures. The learning curve is steep, with potentially high strategic costs for misjudgments. Finding the appropriate and practical balance is where the challenge lies.

In 2008, Ambassador Eric Edelman, former undersecretary of defense for policy, put forward the U.S. position on kinetic versus nonkinetic operations in Afghanistan, citing a ratio of national effort he attributed to David Galula (who, in turn, got his formulation from Mao): "Eighty percent . . . ought to be on the development, social assistance, political and economic sides, not just on the military side."[45] Ideally, a great deal of that effort would fall to civilians, but this is often impossible not only because of ongoing violence but because civilian agencies are not designed or resourced to undertake large-scale nation-building missions. Even adaptations intended to boost civilian capabilities thus far have failed to produce the intended civilian complement. The several initiatives under Clinton, Bush, and Obama to promote civilian "uplift" did not significantly increase civilians' relative role in either Iraq or Afghanistan. In the meantime, the military is left as the only institution ready and able to assume responsibility for the full range of Phase Five operations. In practice, this means that the military becomes responsible not only for security but for traditionally civilian tasks as well.

Lieutenant Colonel Guy Jones, commander of the 82nd Airborne Division's Second Battalion, 508th Parachute Infantry, was on his fourth tour of Afghanistan when he told a reporter: "I almost never do kinetic operations."[46] He, like so many U.S. military personnel in Afghanistan, is involved in diplomatic initiatives with local leaders as well as in development projects and in siphoning funds into communities in an effort to offset the Taliban's influence. One Army Reserve officer who was in Afghanistan observing operations in Ghazni province described the "hold" and "build" phase of operations that follows the clearing out of insurgents and terrorists. She wrote that in a period of just eight months, the military unit she observed had "spent over $150,000 in economic development, basic service provision, and jobs program efforts to rebuild Khezer Khell School, support Mata Khan Clinic, and institute other important capacity building efforts to empower the sub-district governors."[47] More generally, as the *Washington Post* reported in January 2011, "U.S. troops in Afghanistan have spent $2 billion over six years on 16,000 humanitarian projects through the Commander's Emergency Response Program."[48] Less interesting than the amount of money spent is the nature of the projects—economic development, support to vulnerable local political institutions—that the military was undertaking. The deputy assistant secretary of defense explained in his March 2010 testimony before the Senate Armed Services Subcommittee on Emerging Threats and Capabilities that the U.S. military's role during the "hold phase" in Afghanistan necessarily includes such development initiatives. They are intended to support the Afghan government's efforts to solidify gains and involve not just CERP projects but also deploying U.S. "Civil Affairs capabilities, fielding medical and dental assistance teams, conducting information support operations, and . . . manning and leading Provincial Reconstruction Teams."[49]

The story in Iraq is similar. As part of the transition out of Iraq, U.S. troops were formally shifted from combat missions to stability operations. Their actual day-to-day was not affected, however. As Major General Lanza, the U.S. Army spokesperson in Iraq said in July 2010, "In practical terms, nothing will change. We're already doing stability operations."[50] Indeed, from the point at which victory was declared in May 2003, U.S. forces found themselves doing stability operations: undertaking COIN, advising and training Iraqi soldiers and police, and supporting—and often running—civilian reconstruction efforts. That year, Frederick Kagan of the American Enterprise Institute disparagingly described this use of American military personnel as the "new new thing," in which "conventional troops [were turned] into a sort of "Special Forces Lite." He wrote that, "to the exclusion of many other vital tasks . . . armored battalions now train Iraqis and conduct economic reconstruction and political redevelopment at the lowest level."[51] Two years later, Major General Peter Chiarelli and Major Patrick Michaelis published a 2005 *Military Review* article in which they asserted: "Task Force Baghdad's campaign to 'win the Peace' in Iraq has forced us, as an instrument of national power, to change the very nature of what it means to fight. . . . Although trained in the controlled application of combat power, we quickly became fluent in the controlled application of national power."[52] And four years after that, as operations in Iraq began to wind down, Company A, 1st Battalion, 8th Cavalry Regiment, 2nd Brigade Combat Team, 1st Cavalry Division was praised in the *Army Times* as a key example of such new modes of employing troops. Company A not only oversaw Iraqi Army checkpoints but was responsible for paying the Sons of Iraq for their contributions in the fight against al Qaeda and worked on building relations with the local community. Their executive officer said of them: "Our soldiers understand the overall concept of what they are doing in the region. They realize they are helping the Iraqis set up their government, and they are improving the quality of life in the towns in the region."[53]

Fill-the-gap militarization also can extend beyond local projects, however, to the big-picture planning and implementing of U.S. policy. The author of the 2010 *Rolling Stone* article that led to General McChrystal's ouster from Afghanistan observed, for example, that McChrystal's team in Afghanistan represented "the most powerful force shaping U.S. policy in Afghanistan," because of the lack of a civilian equivalent.[54]

These kinds of fill-the-gap militarization are a function of changing strategic priorities and the related shift from involvement in big wars with clear ends to messier, ongoing conflicts where "victory" has been redefined to mean establishing adequate stability to justify withdrawal of American forces. Militarization under these conditions is of a different sort than militarization under Phase Zero; rather than deliberate military extension, it tends to be a direct reflection of the mismatch between policy objectives and civilian capabilities, with the military as the go-to solution. Bringing the military in becomes necessary because there are simply too few trained, deployable civilians, functioning with limited resources, and working from within a structure designed for other ends. When the military undertakes these kinds of development and governance operations, it is usually because policy makers have decided that such efforts are in the U.S. national interest but that only the military has the capacity to do them. The 2010 Quadrennial Defense Review addressed this issue as euphemistically as possible by asserting DOD's commitment to whole-of-government operations while noting:

> America's civilian instruments of statecraft were allowed to atrophy in the post–Cold War era, and the lack of adequate civilian capacity has made prevailing in current conflicts significantly more challenging. Unfortunately, despite a growing awareness of the need and real efforts throughout the government to address it, adequate civilian capacity will take time and resources to develop and is unlikely to materialize in the near term. The Department will therefore continue to work with the leadership of civilian agencies to support the agencies' growth and their operations in the field, so that the appropriate military and civilian resources are put forth to meet the demands of current contingencies.[55]

IMPLICATIONS FOR THE ARMED FORCES, CIVILIAN AGENCIES, AND U.S. FOREIGN RELATIONS

Although DODD 3000.05 and subsequent actions would seem to signal a strong trend in the military's embrace of stability operations, the institution is far from unified on whether or not this is the best strategy. Some in the military definitely see the organization's expansion into traditionally civilian roles as not just an opportunity but a necessity. This assessment is based, depending on their views, on the new security environment, policy makers' demands and civilians' limitations, and the decreasing national interest in the military's traditional missions and the need to justify the forces' structure and budget. Others, however, perceive such a trend as entailing potentially serious real and institutional costs. Phase Five operations, in particular, raise grave concerns because they arguably affect the military's balance of capabilities in ways that peacetime extension does not. This is because the stability operations that can take place during Phase Five—COIN, training and assistance for foreign militaries and police, and support to nation building—are messy, prolonged, and politically ambiguous; can require a great deal of manpower; rely on basic technologies like MRAPs rather than on technology in which the United States has a comparative advantage; involve often disturbing and even morale-reducing compromises and concessions (allying with the Sons of Iraq, for example, or working during the day with Afghan men who enjoy *bacchá*—pederasty—in the evenings); and do not tend to culminate in the kind of measurable, satisfying, ticker tape–parade success that a victory in war brings.[56] Without adequate preparation, the political, institutional, and resource costs can simply be unsustainable.

The often heated debate about the elevation of these kinds of stability operations to a primary mission revolves around questions of whether the armed forces' roles and responsibilities have changed qualitatively and substantially. In debates on this subject, experts are offering redefinitions of war and the armed forces' functions in it. At the Army War College's Spring 2010 conference, civilian and military experts sat on panels titled: "How Do We Know That We Are at War?" "How Do We Know When a War Is Over?" and "Who Participates in War?"[57] Both progressives and traditionalists were represented. Each panel attempted to hash out not only their specific topics but also how to contribute to the broader redefinition of security and military responsibilities as functions of the U.S. government. At the heart of the debate is the question of what is best for the U.S. military. As with any institution seeking to protect its organizational interests, the military must persuade those who fund it of its relative value, in this case as an instrument for achieving American objectives abroad. And the military has been able to take advantage of the nexus of securitized instability and institutional privileging in order to protect its budget and staffing. Although policy makers deployed troops for stability operations even before the military itself had recognized that the tides had changed, DOD and the services have since caught up to their civilian leaders. They have decided that it is in their interest to adopt and prepare better for missions that they would have previously assumed civilians would take on.

There are real benefits to this. It meant that when Secretary Gates began to pare back the military under budgetary pressure, he was doing so from a military already larger than the one he'd inherited. It means that even as Americans' threat perceptions change, the military will have a job. It helps ensure that the problems that plagued the military in Iraq—before the troops had adequate body armor, before the deployment of MRAPs, before the surge—will not be repeated. It gives the military a voice at the table in almost every foreign policy decision. From an institutional perspective, at least in the short term, the embrace of stability operations has been a smart move.

Yet stability operations—and fill-the-gap operations, in particular—can have tremendous potential costs for the military. As chapter 3 shows, although most stability operations can be undertaken by a military prepared for conventional warfighting, peace operations, support to nation building, and COIN require specialized training, force structure, and equipment and entail high operational tempos over prolonged periods. Forces have to be trained and prepared to work with, alongside, and in support of civilians, and they have to coordinate their efforts with other agencies and foreign governments and militaries. Troops will be war fighters but also developers and diplomats. Their self-image will necessarily shift to accommodate the new requirements. This is something that can take years to inculcate—consider the training period for special operators—and, moreover, in the event the perception of the security environment shifts, it is not readily reversible.

Fill-the-gap operations also are far different from traditional operations: rather than victory through the battlefield defeat of their opponents or deterrence through shows of force, troops deployed for peace operations, COIN, and/or nation building are battling for the support of local populations in complex political, social, and cultural environments further complicated by instability and often violent competition. Not only will they require a different approach and, therefore, different skills, knowledge, and self-image, but the likelihood for success is limited, and the likelihood of second-guessing, criticism, and loss of public support is high.

Furthermore, military objectives in fill-the-gap operations are also prolonged operations, so U.S. military personnel will likely experience serial deployments. One study published in the *American Journal of Public Health* showed that multiple deployments adversely affected troops' mental health, placing them at higher risk for post–traumatic stress disorder, severe depression, and alcohol and drug abuse.[58] Indeed, the wars in Iraq and Afghanistan have raised concerns about suicide and postdeployment domestic violence. In 2010, nearly as many U.S. troops were lost to suicide as to deaths in battle in Iraq and Afghanistan; in 2009, more troops died by their own hand than in fighting.[59] Multiple deployments also correlate with spouse suicides.[60] Deployments for these kinds of operations clearly also have implications for morale and retention. In describing the troubling phenomenon of the exodus of young officers from the Army, for example, Andrew Tilghman wrote:

> While many officers don't oppose the war itself, returning repeatedly to serve in Iraq is a grueling way to live. One of the many reasons for this is that it corrodes their families; the divorce rate among Army officers has tripled since 2003. Internal surveys show that the percentage of officers who cite "amount of time separated from family" as a primary factor for leaving the Army has at least doubled since 2002, to more than 30 percent. And family is a factor even for officers who don't have one yet. One young soldier I met at Fort Bragg, North Carolina, said his primary

problem with military life was the difficulty of finding a girlfriend while spending more than half his time in Iraq. As officers prepare for a third or even fourth deployment, a new wave of discontent is expected to wash over junior leaders. Studies show that one deployment actually improves retention, as soldiers draw satisfaction from using their skills in the real world. Second deployments often have no effect on retention. It's the third deployment that begins to burn out soldiers. And a fourth? There's no large-scale historical precedent for military planners to examine—yet.[61]

Finally, involvement in these operations also can erode the military's domestic and international reputation in several ways. First, whereas rapid victories with few American deaths and the gee-whiz factor of high-tech military equipment enhance foreign respect for, and domestic pride in, the U.S. military, slogging complex contingencies with no obvious gains and continuous attrition have the opposite effect. Former Air Force Secretary Michael Wynne remarked on the first point with some irony: "I am sure the North Koreans fear the MRAP and the Iranians are cringing in their boots about the threat from our stability forces."[62] But complex stability operations also are a veritable minefield of potential missteps that can tarnish the U.S. military's image, from accidental drone attacks on civilians to the negative political ramifications of providing support or assistance to officials later found to be knee deep in corruption.

Thus, even as the military has been adjusting to the demands (and opportunities) of Phase Five, it has been trying to mitigate its costs. Such an approach requires distinguishing between appropriate military tasks and those foisted upon the armed forces because only they can do them. Therefore, in addition to making internal adjustments to be better prepared for stability operations, as outlined in chapter 3, military leaders have also staunchly supported a stronger civilian capability and greater awareness among policy makers of the problems with fill-the-gap operations. In July 2008, a Center for Global Engagement poll found that "Eighty-four percent (84%) of officers say that strengthening non-military tools such as diplomacy and development should be *at least* equal to strengthening military efforts when it comes to improving America's ability to address threats to our national security."[63] Six months later, Admiral Mike Mullen, chairman of the Joint Chiefs of Staff, similarly cautioned against further militarization of U.S. foreign policy.[64] And soon thereafter, nearly fifty retired generals and flag officers released a letter to Congress calling for adequate funding of civilian agencies, noting that the requirement for robust civilian leadership in foreign policy is too often undermined by limited resources.[65] More specifically, the U.S. military has been supportive of the State Department's Office of the Coordinator for Reconstruction and Stabilization (S/CRS) and its mission of identifying states at risk of failing and promoting healthy democracies. In his prepared statement for testimony before the armed services committees in February 2005, General Richard B. Myers, chairman of the Joint Chiefs of Staff, cited the creation of S/CRS as "an important step" in helping "post-conflict nations achieve peace, democracy, and a sustainable market economy." He continued, "In the future, provided this office is given appropriate resources, it will synchronize military and civilian efforts and ensure an integrated national approach is applied to post-combat peacekeeping, reconstruction and stability operations."[66]

The civilian lacuna has been an ongoing source of concern in many regards. The military's frustration with limited civilian capacity is nothing compared to State's and USAID's own dissatisfaction. Yet, just as "the U.S. military was designed to defeat other armies, navies, and air forces, not to advise, train, and equip them . . . the United States' civilian instruments of power were designed primarily to manage relationships between states, rather than to help build states from within."[67] The State Department's country teams are composed of diplomats who express American interests to their local counterparts using established protocols; depending on the team and country, there is one person responsible for liaising with the press, another who meets with local military leaders, another who might work with his or her counterpart on trade, and so forth. But country team members are not trained or equipped to stand up new governments from scratch or to assist in the day-to-day minutiae involved in the creation of institutions. USAID experts, for their part, have not been involved directly in development efforts for decades; they are organized to identify what development projects should be done and to fund local and international NGOs to do the work. They are not trained or resourced to put in place—or even to help put in place—the agencies, practices, and rules of entire national economies. The oft-denigrated civilian capacity for nation building has thus been a function not only of persistent underfunding but also of a structure formulated to achieve very different ends than those for which civilian agencies today are being deemed responsible.

In recognition of this, President Clinton began a push to grow civilian capacity in 1997, with his release of Presidential Decision Directive (PDD) 56. The PDD was intended to help regularize interagency planning and coordination for complex contingencies, but it met resistance within the bureaucracy and was never implemented. In fact, it was not until the United States became mired in the nation-building efforts in Iraq and Afghanistan that enough political room was created to allow for another attempt at reorganizing for improved interagency cooperation. By that time, several legislative and academic studies had been written, many of which focused on the challenges of reconstruction, the shortfalls of civilian agencies, and the need for a deployable civilian corps.[68] In this new context, President Bush established the S/CRS in 2004 and tasked it to "lead, coordinate and institutionalize U.S. Government civilian capacity to prevent or prepare for post-conflict situations, and to help stabilize and reconstruct societies in transition from conflict or civil strife, so they can reach a sustainable path toward peace, democracy and a market economy."[69] Its creation was a direct response to concerns about civilian shortfalls in stabilization and reconstruction, subsequent militarization, and consequent problems. The office was organized to help the State Department take the lead on S&R, both in policy forums and in the field. The S/CRS staff in Washington, D.C., reflects the interagency more broadly, with representatives from not only the State Department and USAID but also the Office of the Secretary of Defense as well as the Central Intelligence Agency, Army Corps of Engineers, Joint Forces Command, Joint Chiefs of Staff, and Treasury Department. A year after standing up the S/CRS, the Bush administration released National Security Presidential Directive (NSPD) 44, supplanting PDD 56 and intended to provide for the management of interagency stabilization and reconstruction operations. In the same year, the administration also undertook an initiative called "transformational diplomacy," aimed at further restructuring the State Department. As Secretary of State Condoleezza Rice said at the time, U.S. foreign policy needed to take into account the "intersections of diplomacy, democracy promotion, economic reconstruction and military security."[70]

In addition to the S/CRS, which is intended to address coordination problems, there has been a larger initiative to extend civilians' reach and authority into field operations. One aspect of this was the establishment of the Civilian Response Corps (CRC), intended to become a truly deployable, expeditionary State Department element. The CRC is organized into active, standby, and reserve components. These are composed of, respectively, full-time government employees trained and prepared for S&R and deployable within forty-eight hours, full-time government employees with relevant experience and expertise who are deployable within thirty days, and U.S. citizens who can take on S&R responsibilities and who are deployable within forty-five to sixty days. The active component is anticipated ultimately to have 250 members. It and the standby component are up and running, though not fully funded or staffed; the reserve component is planned but not yet funded. Until the CRC is completely manned, the State Department will continue to rely on contractors and on the military.[71]

Another major effort to field civilians includes the PRTs in both Afghanistan and Iraq. As discussed in chapter 3, PRTs are intended to provide civilians access to the field even in nonpermissive environments by having military personnel clear and hold an area so that the civilians can safely begin work with local counterparts to establish stability and help improve governance. The United States set up the first PRT in Afghanistan in 2002 and within a few years had encouraged other International Security Assistance Force (ISAF) partners to adopt variations on the model. By spring 2010, there were twenty-six PRTs in Afghanistan, twelve of which were U.S.-led (one jointly with Romania).[72] There were also twenty-three U.S.-led teams in Iraq, including seven "embedded" PRTs (ePRTs) working with the military at the brigade level.[73] Refinements of the PRTs include additional organizations like District Support Teams (DSTs) and Agribusiness Development Teams (ADTs).[74] Today, American PRTs come in three models: the civilian-led teams in Iraq, the military-led teams in Afghanistan, and embedded PRTs in both countries. The PRTs in Iraq and Afghanistan both run from thirty to one hundred members, with troops heavily outnumbering civilians (civilians make up 10 percent or less of PRT membership). Embedded PRTs (ePRTs) were introduced as part of the surge in Iraq and later put in place in Afghanistan, as well. They differ from the regular PRTs in that they are small, four-person interagency teams embedded in brigades to help draft operational plans that take development and diplomacy into account.

Although all of these efforts—the changes to the civilian bureaucracy and improvements in civilian deployability—are intended to enhance civilian capabilities and offset militarization, they have so far failed to live up to their potential. For example, though the S/CRS may be tasked to lead on S&R, it has no means by which to hold even other State Department offices to account, much less members of other departments and agencies, many of which see themselves in direct competition with State for resources and influence. Wielding neither carrots nor sticks, the S/CRS cannot make the interagency come to attention, cannot elicit support, and cannot hold others in the executive branch responsible. The combination of underfunding, competition, and an authority void has hampered policy coordination on S&R at the highest levels, undermining S/CRS's ability to ameliorate militarization.[75] Indeed, the office's future is now in doubt.[76] Nor has the CRC reached its potential. Congress authorized the corps in October 2008. Within two years, its active and standby components combined had grown to a much-heralded thousand members, and CRC personnel had deployed to over twenty-eight countries worldwide. But although this is a solid start, it is far from the number of personnel needed. The military analyst Steven Metz laid out the numbers, explaining that at full strength the CRC would need 4,500 members, a difficult ideal to achieve, and that even this would only allow for one CRC advisor per several tens of thousands of people in countries like Pakistan and Nigeria.[77]

Meanwhile, although PRTs are in high demand and considered an effective way to place civilians where they are most needed, their implementation has been plagued by a paucity of nonmilitary personnel. In a U.S.

Institute of Peace exit interview with an officer who commanded PRTs in Afghanistan for a year, the officer observed:

> The problem we had, I had nine provincial reconstruction teams and we had about five State reps, so we had gaps. What we, I had places where I really needed a State rep very badly. One was in Paktika Province, which was the last one that he [the U.S. embassy civilian in charge of staffing PRTs] wanted filled. I didn't have a rep either. I spent my first three months with no State rep at all and no AID rep. I'll tell you I didn't know what I was missing until I finally got one.[78]

In late 2008, Eliot Cohen, then counselor to Secretary of State Rice, said that the DOD's "appetite is unlimited" for State Department personnel to join the understaffed PRTs, but he also noted that with only 5,500 diplomats available worldwide, demand outpaced supply dramatically.[79] In the same time period, the U.S. House of Representatives Armed Services Committee "found that PRTs are often unevenly staffed and led, and lack strategic guidance or oversight."[80] In Afghanistan, PRTs often have had fewer than a dozen nonmilitary civilian professionals and have frequently been led by Air Force or Navy officers unlikely to have relevant skills and expertise.[81] The problems staffing PRTs in Afghanistan mirror similar issues in Iraq, a problem explained in a congressional report as resulting from the limited number of civilians qualified by skills and experience.[82] Another report found that because of the shortage of civilians for the PRTs in Iraq, DOD provided civil affairs personnel to fill the gap. This still left unmet requirements for people skilled in "local government, city management, business development, and agricultural advisers . . . [and] many PRTs were at half-capacity, there was a mismatch of skills to requirements, and there were only 29 bilingual Arabic-speaking cultural advisers of 610 personnel."[83]

PRTs are also plagued by a lack of standardization: they have no standard size and no standard allotment of positions to different agencies and departments. PRTs in Iraq are very different from those in Afghanistan. Each country runs its PRTs entirely differently, but even among U.S.-led PRTs there is no continuity. This is not a deliberate outcome of matching form to function but rather a byproduct of ad hocery and interagency competition. A January 2008 study produced by Princeton's Woodrow Wilson School of Public and International Affairs found, unsurprisingly, that DOD, State, and USAID each has a very different agenda for the PRTs. DOD's priority is COIN, and PRTs are excellent contributors to winning hearts and minds. DOD therefore prefers to use the PRTs for quick impact projects (QIPs), "small-scale short-term projects aimed at pacifying local populations and building trust."[84] The State Department, in contrast, views the PRTs as platforms for reconstruction and stabilization, and USAID is focused on development and long-term projects in more permissive areas. The Princeton team conducted interviews in which "former PRT members . . . commented that the divergent mandates officials bring from their home agencies [created] friction in the field—a dynamic made worse by the largely consensus-based decision making process."[85]

In fact, although PRTs are supposed to be one of the key answers to militarization, the shortage of civilian personnel, the PRTs' heavily military structures, and DOD's dominance in nonpermissive environments mean that PRTs end up being mostly military organizations that primarily undertake tasks that are military priorities. This is exacerbated by the fact that PRTs have no funds of their own and tend to rely on CERP funding. In practice, the projects go where the money goes, giving the military tremendous influence over PRTs' efforts. The Princeton study found that the "wide disparity in resources generates disproportionate DOD influence over both the policy planning process in Washington and field-level operations."[86] Hillary Clinton remarked on CERP during the hearings on her nomination to be secretary of state. Referring to her first trip to Iraq in 2003, she said she returned a believer in CERP but was also concerned about the disparity of funding for warriors versus the State Department experts or USAID development officers who might better promote political and economic advances in our national interest.[87]

Although there have been setbacks, efforts to reinvigorate civilian capabilities are ongoing. With the Quadrennial Diplomacy and Development Review (QDDR),[88] the State Department hoped to present a persuasive accounting of the civilian agencies' capabilities and a sense of the extent and costs of their requirements. It also hoped to develop support in Congress by opening lines of constructive communication. While the military has been hugely successful in defining its advantages to legislators and has effectively used its own Quadrennial Defense Review, on which the QDDR is patterned, to further articulate its needs, the civilian agencies have not, until now, made the same effort. The QDDR is intended to change that.[89] Although the document was hampered by delays and concerns about the extent to which it had to be watered down to achieve buy-in from the various departments and agencies, compiling the data for the QDDR was a valuable exercise. It shined light on where the civilian agencies best contribute to achieving U.S. foreign policy goals and, with empirical data, clarified in what dimensions they need to improve. These are important steps in strengthening the beleaguered diplomatic and aid institutions.

While the civilian shortage for nation building has become a familiar theme, less remarked upon is the fact that the shortage is a function of a new interpretation of civilian roles that, in turn, is rooted in the securitization of instability. Diplomacy and development programs always have been used to achieve American goals—including security objectives—internationally; when American goals began to include a very broad interest in the reduction of instability, however, and when that became strongly associated with U.S. security, the expectations of civilian agencies changed significantly. Their efforts became, to a greater extent than ever, quick fixes to current security concerns. This created greater demands on civilian institutions while also forcing them to shift their resource allocations from long-term programming worldwide to shorter-term efforts in conflict zones. The QDDR, for example, proudly touts civilian utility in the new security environment by citing statistics on precisely this shift in resources: "We have already begun to address these trends; today more than a quarter of State and USAID's personnel serve in the 30 countries that are at the highest risk for conflict. More than 2,000 civilian personnel are deployed to Afghanistan and Iraq alone."[90]

The extreme example of this was in the militarization of the civilian responsibilities in Iraq as U.S. troops withdrew from that country. By the end of 2011, according to the 2008 status-of-forces agreement, all American forces had to leave. In their stead were unprecedented numbers of U.S. diplomats and, to provide security for them, thousands of civilian security contractors (estimates range from four thousand to seven thousand). The State Department, in preparation for these unusual conditions, requested MRAPs, Black Hawk helicopters, and other military equipment for dispersal to the contractors. Members of Congress, with the security contractor firm Blackwater's politically devastating behavior in Iraq fresh in their memories, denied most of the State Department's requests.[91] Ultimately, however, State and other civilian agencies became responsible for arranging private security, one way or the other, for their personnel in Iraq. They are in Iraq conducting nation building as the final stages of a military mission, in the name of U.S. security interests, and with responsibility for the only U.S. defense forces—private soldiers—in the country.[92] State's Bureau of Diplomatic Security is therefore now facing unprecedented demands even as it struggles with staffing and funding shortfalls.[93] This actual militarization of civilian responsibilities is as much a function of securitized instability as is fill-the-gap militarization. It also shows that, despite the apparent impression that the military can do everything, diplomats and aid personnel—whether for practical or political reasons—still can do things that the armed forces cannot.

Nonetheless, civilian agencies recognize the threat that new expectations and the military's comparative advantages in fulfilling them presents to their own institutional heft. The military's increased assumption of traditionally civilian roles has not gone unremarked or unchallenged. It has raised debates about the relative distribution of resources as well as concerns about the effects of militarization on broader U.S. interests. There has been tremendous internal and interagency debate about each executive agency's appropriate role, civil-military relations, and U.S. foreign policy priorities. In particular, and despite improved funding since the Iraq war, USAID and State are struggling to demonstrate their continued relevance and are competing with each other and with DOD for responsibilities, resources, and influence. As mentioned earlier, Secretary of State Clinton instituted the Quadrennial Diplomacy and Development Review precisely because the civilian agencies need both to clarify and assert their relative value. It is notable that the QDDR is based on the U.S. military's Quadrennial Defense Review, and thus the armed forces are the standard to which the civilian agencies aspire. As Clinton put it, the QDDR will help "create a global civilian service of the same caliber and flexibility of the U.S. military."[94]

The civilian agencies have expressed particular concern about the military's role in reconstruction. The potential problems with this form of militarization are multifold. Because the military is neither a diplomatic nor a development organization, the wells it digs or the schoolhouses it constructs are intended to achieve U.S. military purposes: to provide access to strategic locations or to develop relations with specific leaders or populations. Such projects are not designed to be sustainable, are not organized for long-term effect, are not the result of development planning processes, and do not conform to civilian agencies' assessments and programming. American troops will not place a well where it is most needed either for local use or for broader U.S. strategic and political interests; they will place a well where they need it. They will not go into a village and determine what it most needs or consider how their presence affects the local balance of power; they will provide what will benefit themselves. The wells might be helpful and the schoolhouses might be valuable, but the military is not designed to assess what is best for an area, nor to evaluate the larger political and social impact of what it provides, nor to ensure that whatever it builds or offers is sustainable in the long run.[95]

Military development efforts also can taint civilian projects by creating confusion. When U.S. military personnel wear civilian clothing while conducting civic actions, for example, they can be mistaken for civilian actors. Their efforts—driven by military interests and priorities—can be taken to represent more general U.S. interests, thus bringing into question Americans' commitment to sustainable political and economic development. Such military projects also can lead to misunderstandings and even prove counterproductive if they are not coordinated with civilian efforts. They can privilege different local actors, upend local political dynamics, and contribute to corruption. In effect, they can provide short-term military benefits at long-term development costs. Furthermore, where troops are active in traditionally civilian roles or are working with their civilian counterparts, locals can perceive the civilian governmental and nongovernmental programs as fronts for military action or intelligence gathering and become distrustful. In these ways, military encroachments into traditionally civilian roles can produce jobs poorly done in development or political terms while compromising civilian agencies and increasing their challenges.[96]

These concerns seemed to be borne out in Afghanistan, where the military's nation-building efforts have had, at best, mixed results. The U.S.-led NATO offensive in Marja, in particular, reflected the problems of military solutions to political problems. There the American military had, as General McChrystal described it, a "government in a box, ready to roll in" after the troops.[97] But the planning for civilians' needs was still inadequate in terms of support for refugees and aid to noncombatants. One study found that, far from winning over the population, the operation in Marja alienated the locals. Sixty-one percent felt more negative toward NATO than prior to the offensive, 67 percent did not support a strong NATO-ISAF presence in their province, and 71 percent wanted the NATO forces to leave.[98] Soon after the offensive, the province reverted to Taliban control.

Unfortunately, civilians cannot yet do much better. The military acknowledged the failure in Marja and, in the summer of 2010, attempted to implement "lessons learned" in Kandahar, bringing civilians' role to the fore. The intent became not to pacify and then build but to begin with civilian outreach efforts in order to win over the population. One soldier explained: "Kandahar, it is a different type operation, it is not like Marja, it is not going to be that kinetic." The focus became reliance on PRTs in six districts around the province, with the hopes that the civilians could win hearts and minds and either forestall or diminish violence. Yet, although about four hundred American diplomats and governmental development experts went into Kandahar and other provinces to help promote local governance and to create economic opportunities, they represented only about a third of the American civilian governmental personnel in Afghanistan; most remained in Kabul, where their security could be better ensured. Of those who ventured into the countryside, most undertook projects intended to provide short-term benefits rather than long-term development, and most of these were undertaken without close coordination with local officials or the establishment of local institutions. Indeed, the Americans—both govern-ment workers and NGOs—snapped up the most educated and competent Afghans to serve as translators, offering higher salaries and greater security than local administrative jobs would entail. To the U.S. military's chagrin and deep frustration, American civilians thus undermined the potential for the development of an effective Afghan civil service even as they nominally promoted such improvements.[99]

Anthony Cordesman anticipated precisely this kind of outcome to a "civilian surge," arguing that there was a fundamental disconnect between the military's optimistic and unrealistic assumptions about what civilians could achieve in COIN and stability operations and civilians' actual capa-bilities. He wrote:

> It was all too easy to formulate a new strategy based on "shape, clear, hold, build, and transition" as long as the civil side of "hold, build, and transi-tion" was conceptual, and did not have to be implemented in rural areas like Marjah . . . and the far more challenging conditions of a largely urban area like Kandahar. It was clear from the start, however, that any practical appli-cation of this strategy lacked operational definition on the civil side, that the aid community was not ready to implement it and any civilian "surge" would still leave civil activity highly dependent on the US military, and that building Afghan capabilities would be a slow effort that had to occur at every level from local to central government. In short, implementation was never a military-driven exercise in finding the right troop to task ratio, but always a politico-economic exercise in resource to experiment ratio.[100]

In effect, civilians find themselves squeezed between a lack of support and high expectations in a world in which the causes of instability are them-selves considered security risks. Institutional privileging has absolutely lim-ited civilian capacity and is itself a reflection of legislators' limited trust of and confidence in civilian agencies:

> One of the biggest questions facing the United States is whether Con-gress will foot the bill for a civilian-led nation-building effort. Although

lawmakers have been reluctant to cut funding to U.S. combat troops, they seem far more willing to cut aid to the Iraqis. The Obama administration's request for $2 billion to train and equip Iraqi army and police forces was recently cut in half by the Senate.[101]

Finally, fill-the-gap militarization both reflects and affects policy makers' foreign policy options. They are caught, in responding to international events and in promoting U.S. interests abroad, between underfunded and undermanned civilian agencies and a military that, while a jack of all trades, remains really a master of one: warfighting. As the Council on Foreign Relations senior fellow Stephen Biddle warns, relying on the military in lieu of civilian capabilities, as happens in fill-the-gap operations, "jeopardizes the mission." Further, he argues, "the military cannot by itself create governance reform."[102] Without adequate numbers of adequately trained civilian personnel, situations like that in Kandahar will be all too common. American policy makers and legislators therefore have a judgment call to make. They can forgo operations for which they do not have the appropriate instruments, they can refocus on building civilian capacity to complement existing military capabilities in order to achieve their very broad goals, or they can continue what they're doing, which is retaining their ambitious agenda and turning to the military to accomplish it, regardless of the costs to the military, to civilian agencies, and to their chances for success.

COIN: A MICROCOSM

One of the most significant outcomes of elevating stability operations has been the simultaneous and related elevation of COIN. The high-profile 2006 release of the new U.S. counterinsurgency (COIN) doctrine, Army Field Manual 3-24/Marine Corps Warfighting Publication 3-33.5, reflected the new cachet that COIN as a mission gained after its tenets, as applied during the surge in Iraq, appeared to rescue the American efforts to stabilize that country. The efforts in Iraq were followed by an active COIN campaign in Afghanistan. COIN is a subset of stability operations and arguably the most challenging of them, requiring intensive efforts for the duration of the contingency. The implications for the military of this renewed focus on COIN are not to be underestimated. It was no coincidence that the U.S. military abandoned COIN after Vietnam. The devastating effects on the military, especially the Army, of involvement in that conflict lasted for decades and included low morale, poor public image, reduced funding, and terrible civil-military relations. By promulgating COIN doctrine and preparing the troops for such operations, the military is handing policy makers a ready-made instrument of foreign policy that they will therefore be more likely to use. For the military, this is a tremendous risk, given the real potential for Vietnam-like costs of deployment for COIN.

But there are also implications for civilian agencies and for U.S. foreign policy more generally. The first is, simply, further fill-the-gap militarization. In COIN, kinetic operations to combat insurgents must be balanced against the possibility of alienating the local population. COIN requires fighting and winning against rebels while wooing the population. And wooing the population requires diplomacy and development. The COIN manual states: "Military actions executed without properly assessing their political effects at best result in reduced effectiveness and at worst are counterproductive. Resolving most insurgencies requires a political solution; it is thus imperative that counterinsurgent actions do not hinder achieving that political solution," and an "operation that kills five insurgents is counterproductive if collateral damage leads to the recruitment of fifty more insurgents."[103] U.S. military leaders have become wont to repeat Lieutenant General James Dubik's comment that "you can't kill your way out of this kind of war."[104] In keeping with this, the COIN manual, like DODD 3000.05 and the 2010 Army Posture Statement, tasks the military to work with and in support of civilians. If there are not enough civilians to do the jobs, however, or if their training and the structure of their agencies are not well matched to the demands of a postconflict environment (as proved to be the case in both Afghanistan and Iraq), the military will find itself deeply involved in the more characteristically civilian aspects of stability operations. Indeed, the COIN manual also includes the following caution:

Durable policy success requires balancing the measured use of force with an emphasis on nonmilitary programs. Political, social, and economic programs are most commonly and appropriately associated with civilian organizations and expertise; however, *effective implementation of these programs is more important than who performs the tasks. If adequate civilian capacity is not available, military forces fill the gap.*[105]

In practice, this means that the military will prepare itself to assume responsibility for political, economic, and social programs in COIN for circumstances when civilian agencies cannot fulfill the need. And, as Defense Secretary Robert Gates made clear, the expectation is that civilian agencies will not be ready:

> even with a better-funded State Department and U.S. Agency for International Development, future military commanders will not be able to rid themselves of the tasks of maintaining security and stability. To truly achieve victory as Clausewitz defined it—to attain a political objective— the United States needs a military whose ability to kick down the door is matched by its ability to clean up the mess and even rebuild the house afterward.[106]

COIN—now and as a future prospect—serves as yet another reason for the military to ready itself for diplomacy and development responsibilities.

CONCLUSION

The military's embrace of stability operations ideally would provide policy makers with a broader set of tools for protecting U.S. interests abroad. Unfortunately, the reverse has been the case. As the military has adapted itself to assume traditional civilian roles in peacetime and postconflict, it has contributed to the accelerated reduction of civilian capabilities and the refocusing of civilian attention to a limited number of strategically important areas. Overreliance on the military and the further weakening of the civilian agencies each contribute to the other in a vicious cycle. The unrealistic demands on civilians, who then cannot meet them, enhances the military's appeal as a tool of foreign policy; the military's capacity and reliability make further reductions in civilian agencies possible. The outcome for policy makers is a more limited set of instruments than they have had in the past, with long-term development and diplomatic tools being stripped out in favor of short-term security-oriented options. This is militarization in several senses: greater reliance on the military relative to civilian agencies, the securitization of political and economic concerns, and the resulting reorientation of diplomatic and development tools toward achieving security outcomes.

Ironically, both of the current responses to militarization serve to further entrench it rather than ameliorate it.[107] In the first case, civilian capabilities are being ramped up to improve coordination and deployability. The cavalcade of acronyms (S/CRS, CRC, PRTs, ePRTs, DSTs) represents the efforts to restructure for greater interagency cooperation and civilian leadership. This effort has been plagued with problems, however, many of them rooted in bureaucratic and interagency competition. This is true in concrete form as civilians are seconded to brigades and the military dominates both the staffing and the deployment of PRTs. It is also the case in terms of civilian agencies' priorities. USAID and the State Department are rapidly increasing their capacities not for global involvement but for action in critical-priority countries like Afghanistan and Iraq. Their focus is shifting to accommodate demand for diplomats and aid administrators in war zones. This necessarily means shifting their resources and attention from long-term efforts in the rest of the world. As Defense Secretary Gates observed: "although there have been significant increases in the State Department budget over the last four or five years, and we have a billion-dollar embassy in Baghdad, and you have so many Foreign Service officers concentrated in Iraq and Afghanistan, the rest of the world hasn't seen much of an increase."[108] Finally, the effort to bring civilians into S&R leads, counterintuitively, to militarization insofar as traditionally civilian responsibilities—humanitarian assistance and development aid, for example—are being perceived not as ends in themselves but as means to achieve security outcomes. In other words, they are becoming instruments of conflict management. This dynamic was described in an article in the *International Review of the Red Cross* that decried the blurring of the distinctions between humanitarian, political, and military action that takes place "when civilians are embedded into military structures, and when the impression is created that humanitarian organizations and their personnel are merely tools within integrated approaches to conflict management."[109] Overall, the effort to ensure State Department and USAID leadership on critical reconstruction and transition tasks has had some notable successes[110] but so far has proved to be counterproductive in reducing militarization.

The second approach involves military preparation to assume these responsibilities in the event that civilians do not or cannot step up; it does not reduce militarization. Rather, it is an effort to control militarization, reduce its negative effects on security and military readiness, and improve the military's abilities in this realm. Doctrinal changes, with concomitant changes in training, education, and organization, are setting the stage for the military to undertake more readily and consistently traditionally civilian responsibilities for reconstruction and transition. Thus, this latter approach is institutionalizing militarization, instead of reducing it, and shifting responsibilities in a deliberate and likely permanent way.

Chapter 6 addresses the dynamic created when, on the one hand, U.S. policy makers' ambitions exceed the tools at their disposal and, on the other hand, the military attempts to meet the need. The chapter examines whether, in light of American interests, international conditions, and U.S. military and civilian capabilities, the current path of securitized instability and increasingly militarized foreign policy is a reasonable one and, if not, what possible alternatives might be.

SIX
A NEW WORLD ORDER?

I n early 2011, as the Arab Spring swept across the Middle East, the governments in Egypt and Tunisia fell relatively peacefully in the face of popular uprisings. But the alternative to capitulation was violence, and Muammar Qaddafi in Libya demonstrated quickly that he would resist any effort to overthrow his government with massive retaliation against protestors and rebels. Setting a precedent for subsequent violent repressions of opposition in Bahrain, Yemen, and Syria, Qaddafi mustered forces against antigovernment activists and turned his response into a military campaign, using planes, helicopters, tanks, and artillery to punish the rebels. The international community reacted with disapprobation and, fearing a massacre, the United States and its NATO allies, acting under the auspices of UN resolutions 1970 and 1973, enforced an arms embargo and set up a no-fly zone over Libya in an effort to prevent Qaddafi from using aircraft in his attacks. The United States led the initial military response to Qaddafi but quickly turned control over to NATO. Americans nonetheless continued to contribute support to the campaign by using drones to target Qaddafi's forces and strongholds, providing aerial refueling and reconnaissance, and dispatching CIA advisors to assist the rebels. As the conflict in Libya shifted from its early stages as a continuation of the Arab Spring to a more tenacious revolution against the long-standing strongman, the NATO and U.S. efforts lost their focus. Though initially justified as a humanitarian intervention to prevent the slaughtering of civilians, by June 2011, over three months into the international effort in Libya, NATO had bombarded Qaddafi's personal compounds, dropped bombs on Tripoli, extended the anticipated duration of its operation, and made Qaddafi's relinquishment of power a condition for a NATO ceasefire. This expansion of purpose is an example of mission creep.

In the 1990s, as U.S. forces were deployed for serial peace operations and support to humanitarian assistance missions in northern Iraq, Somalia, Bosnia, Haiti, and Kosovo, concerns about mission creep became common. The term referred to an extension of the armed forces' role beyond their original charge, an extension attributable, variously, to mutating political guidance, changing circumstances on the ground, and inadvertent military actions. Mission creep was deemed most likely to occur when, among other things, military operations were guided by unclear political objectives or strategy.[1] Such unintentional expansion of the armed forces' role in any given operation was considered problematic both because it reduced the likelihood of operational success and because of the potentially negative effects on the armed forces. The first concern proved well founded. American actions in Somalia technically were deemed successful, but the objectives had been deliberately extremely limited, and any positive outcomes were ephemeral. One cannot downplay the benefits of lives saved through the provision of food aid protected by American forces, but such gains lasted only as long as U.S. troops remained in the country. Meanwhile, the negative consequences of the U.S. actions included Osama bin Laden's interpretation of the U.S. withdrawal after American troops were killed in what became known as Black Hawk Down as a lack of stomach for casualties and thus an invitation for a large-scale attack. The Clinton administration made the decision not to respond in Rwanda on the basis of U.S. experiences in Somalia, a judgment that Clinton repeatedly cited, in retrospect, as his biggest regret. After international troops withdrew, Somalia spiraled out of control domestically, becoming a completely failed state. American efforts in Haiti likewise achieved, in the short term, some narrow goals, but these failed to translate into enduring returns. As in Somalia, the United States offered band-aids—very expensive band-aids—where major surgery was needed. And, as in Somalia, the overall conditions in Haiti were little improved and then only temporarily. Even in Bosnia, though American involvement helped broker the end of the conflict, the ongoing political and social instability in the territory reflects the challenges of effectively resolving such hostilities at their roots. In each instance, deployed troops encountered complex local dynamics for which their policy guidance was inadequate. In each case, troops were asked to respond flexibly, make rapid and sophisticated judgment calls, and ultimately provide fixes for situations that were completely foreign to them, whether it was brokering negotiations between Somali warlords or determining the quality of meat that should be provided as part of short-term humanitarian assistance to Haitians. The military adapted to the requirements as well as it could, though not without grumbling about being deployed beyond its purview and with negative implications for morale, retention, and readiness.

In many respects, what we see today in terms of the securitization of instability and the militarization of foreign policy are simply mission creep writ large. U.S. policy makers are doing, on a global scale, what they did in a more limited way in each post–Cold War operation; they are demanding ambitious outcomes—both broad and deep—with inadequate guidance as to priorities and constraints and without clear, definable, measurable goals.[2] And the U.S. military is doing, on a global scale, what it did in each post–Cold War operation; it is stepping up, demonstrating its utility, and attempting to fill in the blanks in guidance and capabilities.

Between the immediate post–Cold War and now, however, a significant change has taken place: for reasons laid out in detail in chapter 4, the military has embraced such a role. Gone, for the most part, are the cautions of Weinberger and Powell, replaced by the wholehearted enthusiasm of notable military officials including Gates, William Caldwell, William Wallace, Anthony Zinni, and John Abizaid. Rather than placing a check on the policy makers' limitless agenda, as previous military resistance had done, the armed forces' adoption of stability operations reinforces the strategic mission creep currently taking place. In critiquing the 2010 QDR and DOD budget request, Gordon Adams made precisely this point:

Defense Secretary Robert Gates argued that the two documents were "shaped by a bracing dose of realism" with regard to risk and resources.

> I respectfully disagree. The QDR's risk assessment piles on missions like a short-order cook stacks pancakes at IHOP, setting no priorities between near-term challenges and long-term requirements. And the budget continues to accommodate such a limitless agenda. The bottom line: This lack of discipline will broaden the country's defense requirements and expand military spending in ways that will make establishing budget and mission discipline in the future even more difficult.[3]

This culmination of institutional privileging and securitized instability in the expansion of the military's role into efforts to address the roots of conflict across the entire spectrum of operations means that soon there will not be a process of militarization; instead, U.S. foreign policy will simply be militarized. Mission creep will have taken place both in terms of the American foreign policy agenda and in terms of the scope of military responsibilities. The military has shown that it will, given the opportunities created by securitization and institutional privileging and the downplaying of conventional threats, choose to prepare for and proactively participate in stability operations. Yet it is already finding itself mired in unwinnable contingencies, spread thin, with reduced overall readiness. Nonetheless, the armed forces will dominate not just in terms of manpower and budget but influence as well, at least in areas considered of strategic importance to the United States. Civilian tools of policy will be perceived as means to achieve security ends rather than broader objectives, with a cascade of effects. Civilian agencies' resources will be redesignated for short-term contingency efforts and away from ongoing, long-term processes. The effects of this will be felt worldwide, because—as is happening today, with the preponderance of State and USAID personnel in Iraq and Afghanistan—civilian resources and attention will be drawn away from all but the most immediately significant countries. Civilian agencies, designed for very different purposes, will be unable to fulfill the demands of stability operations but, having refocused their energy toward those in order to curry legislative favor and funds, they will also be unable to sustain longer-term programs and efforts. Civilians will be reliant on the military in conflict zones, limiting their independence of action and movement. The civilian agencies will thus be in a position in which they contribute expertise and knowledge, but they will not lead U.S. involvement abroad. American foreign policy will become little more than the implementation of short-term security measures and responses. Long-term processes of diplomacy and development will fall by the wayside. Policy makers thus will be faced with involvement in unwinnable contingencies that undermine American legitimacy internationally, exhausted military forces, overstretched civilians, and declining public support at home—and only short-term foreign policy instruments at their disposal.

Many people see this happening, but the obstacles to halting militarization are extraordinarily high and fraught with political challenges. What needs to happen is the reversal of the process of securitization that led Americans to define their security interests to include the world's economic and social woes. As long as there is consensus that U.S. security interests include addressing instability and its causes, militarization will remain an issue. Yet securitization is not easily undone. Once people perceive the world in one light, adjusting their understanding is incredibly hard, especially if their security or national prestige is at stake. Michael Parenti describes the progression of securitization as disingenuous:

> For decades we were told that a huge U.S. military establishment was necessary to contain an expansionist world Communist movement with its headquarters in Moscow (or sometimes Beijing). But after the overthrow of the Soviet Union and other Eastern European Communist nations, Washington made no move to dismantle its costly and dangerous global military apparatus. All Cold War weapons programs continued in full force, with new ones being added all the time, including plans to militarize outer space. Immediately the White House and Pentagon began issuing jeremiads about a whole host of new enemies—for some unexplained reason previously overlooked—who menace the United States, including "dangerous rogue states" like Libya with its ragtag army of 50,000. The elder George Bush, as Richard Barnet noted, even "proclaimed the new American enemy to be 'instability,' a vague but ominous political science metaphor." . . . These claims were swiftly and uncritically embraced by defense establishment academics and media pundits who pretend to an expertise on foreign affairs.[4]

The U.S. congressmen Barney Frank and Ron Paul see deeper roots to securitization. They pointed out in an editorial that the United States has long seen itself as the world's policeman. Because of that self-perception, the Pentagon budget accounts for more than all other discretionary spending programs combined. In fact, "American military spending makes up approximately 44% of all [military expenditures] worldwide." Americans believe that "as a superpower it is our duty to maintain stability by intervening in civil disorders virtually anywhere in the world." The two legislators point out, however, that such a stance "often generates anger directed at us and may in the end do more harm than good."[5]

It will do the United States more harm than good not only in terms of its foreign relations but in terms of its own foreign policy architecture as well. If the United States does not perceive poverty, instability, crime, and other quality-of-life issues worldwide as immediate threats to security, then it can step back and reevaluate the foreign policy path it has hurried down. Indeed, in the long run, precisely those kinds of problems will be much more effectively and fundamentally addressed through long-standing civilian programs than through short-term militarized fixes. If this reevaluation does not take place soon, however, militarization will be entrenched, civilian agencies will be undermined, and the long-term programs in place will fade into history.

Reversing the processes of securitization and militarization would require not only critical thinking but a deliberate redirection of policy. The first requires rejecting the visceral response to 9/11 and the received wisdom about the changing security environment to consider the costs and benefits of certain policies in light of U.S. interests. As Steven Metz and Frank Hoffman point out, "The key is to identify the point at which the expense of building and sustaining capability outweighs the expected strategic utility."[6] Phoebe Marr questioned, even more broadly, American involvement in the most challenging stability operations. She wrote, in a 2005 *Foreign Affairs* article:

Given such daunting difficulties, the best advice to draw from these books may be this: if you cannot garner adequate resources—and public opinion at home and abroad—to rebuild a nation, do not start. Rather than ponder the dos and don'ts of nation building, as Diamond and Phillips do, perhaps it would be wiser to weigh the whys and why nots of engaging in it in the first place. If the U.S. experience in Iraq holds any lesson for the future, it may be that Washington should exercise extreme caution before launching another such operation. In the meantime, it should look harder for ways to shore up or bring change to failing states before they warrant intervention at all.[7]

Such cautionary statements are not new. In the 1980s, Robert Johnson warned in *International Organization* that America was inflating the threats from the developing world and, even then, securitizing global instability. He wrote:

> The invocation of world order principles inflates the stakes in a conflict by suggesting that, not just immediate U.S. interests, but values that we hold to be of universal significance, are at stake. . . . We have an interest in a world order in which nations determine their own futures and in which the use of force is minimized because such an order is likely to be congenial to the achievement of other U.S. values. However, because of the difficulty of applying these principles and because there is no necessary connection between them and American security, we should be extremely cautious about using such vague rationales to justify U.S. intervention in particular conflicts.[8]

Redirecting policy requires just this kind of careful decision making about goals, means, and capabilities. These are intrinsically related. The most critical question to ask is whether this new operating environment is unavoidable. U.S. decision makers, both civilian and military, are assuming that the past two decades presage the future. Such internal pressures have given rise to the dual ideas that the military should be involved in shaping permissive environments and that often it is the only reliable institution for shaping nonpermissive postconflict environments. One could make a strong argument, however, that the past two decades are functions of policy decisions that created involvement in stability operations, rather than that stability operations have been a necessary response to pressing international events. U.S. expeditionary efforts arguably are driven more by internal pressures than by external imperatives. This basic question under-pins debates about the United States' role and responsibilities in Iraq, Afghanistan, Libya, and Pakistan, to name but a few examples. America is pouring resources—money and manpower—into each of these countries in the hopes of creating stability, of successfully building nations, and of over-coming local tensions and conflicts and political dynamics to install demo-cratic regimes, healthy economies, and stable societies. Progressives see this as America's future as well as its present and advocate for a crucial role for the military in these ambitious endeavors. Traditionalists, in contrast, see these as engagements of choice, not necessity, and ask policy makers and observers to question whether the choices have been good ones.

Ironically, just as the American policy makers and military leaders stake their institutions' future on the need to prevent, respond to, and rectify failing states and the many threats that emanate from them, more careful analysis of failed and failing states indicates that they may not present quite the secu-rity challenges that have been attributed to them. Stewart Patrick's extremely detailed book *Weak Links: Fragile States, Global Threats, and International Security* provides evidence that only under some conditions will failed or fail-ing states pose security threats to the United States and, moreover, that a militarized response will not help mitigate the problems that do exist:

> Unfortunately, the U.S. government's recent approach to state fragil-ity has been reactive, fragmented, militarized, under-resourced, and self-contained. [To better deal with the problem,] the U.S. government should adapt its conventional development aid and policy to the reali-ties of fragile states; invest in the civilian U.S. capabilities necessary to advance good governance and security in such contexts; and rebalance the military, diplomatic, and development components of its engagement.[9]

Yet what will matter is not the actual threat but rather where decision mak-ers come down on this issue, how they perceive or choose to depict the threat, and how they identify their best options in response to that. It will be the policies that will have tangible repercussions in terms of future U.S. capabilities. As Benjamin Fordham points out:

even if policy choice is, in part, a function of capabilities, capabilities are also a function of policy choice. Decision makers build military (and other) capabilities based on the policies they expect to pursue and the international conditions they expect to face. State leaders who expect to use force more frequently will build more military capabilities. . . . Although choices about capabilities must be made long before force is actually used, it is important to consider the extent to which any observed relationship between capabilities and policy choice stems from the decision makers' anticipation of their future needs and their resulting decisions about military spending and procurement.[10]

Consider, for example, how changing military concepts can reinforce securitization. Adding stability operations as a legitimate and primary mission—and reconfiguring the spectrum of conflict to include phases Zero and Five—creates a new way of thinking that, once accepted and institutionalized, is incredibly difficult to reverse.[11] In recognition of this, the traditionalists are trying to keep precisely this discussion alive. Gentile and Bacevich and others are attempting to inculcate doubts about this new direction before the mindset hardens and becomes irreversible. They want military and civilian leaders to consider the costs of securitized instability and militarized foreign policy in terms of the armed forces' efficacy and interests and more general U.S. policy concerns. Their efforts have been unflagging, but they are persistently undermined by political reality: embracing stability operations broadens the military's purview and provides the armed forces with a new raison d'être just as it appears to have maxed out its old one, at least politically. Legislators and policy makers alike have a history of privileging military solutions over civilian ones. And concerns about instability worldwide have been reified through repetition.

Securitization of instability is likely to last only until the next existential threat comes along; militarization of U.S. foreign policy will decline when budgets or circumstances force hard decisions about military priorities. In the meantime, however, both of these trends have momentum, and neither bodes well for the military, for civilian agencies, or for U.S. foreign policy.

NOTES

INTRODUCTION. MISSION CREEP WRIT LARGE: THE U.S. MILITARY'S EMBRACE OF STABILITY OPERATIONS

1. Department of Defense Directive, Number 3000.05, November 28, 2005, Subject: Military Support for Stability, Security, Transition, and Reconstruction (SSRT) Operations, http://www.usaid.gov/policy/cdie/ssso6/sss_1_080106_dod.pdf.
2. Ibid., 2.
3. The Goldwater-Nichols Department of Defense Reorganization Act of 1986 was the biggest change in the U.S. military's structure since the 1947 National Security Act, which created the National Security Council, Central Intelligence Agency, and the Department of Defense, among other things. Goldwater-Nichols centralized operational authority through the chairman of the Joint Chiefs of Staff rather than, as previously, through the service chiefs and designated the CJCS as the principal military advisor to the president, the NSC, and the secretary of defense. It also streamlined the operational chain of command from the president, through the defense secretary, to the unified commanders. The intention of the reorganization was to enhance joint coordination and cooperation, which under the previous structure had suffered from interservice competition and lack of communication.
4. "Full-Spectrum Operations in Capstone Doctrine," Information Papers, 2008 Army Posture Statement, http://www.army.mil/aps/o8/information_papers/transform/Full_Spectrum_Operations.html.
5. Nathan P. Freier, "Shifting Emphasis: Leaders, Strategists, and Operators in an Era of Persistent Unconventional Challenge," Center for Strategic and International Studies, September 2008, http://www.csis.org/media/csis/pubs/090305_shifting_emphasis.pdf; Freier, "The New Balance: Limited Armed Stabilization and the Future of U.S. Landpower," Strategic Studies Institute, U.S. Army War College, April 6, 2009, http://www.strategicstudiesinstitute.army.mil/pubs/display.cfm?PubID=915. In "Mapping the Global Future," the National Intelligence Council refers to "pervasive insecurity." See http://www.dni.gov/nic/NIC_globaltrend2020_s4.html. FM 3-0 (2008)

begins on p. 1-1 with a section titled "Instability and Persistent Conflict," http://www
.cspan.org/Content/PDF/fm3_2008.pdf. Also see William S. Wallace "FM 3-0 Operations: The Army's Blueprint" (U.S. Army), *Military Review* (March–April 2008):
3, where the general writes that the current edition of FM 3-0 "reflects Army thinking
in a complex era of persistent conflict."

6. Unconventional warfare is defined as "operations conducted by, with, or through
irregular forces in support of a resistance movement, an insurgency, or conventional military operations." See *Special Forces Unconventional Warfare*, Field Manual
3-05.201, September 28, 2007. Foreign internal defense is defined as "the participation by civilian and military agencies of a government in any of the action programs
taken by another government or other designated organization, to free and protect its
society from subversion, lawlessness, insurgency, terrorism, and other threats to their
security." See *Foreign Internal Defense*, Joint Publication 3-22, July 2010, ix, http://
www.dtic.mil/doctrine/new_pubs/jp3_22.pdf.

7. Although IW was not as broad a category of operations as "operations other than
war" (OOTW) or "low-intensity conflict" (LIC), it suffered from many of the same
problems as those earlier groupings. Despite its prominence in the 2006 QDR, IW,
like its predecessors, merely lumped together a set of operations other than conventional war. Such operations had, in the past, been considered either unwelcome
distractions that reduced readiness or bonus operations reflecting the benefits of
having a large and extraordinarily capable military. Either way, they had long been
marginal to the armed forces' primary mission. Being rolled under a single category as IW did little to illuminate how each contributes to U.S. national security
interests and did much to obscure crucial differences among them. UW and FID,
for example, are mutually exclusive; COIN is usually conceived of as a subset of
FID; and CT is often a completely standalone activity, though it can be conducted
as part of a broader contingency. Each of these can run as a complement to a
conventional war (UW was an important part of the U.S. effort in World War II,
for example). All of these incorporate stability operations. Though IW as a term
is in the process of being excised, references to IW persist in doctrine as well as in
the names of several military institutions, including the Marine Corps Center for
Irregular Warfare (CIW).

8. This last is often referred to as stabilization and reconstruction (S&R), or stabilization, security, transition, and reconstruction (SSTR) efforts.

9. DOD 3000.05 reflects a maturation from the assumptions underlying the RMA to
those underpinning stability operations, i.e., conflict does not end when combat is
over. Understanding the requirement for establishing peace after war is not new; it
is just newly embraced. For an early advocate of this logic, see: B. H. Liddell Hart,
Strategy (London: Faber & Faber, 1967), 322.

10. "Rumsfeld Foresees Swift Iraq War," *BBC News*, February 7, 2003, http://news.bbc
.co.uk/2/hi/middle_east/2738089.stm. Rumsfeld liked to say this. CBS News quoted
him predicting the length of the incipient war in 2002, "Five days or five weeks or

five months, but it certainly isn't going to last any longer than that." John Esterbrook, "Rumsfeld: It Would Be a Short War," *CBS News*, November 15, 2002, http://www.cbsnews.com/stories/2002/11/15/world/main529569.shtml.

11. One reviewer of this chapter pointed out that "the American leadership conceived of the Iraq war in Jominian/Napoleonic terms—an attack to defeat the classical 'center of gravity' (the Iraqi military), then to capture the capital and install a new government. Within those conceptual parameters (but those only), OIF was an unqualified success. The conceptual failure of the Bush administration was the unwillingness to think outside those narrow confines and to imagine the second-order consequences and 'cascading', the unexpected outcomes. This was the result of linear rather than non-linear thinking." The author could not have said this better herself.

12. U.S. Army Field Manual (FM) 3-0, *Operations*, February 2008. "The 2008 publication of Field Manual 3-07, *Stability Operations and Support Operations*, provides a proven framework for discussing stability operations and should be used as a model for development of a joint publication. The USJFCOM FEA findings concluded the subject warranted a more detailed discussion in joint doctrine. The JDPC members unanimously agreed to accept the proposal for a JP on stability operations. USJF-COM was designated as the lead agent and began development in the first quarter of calendar year 2009." "Joint Doctrine Update," *Joint Force Quarterly* 53 (2nd quarter of 2009): 128; William B. Caldwell IV, "Evolution vs. Revolution: FM 3-0," blog entry, *Small Wars Journal*, February 15, 2008, http://smallwarsjournal.com/blog/2008/02/evolution-vs-revolution-fm-30/; William S. Wallace, "Full Spectrum Operations: FM 3-0: Resetting the Capstone of Army Doctrine," *Army* (March 2008).

1. STABILITY OPERATIONS IN CONTEXT

1. Department of Defense Directive, Number 3000.05, November 28, 2005, Subject: Military Support for Stability, Security, Transition, and Reconstruction (SSRT) Operations, http://www.usaid.gov/policy/cdie/ssso6/sss_1_080106_dod.pdf.

2. *Department of Defense Dictionary of Military and Associated Terms*, Joint Publication 1-02, 2009, 517.

3. *Operations*, U.S. Army Field Manual 3-0 (Washington, D.C.: Headquarters, Department of the Army, 2008), 1-15.

4. FM 3-0 (2008), 9-1; for the lists of tasks within OOTW, see *Operations*, U.S. Army Field Manual 100-5 (Headquarters, Department of the Army, June 1993), 13-0. Only disaster relief, which was included under OOTW, is not subsumed within stability operations.

5. Some of the tasks that fall within the category of stability operations—such as support to insurgency and shows of force—are less intuitively consistent with the concept of promoting stability, since they may well contribute to instability in the short term. Just as war is intended to culminate in peace, however, these are intended to contribute, ultimately, to greater stability.

6. Specifically, Clausewitz wrote: "We see, therefore, that war is not merely an act of policy but a true political instrument, a continuation of political intercourse, carried on with other means." Carl Von Clausewitz, *On War* (Oxford: Oxford University Press, 2007), 28.

7. There is a school of literature on the subject that emphasizes *security cooperation* instead of stability operations and, within that, the importance of military assistance. The focus is thus on military-to-military relations and, specifically, on training (through security assistance [SA], security force assistance [SFA], and international military education and training [IMET]) and foreign military financing (FMF). SA, IMET, and FMF are paid for by Congress, overseen by the State Department, and implemented by DOD. The Special Operations Command (SOCOM) has proponency for SFA, which is basically SA with even less of a civilian stamp on it. All of these are means of influencing and advising foreign militaries while maintaining open lines of communication and leverage. Though not synonymous with stability operations nor as broad a concept, security cooperation does encapsulate much of the U.S. military's role in stability operations and is relevant across the full spectrum of conflict. For an excellent overview of the role of military assistance in U.S. foreign policy, see Derek S. Reveron, *Exporting Security* (Washington, D.C.: Georgetown University Press, 2010).

8. FM 3-0 (2008), 9-1.

9. *Stability Operations,* U.S. Army Field Manual 3-07 (Washington, D.C.: Headquarters, Department of the Army, October 6, 2008), 1-1.

10. Matt Wulffe, *Robert Rogers' Rules for the Ranging Service: An Analysis* (Westminster, Md.: Heritage Books, 2009).

11. These included the "Little Belt" Affair, the three Seminole Wars, the Black Hawk War, the Cayuse War, and many others.

12. Adrian R. Lewis, *The American Culture of War* (New York: Routledge, 2007), 40.

13. Brent C. Bankus, "We've Done This Before," *Small Wars Journal* 4 (February 2006): 34.

14. James Kurth, "Variations on the American Way of War," in *The Long War: A New History of U.S. National Security Policy Since World War II*, ed. Andrew J. Bacevich (New York: Columbia University Press, 2007), 55. Of course, though the Americans embraced this "way of war," it was not uniquely American. Napoleon's methods were consistent with this approach, for example.

15. Brian McAllister Linn, *The Philippine War, 1899–1902* (Lawrence: University of Kansas Press, 2000).

16. "Chronology of U.S. Military Actions and Wars," *American Experience*, PBS, http://www.pbs.org/wgbh/amex/warletters/timeline/index.html.

17. Thomas Aiello, "Constructing 'Godless Communism:' Religion, Politics, and Popular Culture, 1954–1960," *Americana* 4, no. 1 (Spring 2005).

18. It is worth noting that during World War II, Army Chief of Staff General George C. Marshall (of the famed Marshall Plan) anticipated that the military would need to prepare for postcombat stability operations. Early in the U.S. engagement in the war, Marshall charged Major General John Hilldring with preparing occupation plans

for those countries the allies were going to liberate. This understanding that there would be a prolonged transition period from war to peace was one of the factors that differentiated the American approach to victory in World War II from the planning for the wars in Iraq and Afghanistan. For more on this, see Richard E. Neustadt and Ernest R. May, *Thinking in Time: The Uses of History for Decision Makers* (New York: The Free Press, 1986), 247–248.

19. "Chronology of U.S. Military Actions and Wars."

20. George C. Herring, "America and Vietnam: The Unending War," *Foreign Affairs* 70, no. 5 (Winter 1991): 104–119.

21. Ibid., 112.

22. "A Strong but Risky Show of Force," *Time* (May 26, 1975).

23. "Debacle in the Desert," *Time* (May 5, 1980).

24. Richard W. Nelson, "The Multinational Force in Beirut," in *The Multinational Force in Beirut, 1982–1984*, ed. Anthony McDermott and Kjell Skjelsbaek (Board of Regents of the State of Florida, 1991), 95.

25. Julie Wolf, "The Invasion of Grenada," *Reagan, the American Experience*, PBS, http:// www.pbs.org/wgbh/amex/reagan/peopleevents/pande07.html.

26. S. J. Labadie, "Jointness for the Sake of Jointness in 'Operation Urgent Fury,'" Naval War College, May 17, 1993.

27. "Operation Urgent Fury," Globalsecurity.org, http://www.globalsecurity.org/military/ ops/urgent_fury.htm.

28. In El Salvador in the 1980s, for example, the Reagan administration was distressed by the coalition of leftist groups that rose in opposition to the government. When civil war broke out, the United States supported the Salvadoran leadership, providing tremendous financial aid, military education, training, and hardware to the Salvadoran armed forces over a period of twelve years. The U.S. Congress limited to fifty-five the number of American military advisors who could deploy to El Salvador, and though that may have been exceeded, there were never more than 150 U.S. troops in the country; instead, Salvadoran military officers were trained in the United States, at the School of the Americas in Georgia. With American support, the Salvadoran government was able to resist the rebels, but at a terrible price. Seventy-five thousand people died in the war, and the U.S.-backed armed forces, intelligence services, and government-supported militias were responsible for massive human rights abuses, including massacres. During the entire period, the United States infused the Salvadoran economy with funds, but the stability element of the FID in El Salvador was stunted and incomplete, with no real pressure on the government to address the underlying problems that led to and sustained the conflict. After UN-mediated peace negotiations were concluded in 1992, U.S. aid transitioned into redevelopment assistance and the real stability operation in the country—mostly civilian run—began.

29. Ivo H. Daalder, "Knowing When to Say No: The Development of U.S. Policy for Peacekeeping," in *UN Peacekeeping, American Politics, and the Uncivil Wars of the 1990s*, ed. William J. Durch (New York: St. Martin's Press, 2006), 39–40.

30. Remarks by the President, National Defense University, Ft. McNair, Va., January 29, 1998.

31. "Military Operations: Impact of Operations Other Than War on the Services Varies," Report to the Chairman, Subcommittee on Readiness and Military Management Support, Committee on Armed Services, U.S. Senate (Washington, D.C.: United States General Accounting Office, 1999), GAO/NSIAD-99-69, 38, http://www.gao.gov/archive/1999/ns99069.pdf.

32. Ibid.

33. John Shalikashvili, "Shalikashvili: Focus Remains on Warfighting, Not Peacekeeping," *Defense Daily* (September 2, 1994).

34. Eric Shinseki, "Shinseki: Division Readiness Problems Due to Deployments," *Defense Daily* (November 12, 1999): 1.

35. James M. Inhofe, "Challenges of Military Readiness," *Military Review* (March–April 1999): 15–16.

36. "Military Operations: Impact of Operations Other Than War on the Services Varies."

37. John Shalikashvili, *NewsHour* transcript, September 25, 1997.

38. Daalder, "Knowing When to Say No," 41–42.

39. Michael O'Hanlon, "Transformation Reality Check," *Armed Forces Journal* 144, no. 8 (March 2007), http://www.armedforcesjournal.com/2007/03/2515135/.

40. Thomas E. Ricks, *Fiasco: The American Military Adventure in Iraq* (New York: Penguin, 2006), 78.

41. Ibid., 79.

42. Michael R. Gordon and Bernard E. Trainor, *Cobra II: The Inside Story of the Invasion and Occupation of Iraq* (New York: Vintage, 2007), 176.

43. Ibid., 52, 180.

44. "Beyond Nation Building," Remarks as Delivered by Secretary of Defense Donald H. Rumsfeld, Eleventh Annual Salute to Freedom, Intrepid Sea-Air-Space Museum, New York City, Friday, February 14, 2003.

45. Ibid.

46. Kevin H. Govern, "Paving the Road to the Warfighter: Preparing to Provide Legal Support on the Battlefield," *Army Lawyer*, DA PAM 27-50-350 (Washington, D.C.: Headquarters, Department of the Army, March 2002), 62.

47. Bob Woodward, *Plan of Attack* (New York: Simon & Schuster, 2006), 106.

48. John D. Banusiewicz, "'As Iraqis Stand Up, We Will Stand Down,' Bush Tells Nation," *Armed Forces Press Service* (June 28, 2005), http://www.defenselink.mil/news/newsarticle.aspx?id=16277.

49. Although DODD 3000.05 was released while Rumsfeld was still secretary of defense, he himself never signed it. Instead, Gordon England signed it as acting secretary of defense: http://www.usaid.gov/policy/cdie/sss06/sss_1_080106_dod.pdf. The instruction for DODD 3000.05, issued in 2009, was signed by Michele Flournoy, undersecretary of defense for policy: http://www.dtic.mil/whs/directives/corres/pdf/300005p.pdf.

50. Michael Howard, *Clausewitz* (Oxford: Oxford University Press, 1983), 34.

51. Charles W. Ostrom Jr. and Brian L. Job, "The President and the Political Use of Force," *American Political Science Review* 80, no. 2 (June 1986): 541–542.

52. Barry M. Blechman and Stephen S. Kaplan, *Force Without War: U.S. Armed Forces as a Political Instrument* (Washington, D.C.: The Brookings Institution, 1978), 3. On p. 12, the authors offer a more detailed definition: "political use of the armed forces occurs when physical actions are taken by one or more components of the uniformed military services as part of a deliberate attempt by the national authorities to influence, or to be prepared to influence, specific behavior of individuals in another nation without engaging in a continuing contest of violence."

53. Nadia Schadlow, "War and the Art of Governance," *Parameters* (Autumn 2003): 85.

54. Richard M. Saunders, "Military Force in the Foreign Policy of the Eisenhower Presidency," *Political Science Quarterly* 100, no. 1 (Spring 1985): 97.

55. Samuel Huntington, as cited in ibid., 97.

56. Ibid., 116.

57. Robert R. Bowie and Richard H. Immerman, *Waging Peace* (New York: Oxford University Press, 1998), 190–191. The president's stance was limited to what he perceived as peripheral countries, however. In fact, he put forth the Eisenhower Doctrine in a speech in 1957, asserting that the United States would protect Middle Eastern regimes threatened by communism. This doctrine guided the decision to deploy U.S. forces to Lebanon in 1958 in defense of that country's pro-Western government. "The Eisenhower Doctrine: A Message to Congress, January 5, 1957," *Department of State Bulletin* 36, no. 917 (January 21, 1957): 83–87, http://www.fordham.edu/halsall/mod/1957eisenhowerdoctrine.html.

58. Bowie and Immerman, *Waging Peace*, 65. Of course, neither Dulles nor his CIA director brother Allen were averse to imperialistic behavior, just the image. The two were responsible for covert operations that overthrew democratic governments in both Iran and Guatemala.

59. Richard A. Melanson, *American Foreign Policy Since the Vietnam War: The Search for Consensus from Richard Nixon to George W. Bush*, 4th ed. (Armonk, N.Y.: M. E. Sharpe, 2005), 59–60.

60. John S. Sellers, "The Weinberger Doctrine: Useful Compass or Flawed Checklist?" thesis, School of Advanced Airpower Studies, June 2001, 6–7, http://www.dtic.mil/cgi-bin/GetTRDoc?AD=ADA407811&Location=U2&doc=GetTRDoc.pdf.

61. "The Uses of Military Power," Remarks Prepared for Delivery by the Hon. Caspar W. Weinberger, Secretary of Defense, to the National Press Club, Washington, D.C., Wednesday, November 28, 1984, http://www.pbs.org/wgbh/pages/frontline/shows/military/force/weinberger.html. On the third condition, Weinberger in his original formulation of the doctrine referred to Clausewitz: "As Clausewitz wrote, 'no one starts a war—or rather, no one in his senses ought to do so—without first being clear in his mind what he intends to achieve by that war, and how he intends to conduct it.'"

62. Ibid.

63. Ibid.

64. Ibid.

65. Cori E. Dauber, "Implications of the Weinberger Doctrine for American Military Intervention in a Post–Desert Storm Age," in *Dimensions of Western Military Intervention*, ed. Colin McInnis and Nicholas J. Wheeler (Portland, Ore.: Frank Cass, 2002), 88n38.

66. Colin L. Powell, "U.S. Forces: Challenges Ahead," *Foreign Affairs* (Winter 1992), http://www.pbs.org/wgbh/pages/frontline/shows/military/force/powell.html.

67. Of course, those who advocate stability operations often point to the other tenets of *jus ad bellum*, including "just cause," or the use of force to protect innocent lives and "right intention," or use of force to right a wrong.

68. Colin S. Powell, *My American Journey* (New York: Ballantine, 1996), 576.

69. Michael Dobbs, *Madeleine Albright: A Twentieth-Century Odyssey* (New York: Henry Holt, 999), 360.

70. Ibid.

71. Andrew Bacevich refers not to traditionalists and progressives but to conservatives and crusaders, respectively. See Andrew J. Bacevich, "The Petraeus Doctrine," *The Atlantic* (October 2008), http://www.theatlantic.com/doc/200810/petraeus-doctrine. Frank Hoffman offers a slightly different, more nuanced debate between what he terms "counterinsurgents," "traditionalists," "utility infielders," and "division of labor." See "Striking a Balance: Posturing the Future Force for COIN and Conventional Warfare," *Armed Forces Journal* (July 2009), http://www.armedforcesjournal.com/2009/07/4099782.

72. Thom Shanker, "Plan to Shift Military Spending Faces Skepticism," *New York Times* (May 11, 2009), http://www.nytimes.com/2009/05/11/world/asia/11gates.html?adxnnl=1&ref=politicss&adx.

73. Andrew J. Bacevich, *The New American Militarism* (Oxford: Oxford University Press, 2005), 40–41.

74. "Military Operations: Impact of Operations Other Than War on the Services Varies," GAO/NSIAD-99-69, U.S. General Accounting Office, May 1999, http://www.gao.gov/archive/1999/ns99069.pdf; Jennifer M. Taw, David Persselin, and Maren Leed, *Meeting Peace Operations Requirements While Maintaining MTW Readiness* (Santa Monica, Calif.: RAND, 1998).

75. Julian E. Barnes, "Defense Chief Urges Bigger Budget for State Department," *Los Angeles Times* (November 27, 2007), http://articles.latimes.com/2007/nov/27/nation/na-gates27.

76. Lawrence A. Yates, *The U.S. Military's Experience in Stability Operations, 1789–2005*, Global War on Terrorism Occasional Paper no. 15 (Fort Leavenworth, Kan.: Combat Studies Institute Press, 2006), 21.

77. *Special Operations*, Joint Publication 3-05, April 18, 2011, II-6, http://www.dtic.mil/doctrine/new_pubs/jp3_05.pdf.

78. After 9/11, Special Forces personnel were refocused to undertake predominantly DA and CT missions. See Max Boot, Statement Before the Terrorism, Unconventional Threats, and Capabilities Subcommittee of the Committee on Armed Services, House of Representatives, 109th Congress, 2nd session, June 29, 2006, http://www.fas.org/irp/congress/2006_hr/soc.pdf, 3.

79. Derek S. Reveron and Kathleen A. Mahoney-Norris, "'Military-Political' Relations: The Need for Office Education," *Joint Force Quarterly* 52 (1st quarter 2009): 61.

80. Robert C. Shaw, "Integrating Conventional and Special Operations Forces," *Military Review* 77, no. 4 (July/August 1997).

81. It is worth noting that the SOF community itself breaks down between progressives and traditionalists. Although SOF have long deployed for stability operations and are uniquely capable for them, their experiences have not translated into a unified view on the elevation of stability operations to a primary mission. The roots of disagreement go back to the long-standing division with SOF among those who favor foreign internal defense and those who advocate for direct action. For some indication of this cultural divide (often seen as Green Berets versus Rangers, SEALs, and other special operations forces), see Sean D. Naylor, "More Than Door Kickers," *Armed Forces Journal* (March 2006).

82. David Halberstam, *War in a Time of Peace* (New York: Scribner, 2001), 265.

83. "Aspin Criticizes Pentagon's Approach to the Use of Military Force in the Post–Cold War Era," *Jinsa Security Affairs* (October 1992): 7, http://www.securityaffairs.org/archived_site/1992/oct1992.pdf.

84. "Secret Report Urges New Afghanistan Policy," *Politico*, CBS News (February 3, 2009), http://www.cbsnews.com/stories/2009/02/03/politics/politico/main4771546.shtml.

85. Wayne Bert, *The Reluctant Superpower: United States' Policy in Bosnia, 1991–95* (New York: St. Martin's Press, 1997), 18–20.

86. Nathan Freier, "Shifting Emphasis: Leaders, Strategists, and Operators in an Era of Persistent Unconventional Challenge," Center for Strategic and International Studies, September 2008.

2. DOCTRINE AND STABILITY OPERATIONS

1. JP 1-02, 178.

2. Throughout this chapter, the term stability operations and its forbears, LIC, OOTW, and MOOTW will be used as synonyms, with the choice of term determined by the time period under discussion.

3. See, for example, *Operations*, Army Field Manual (FM) 100-5, 1993, vi, http://www.fs.fed.us/fire/doctrine/genesis_and_evolution/source_materials/FM-100–5_operations.pdf. That being said, it is important to concede that doctrine can also reflect changes that have taken place, rather than drive them. It can lag behind changing requirements, and it is affected by politics and the bureaucracy responsible for its

production and maintenance. Nonetheless, whether it is driver or mirror or both, doctrine looked at over time provides a useful gauge of the military's priorities.

4. *Small Wars Manual*, U.S. Marine Corps (Washington, D.C.: U.S. Government Printing Office, 1940), 1, http://www.scribd.com/doc/8218892/Small-Wars-Manual -1940-Edition.

5. Ibid. Capitalization in the original.

6. Indeed, the manual notes that Marines had been referred to as "State Department troops" because of their involvement in small wars.

7. Rod Paschall, "Low-Intensity Conflict Doctrine: Who Needs It?" *Parameters* 15, no. 3 (Autumn 1985): 33.

8. Letter of Instruction, U.S. Army Combat Development Command, July 11, 1966.

9. David J. Dean, *The Air Force Role in Low-Intensity Conflict* (Maxwell AFB, Ala.: Air University Press, October 1986).

10. *Operations Against Guerrilla Units*, FMFM 8-2 (Washington, D.C.: U.S. Government Printing Office, 1964), 1, http://www.vietnam.ttu.edu/star/images/107/1070916001a .pdf.

11. *Counterinsurgency Operations*, FMFM 8-2 (Washington, D.C.: U.S. Government Printing Office, 1967), http://www.vietnam.ttu.edu/star/images/137/1370521001a.pdf.

12. *USMC Professional Knowledge: Gained from Operational Experience in Vietnam, 1965– 1966*, NAVMC 2614 (Washington, D.C.: U.S. Government Printing Office, 1967).

13. The advances that were made in COIN and stability operations doctrine, limited as they were, could in large part be credited to President Kennedy's full-court press for increased civilian and military emphasis on—and preparation for—COIN. Kennedy mobilized the Defense Department, NSC, CIA, and even Congress, promulgating the argument that foreign internal wars required the "same seriousness of purpose as . . . conventional warfare of the past." See Memorandum to the Members of the Special Group, NSAM 124, http://www.jfklibrary.org/Asset-Viewer/qJbe3E_ H7kmxvtbyzSb8pw.aspx; and Michael McClintock, *Instruments of Statecraft* (New York: Pantheon, 1992), chap. 6. The fact that the war in Vietnam was nonetheless undertaken as maneuver warfare and that military doctrine for COIN and stability operations remained low level and relatively underdeveloped reflect the services' resistance to unconventional operations.

14. Kenneth Beebe, "The Air Force's Missing Doctrine: How the Air Force Ignores Counterinsurgency," *Air and Space Power Journal* (Spring 2006), http://www.airpower .maxwell.af.mil/airchronicles/apj/apj06/spr06/beebe.html.

15. "Misreading History?" *Endgame on Frontline*, PBS, http://www.pbs.org/wgbh/pages/ frontline/endgame/themes/misreading.html.

16. Message, 291420Z Sep 82, CINCSOUTH.

17. There is a really interesting story about FM 30-31. The doctrine had a single appendix, supplement A, but was reported by several sources to have a second supplement (FM 30-31B) that was a compilation of super-secret COIN techniques. The Soviets later admitted that they had created FM 30-31B as an act of disinformation.

See "Misinformation About 'Gladio/Stay Behind' Networks Resurfaces," January 30, 2006, http://www.america.gov/st/pubs-english/2006/January/20060120111344atlahtn evelo.3114282.html.

18. For a good overview of how this played out in the Army as it rewrote FM 100-5, see Robert T. Davis II, *The Challenge of Adaptation: The U.S. Army in the Aftermath of Conflict, 1953–2000*, Long War Series, Occasional Paper 27 (Fort Leavenworth, Kan.: Combat Studies Institute Press, U.S. Army Combined Arms Center, 2008), 87–88, http://www.dtic.mil/cgi-bin/GetTRDoc?Location=U2&doc=GetTRDoc.pdf& AD=ADA481031.

19. *Joint Doctrine for Military Operations Other Than War*, JP 3-07 (1995), http://www.bits .de/NRANEU/others/jp-doctrine/jp3_07.pdf.

20. JP 3-07 (1995), vii. Bold in original text.

21. Ibid., I-7. Bold in original text.

22. *Military Operations in Low Intensity Conflict*, FM 100-20/AFP 3-20 (Washington, D.C.: Headquarters, Departments of the Army and Air Force, 1990), chap. 1, http:// www.globalsecurity.org/military/library/policy/army/fm/100-20/10020ch1.htm#s_9.

23. In looking over a draft of this chapter, one reviewer asked whether or not there had ever been any criticism of the U.S. military for producing "too many manuals trying to describe the same thing with different terminology, being written on different timelines, so they're never in synch with each other." Interestingly, in the mid-1990s, when Army General William Hartzog initiated a rewrite of FM 100-5, the Combined Arms Center put together a writing team that eventually included then-Lieutenant Colonel David Fastabend. Fastabend expressed precisely the concern mentioned by the reviewer, saying there was a "doctrine glut," insofar as there were "too many manuals that say too little." Davis, *The Challenge of Adaptation*, 94.

24. *Operations* (1993), 1-4, http://www.fs.fed.us/fire/doctrine/genesis_and_evolution/ source_materials/FM-100-5_operations.pdf.

25. Ibid., 13-0. The ideas contained in *Operations* were reiterated and expanded upon in the 1997 *Quadrennial Defense Review Report*, in which it was asserted that "the Defense Department had an essential role to play in shaping the international se-curity environment in ways that promote and protect U.S. national interests. Our defense efforts help to promote regional stability, prevent or reduce conflicts and threats, and deter aggression and coercion on a day-to-day basis in many key regions in the world." *Quadrennial Defense Review Report* (Washington, D.C.: Department of Defense, 1997), section 3, "Defense Strategy," http://www.fas.org/man/docs/qdr/ sec3.html.

26. *Operations*, U.S. Army Field Manual (FM) 3-0 (Washington, D.C.: Headquarters, Department of the Army, 2001), vii, http://www.dtic.mil/doctrine/jel/service_pubs/ fm3_0a.pdf.

27. William S. Wallace, "FM 3-0 Operations: The Army's Blueprint," *Military Review* (March–April 2008): 4.

28. DODD 3000.05.

29. *Operations and Organization*, AFDD(I) (Washington, D.C.: Headquarters, Department of the Air Force, 2007), 22–34, http://www.fas.org/irp/doddir/usaf/afdd2.pdf.

30. *Irregular Warfare*, AFDD 2-3 (Washington, D.C.: Headquarters, Department of the Air Force, 2007), http://www.fas.org/irp/doddir/usaf/afdd2-3.pdf.

31. *Military Operations Other Than War*, AFDD 2-3 (Washington, D.C.: Headquarters, Department of the Air Force, 2000), http://www.dtic.mil/doctrine/jel/service_pubs/afd2_3.pdf.

32. Oliver Fritz and Gregory A. Hermsmeyer, "The U.S. Air Force and Stability Operations Transformation," *Joint Force Quarterly* (December 2007), http://findarticles.com/p/articles/mi_m0KNN/is_47/ai_n28028077/.

33. *Naval Warfare*, Naval Doctrine Publication 1 (Washington, D.C.: Headquarters, Department of the Navy, 1994), http://www.dtic.mil/doctrine/jel/service_pubs/ndp1.pdf.

34. *Naval Warfare*, Naval Doctrine Publication 1 (Washington, D.C.: Headquarters, Department of the Navy, 2010), http://usnwc.edu/Academics/Maritime—Staff-Operators-Course/documents/NDP-1-Naval-Warfare-(Mar-2010)_Chapters2-3.aspx.

35. *Naval Humanitarian Assistance Missions*, EXTAC 1011 (Washington, D.C.: Headquarters, Department of the Navy, 1996), http://pksoi.army.mil/doctrine_concepts/documents/UN%20Guidelines/Service%20Doctrine/ex1011%20Naval%20HA%20Msns.pdf.

36. *Humanitarian Assistance/Disaster Relief (HA/DR) Operations Planning*, NWDC TAC-MEMO 3-07.6-05 (Washington, D.C.: Headquarters, Department of the Navy, 2005), http://www.au.af.mil/au/awc/awcgate/navy/tm_3-07-6-05_navy_ha&dr_ops_plng.pdf.

37. *Naval Warfare* (1994), 20.

38. *Ground Combat Operations*, MCWP 3-1 (Washington, D.C.: Headquarters, Department of the Marines, 1995), http://www.marines.mil/news/publications/Documents/MCWP%203-1%20Ground%20Combat%20Operations.pdf.

39. *Marine Air-Ground Task Force Civil-Military Operations*, MCWP 3-33.1 (Washington, D.C.: Headquarters, Department of the Marines, 2003), http://www.marines.mil/news/publications/Documents/MCWP%203-33.1%20Marine%20Air-Ground%20Task%20Force%20Civil_Military%20Operations.pdf.

40. The term "progressive" is not used here and throughout in the political sense, where it would indicate liberal beliefs. Rather, the term is used here in reference to those who are proponents of transforming the military to improve its capacity for stability operations.

41. *Operations* (2008), foreword.

42. Ibid., viii.

43. Ibid., 3-1.

44. *Joint Operations*, Joint Publication 3-0, 17 September 2006, Incorporating Change 2, 22 March 2010, http://www.scribd.com/doc/37553840/Joint-Ops-2010.

45. *Stability Operations*, U.S. Army Field Manual (FM) 3-07 (Washington, D.C.: U.S. Department of the Army, 2008), foreword, http://usacac.army.mil/cac2/Repository/FM307/FM3-07.pdf.

46. Ibid., iv.

47. This is made clear in figure 2.1 of *Stability Operations* (2008).

48. See, for example, *Stability Operations and Support Operations*, FM 3-07 (FM 100-20) (Washington, D.C.: Headquarters, Department of the Army, February 2003), 1-2.

49. *Stability Operations* (2008), foreword, 1-17.

50. Ibid., 3-16.

51. James Joyner, "1.5 Million Copies of COIN Doctrine Downloaded," *Outside the Beltway* (January 6, 2007) http://www.outsidethebeltway.com/archives/15_million_copies_of_coin_doctrine_downloaded/.

52. Gian P. Gentile, "A Strategy of Tactics: Population-Centric COIN and the Army," *Parameters* (Autumn 2009): 5, http://www.public.navy.mil/usff/documents/gentile.pdf.

53. Gian P. Gentile, "Our COIN Doctrine Removes the Enemy from the Essence of War," *Armed Forces Journal* (January 2008), http://www.armedforcesjournal.com/2008/01/3207722.

54. One minor example of this was a pair of articles, one by Nagl and one by Gentile, published in the same issue of *Joint Force Quarterly* in 2009: John A. Nagl, "Let's Win the Wars We're In," *Joint Force Quarterly* 52 (1st quarter 2009): 20–26; Gian P. Gentile, "Let's Build an Army to Win All Wars," *Joint Force Quarterly* 52 (1st quarter 2009): 27–33.

55. There is a larger circle of colleagues and mutual friends as well, of course. This becomes apparent reading each book's acknowledgments, where the same names come up time and again.

56. David H. Ucko, *The New Counterinsurgency Era: Transforming the U.S. Military for Modern Wars* (Washington, D.C.: Georgetown University Press, 2009), vii–viii.

57. *Special Operations*, Joint Publication 3-05, April 18, 2011, x.

58. *Civil-Military Operations*, Joint Publication 3-57, July 2008, xiv.

59. *Stability Operations* (2008), 3-9–3-12.

60. Lawrence A. Yates, *The U.S. Military's Experience in Stability Operations, 1789–2005*, Global War on Terrorism Occasional Paper no. 15 (Fort Leavenworth, Kan.: Combat Studies Institute Press, 2006), 1.

61. "Army Doctrine Update," Combined Arms Doctrine Directorate, U.S. Army Combined Arms Center, Fort Leavenworth, Kansas, February 24, 2007, http://asc.army.mil/docs/transformation/Army_Doctrine_Update_FM501_FM30.pdf.

3. PRACTICAL ADJUSTMENTS TO ACHIEVE DOCTRINAL REQUIREMENTS

1. The quotation in the epigraph is from William H. McMichael, "DoD Sets Priorities with 2011 Budget, QDR," *Army Times* (February 1, 2010), http://www.armytimes.com/news/2010/02/military_2011_budget_QDR_020110w/.

2. *Quadrennial Defense Review Report* (Washington, D.C.: Department of Defense, 2010), 89.

3. Ibid., 39–40.

4. 2009 Army Posture Statement, submitted to the Committees and Subcommittees of the U.S. Senate and the House of Representatives, 1st Session, 111th Congress, May 7, 2009, http://www.army.mil/aps/09/2009_army_posture_statement_web.pdf.

5. For more on the Army's transformation, see "2006 and Beyond: What the U.S. Army Is Doing," *Torchbearer National Security Report*, Association of the United States Army, March 2006, http://www.ausa.org/publications/torchbearercampaign/tnsr/Documents/TBear_March_06_optimized.pdf.

6. *Operations* (2008), C-6.

7. Ibid.

8. *Brigade Combat Team*, Army Field Manual (FM) 3-90.6 (Washington, D.C.: Headquarters, Department of the Army, August 4, 2006).

9. Robert D. Morschauser, "The Brigade Combat Team: Stability and Security Force Assistance Operations," Strategy Research Project, U.S. Army War College, Carlisle Barracks, Penn., February 2010.

10. Todd R. Wood, "The Maneuver Enhancement Brigade and Its Role in Stability Operations, Part 1," *Maneuver Support* 29 (Summer 2009): 26–30, http://www.wood.army.mil/engrmag/Maneuver%20Support%20Magazine/PDFs%20for%20Summer%202009/Wood.pdf.

11. Small Wars Council, online discussion forum of the *Small Wars Journal*, "Military Transition Teams (MTTs) in Iraq," http://council.smallwarsjournal.com/showthread.php?t=4260.

12. "Stand Up and Be Counted: The Continuing Challenge of Building the Iraqi Security Forces," U.S. House of Representatives, Committee on Armed Services, Subcommittee on Oversight and Investigations, June 25, 2007, http://democrats.armedservices.house.gov/index.cfm/files/serve?File_id=2bfb0934–1745–4c80–8e21–205915e97cfb; Small Wars Council, online discussion forum of the *Small Wars Journal*, "Military Transition Teams (MTTs) in Iraq," http://council.smallwarsjournal.com/showthread.php?t=4260.

13. Oliver Fritz and Gregory A. Hermsmeyer, "The U.S. Air Force and Stability Operations Transformation," *Joint Force Quarterly* 47 (December 2007): 128–134, http://findarticles.com/p/articles/mi_m0KNN/is_47/ai_n28028077.

14. "The Air Force in Facts and Figures: 2010 USAF Almanac," *Air Force Magazine* (May 2010): 36, http://www.airforce-magazine.com/MagazineArchive/Magazine%20Documents/2010/May%202010/0510facts_figs.pdf.

15. "Aerospace Expeditionary Force (AEF); Air and Space Expeditionary Task Force (ASETF); (Formerly Air Expeditionary Force), Military," Globalsecurity.org, http://www.globalsecurity.org/military/agency/usaf/aef-intro.htm

16. Fritz and Hermsmeyer, "The U.S. Air Force and Stability Operations Transformation."

17. Kevin Henabray, "Air Force Engagement in Expeditionary Warfare," briefing, Headquarters, U.S. Air Force, October 24, 2006, 6.

18. *Operations*, Air Mobility Command Instruction 10-403 (Washington, D.C.: Department of the Air Force, February 22, 2007), 9–10.

19. Jim Fisher, "Troops Project Humanitarian Aid to North Africa," *American Forces Information Service* (March 7, 2011), http://www.militaryconnection.com/news%5Cmarch -2011%5Ctroops-aid-africa.html.

20. Charles Schlegel, Mission Briefing, 435th Contingency Response Group, 2009, 6, http://www.jeaddc.com/2009PresentationsPosted/435%20CRG%20Overview.pdf.

21. Fritz and Hermsmeyer, "The U.S. Air Force and Stability Operations Transformation."

22. Battlefield Airmen include tactical air control party personnel, pararescuemen, security forces personnel, and special operations weathermen.

23. Ronald O'Rourke, "Navy Irregular Warfare and Counterterrorism Operations: Background and Issues for Congress," Congressional Research Service, April 11, 2011, http://www.fas.org/sgp/crs/natsec/RS22373.pdf.

24. Fritz and Hermsmeyer, "The U.S. Air Force and Stability Operations Transformation."

25. Every MAGTF has a command element, aviation element, ground combat element, and combat service support element. A MEF usually totals close to fifty thousand troops and is commanded by a lieutenant general. A MEB's size is usually close to 16,000 troops, though it may vary, and it is commanded by a brigadier general. The MEU is the smallest MAGTF, with two thousand to 2,200 troops, and is commanded by a colonel.

26. "Evolving the MAGTF for the 21st Century," March 20, 2009, http://www.quantico .usmc.mil/MCBQ%20PAO%20Press%20Releases/090430%20CDI%20Docs/CDI _EvolvingMAGTF21stCent.pdf.

27. Karen Parrish, "Special Operations Faces Soaring Demands, Commander Says," *American Forces Press Service* (February 8, 2011), http://www.defense.gov/news/ newsarticle.aspx?id=62737.

28. Ibid.

29. Ibid.

30. "6th Special Operations Squadron," fact sheet, Hurlburt Field, USAF, February 24, 2011, http://www2.hurlburt.af.mil/library/factsheets/factsheet.asp?id=3496.

31. Ibid.

32. U.S. Special Operations Command Web site, http://www.socom.mil/SOCOMHome /Pages/USSOCOM.aspx.

33. Andrew Feickert and Thomas K. Livingston, "U.S. Special Operations Forces (SOF): Background and Issues for Congress," Congressional Research Service, March 28, 2011, 2, http://www.fas.org/sgp/crs/natsec/RS21048.pdf.

34. *Quadrennial Defense Review Report* (Washington, D.C.: U.S. Department of Defense, 2006), 45.

35. Statement of General Bryan D. Brown, Commander U.S. Special Operations Command, Before the House Armed Services Committee Subcommittee on Terrorism, Unconventional Threats, and Capabilities, on the current manning, equipping, and readiness challenges facing special operations forces, January 31, 2007, 4, http://

www.docstoc.com/docs/51014850/HEARING-Before-the-House-Armed-Services
-Committee-Subcommittee-on.

36. Grace V. Jean, "Army Special Forces Gear up for Gray Eagle," *National Defense* (May 2011), http://www.nationaldefensemagazine.org/archive/2011/May/Pages/ArmySpecial ForcesGearUpForGrayEagle.aspx.

37. Grace V. Jean, "Aerial Drones Going Mainstream in Naval Special Warfare," *National Defense* (May 2011), http://www.nationaldefensemagazine.org/archive/2011/May/Pages/AerialDronesGoingMainstreamInNavalSpecialWarfare.aspx.

38. Eric Olson, USSOCOM 2010 Posture Statement, 2, http://www.socom.mil/SOCOMHome/Documents/USSOCOM%20Posture%20Statement.pdf.

39. Author's interview with Ben Moody, CSIS, Washington, D.C., September 20, 2010.

40. "Report to Congress on the Implementation of DoD Directive 3000.05 *Military Support for Stability, Security, Transition, and Reconstruction (SSTR) Operations,* Secretary of Defense, Washington, D.C., April 1, 2007," 7–9.

41. Fritz and Hermsmeyer, "The U.S. Air Force and Stability Operations Transformation."

42. "Report to Congress on the Implementation of DoD Directive 3000.05," 6.

43. "U.S. Army/U.S. Marine Corps Counterinsurgency Center," pamphlet, http://usacac.army.mil/CAC2/coin/repository/COIN_Center_Pamphlet.pdf.

44. *Training for Full Spectrum Operations,* Army Field Manual 7-0 (Washington, D.C.: Headquarters, Department of the Army, 2008), 1-8.

45. *Stability Operations* (2008), 1-8.

46. *Training Units and Developing Leaders for Full Spectrum Operations,* Army Field Manual 7-0 (Washington, D.C.: Headquarters, Department of the Army, 2011), 1-2.

47. Jim Garamone, "Flournoy Calls for Better Interagency Cooperation," *American Forces Press Service* (June 11, 2010), http://www.defense.gov/news/newsarticle.aspx?id=59601.

48. Owen Wood, "Canada: The World's Peacekeeper," *CBC News* (October 30, 2003), http://www.cbc.ca/news/background/cdnmilitary/worldspeacekeeper.html.

49. "Canada Supports Peace Operations Training in Ghana," Government of Canada, http://www.canadainternational.gc.ca/ghana/highlights-faits/PeaceOperations Training-OperationsPaix-March2010.aspx?lang=en.

50. "Peacekeeping: National Defence," chapter 7 of the 1996 May Report of the Auditor General of Canada, http://www.oag-bvg.gc.ca/internet/English/parl_oag_199605_07_e_5038.html.

51. See, for example, Joseph R. Nunez, "Canada's Global Role: A Strategic Assessment of Its Military Power," *Parameters* (Autumn 2004): 75–93. Nunez cites Joseph Jockel's work on the effects of a peacekeeping orientation on Canada's armed forces: "Experts such as Joseph Jockel argue that the country faces hard choices because Canada's peacekeeping orientation has led to a significant degradation of its combat capability, particularly its ability to sustain military operations at brigade level." Joseph T. Jockel, *The Canadian Forces: Hard Choices, Soft Power* (Toronto: Canadian Institute of Strategic Studies, 1999), 113–128. Apparently such concerns extend to public perception as well. A 2003 Gallup poll asking citizens of the United States, Britain, and Canada

to consider their respective militaries' preparedness yielded 83 percent of Americans with confidence in their military, 58 percent of Britons, and only 35 percent of Canadians: http://www.gallup.com/poll/8134/military-readiness-us-canada-britain.aspx.

52. Howard Olsen and John Davis, *Training U.S. Army Officers for Peace Operations: Lessons from Bosnia* (Washington, D.C.: U.S. Institute for Peace Press, October 1999).

53. See, for example, J. Michael Hardesty and Jason D. Ellis, "Training for Peace Operations: The U.S. Army Adapts to the Post–Cold War World," Peaceworks no. 12, U.S. Institute for Peace (Washington, D.C.: USIP Press, 1997); "Peace Operations: Effect of Training, Equipment, and Other Factors on Unit Capability," chapter report, GAO/NSIAD-96-14, October 1995, http://www.fas.org/man/gao/nsiad-96-014.htm; "Making Peace While Staying Ready for War: The Challenges of U.S. Military Participation in Peace Operations," Congressional Budget Office, December 1999, http://www.cbo.gov/doc.cfm?index=1809&type=0&sequence=0.

54. Leigh C. Caraher, "Broadening Military Culture," in *Transforming for Stabilization and Reconstruction Operations*, ed. Hans Binnendijk and Stuart E. Johnson (Washington, D.C.: National Defense University Press, 2004).

55. Derek S. Reveron, *Exporting Security* (Washington, D.C.: Georgetown University Press, 2010), 152–156.

56. Hans Binnendijk and Stuart E. Johnson, *Transforming for Stabilization and Reconstruction Operations* (Washington, D.C.: National Defense University, Center for Technology and National Security Policy, 2004), 90–91.

57. Nathan Hodge, *Armed Humanitarians: The Rise of the Nation Builders* (New York: Bloomsbury, 2011), 136.

58. "Report to Congress on the Implementation of DoD Directive 3000.05," 13–19.

59. Fritz and Hermsmeyer, "The U.S. Air Force and Stability Operations Transformation." "In-lieu-of duties" are tasks that airmen are asked to perform because soldiers are not available.

60. "ATG 101" Information Brief, MAGTFTC Advisor Training Group, April 11, 2011, http://www.marines.mil/unit/29palms/ATG/Documents/ATG%20101%2011%20April%202011.pdf.

61. Chris Heathscott, "Realistic Training Helping to Prepare Arkansas Soldiers for Afghanistan," Arkansas National Guard Public Affairs Office, May 18, 2011, http://www.dvidshub.net/news/70631/realistic-training-helping-prepare-arkansas-soldiers-afghanistan.

62. "Stability Operations: Where We Are and the Road Ahead," Symposium Report, December 13–14, 2004, sponsored by the U.S. Army Peacekeeping and Stability Operations Institute, the U.S. Department of State, and the U.S. Institute of Peace at Carlisle Barracks, Penn., 31.

63. Far from cooperating with the military, NGOs often actively disassociate themselves from military activities in order to maintain their role as neutral actors. In Afghanistan, for example, one PRT commander explained in an interview how the NGOs in his region "were either hostile to the PRT, such as the ICRC, or left the area

in order to avoid appearing to work with the military (Doctors without Borders)."
USIP Interview 45, Afghanistan Experience Project, 1, http://www.usip.org/files/file/
resources/collections/histories/afghanistan/45.pdf.

64. "Beyond Goldwater Nichols: U.S. Government and Defense Reform for a New Strategic Era," Phase 1 Report, Center for Strategic and International Studies (Washington, D.C.: Center for Strategic and International Studies, March 2004), 117.

65. Janine Davidson, "Making Government Work: Pragmatic Priorities for Interagency
Coordination," *Orbis* (Summer 2009): 433.

66. "Another Crossroads? Professional Military Education Two Decades After the Goldwater-Nichols Act and the Skelton Panel," U.S. House of Representatives, Committee on Armed Services, Subcommittee on Oversight and Investigations, April 2010,
Washington, D.C., xiii, http://democrats.armedservices.house.gov/index.cfm/files/
serve?File_id=d4748d4a-b358-49d7-8c9a-aaoba6f581a6.

67. Janet Breslin-Smith and Cliff Krieger, "Strategic Drift? The Future of the National
War College," *Joint Force Quarterly* 55 (4th quarter 2009): 16.

68. H.R. 2207, Interagency Cooperation Commission Act, 111th Congress, 2009–2010,
http://www.govtrack.us/congress/bill.xpd?bill=h111–2207.

69. Leonard Lira, "An Integrative Approach to the Interagency Process," *InterAgency Journal* 1, no. 1 (Fall 2010): 46, http://thesimonscenter.org/wp-content/uploads/2010/11/
IAJ-1-1-pg46–55.pdf. This finding mirrors those from one of the author's publications
more than a decade earlier: Jennifer Taw, *Interagency Coordination in Operations Other
Than War: Implications for the U.S. Army* (Santa Monica, Calif.: RAND, MR-825-A,
1997).

70. Derek S. Reveron and Kathleen A. Mahoney-Norris, "'Military-Political' Relations:
The Need for Officer Education," *Joint Force Quarterly* 52 (1st quarter 2009): 62.

71. *Counterinsurgency*, Army Field Manual (FM) 3-24/Marine Corps Warfighting Publication (MCWP) 3-3.5 (Washington D.C.: Headquarters, Department of the Army/
Headquarters, Marine Corps Combat Development Command, December 2006),
foreword.

72. Daniel Gonzales, John Hollywood, Jerry M. Sollinger, James McFadden, John De-
Jarnette, Sarah Harting, and Donald Temple, *Networked Forces in Stability Operations:
101st Airborne Division, 3/2 and 1/25 Stryker Brigades in Northern Iraq* (Santa Monica,
Calif.: RAND, 2007), 145.

73. "Evolving the MAGTF for the 21st Century," 8.

74. "Building Language Skills and Cultural Competencies in the Military: DOD's Challenges in Today's Education Environment," U.S. House of Representatives, Committee on Armed Services, Subcommittee on Oversight and Investigations, November
2008, 39–52, http://prhome.defense.gov/READINESS/DLO/files/LanguageCulture
ReportNov08_HASC.pdf.

75. Fritz and Hermsmeyer, "The U.S. Air Force and Stability Operations Transformation."

76. "Report to Congress on the Implementation of DOD Directive 3000.05," 5.

77. "Irregular Warfare (IW) Joint Operating Concept (JOC)," version 1.0 (Washington, D.C.: Department of Defense, September 2007), 22–23, http://www.michaelyon-online.com/images/pdf/iw-joc.pdf.

78. This is reflected in the 2005 publication of the notably weak and incredibly ambitious "Defense Language Transformation Roadmap" (Washington, D.C.: Department of Defense, January 2005), http://www.defense.gov/news/Mar2005/d20050330roadmap.pdf.

79. Victor M. Rosello, "Soft Skills for 21st Century Land Dominance," Landpower Essay 09-1 (Arlington, Va.: Association of the U.S. Army, Institute of Land Warfare, January 2009), 2, http://www3.ausa.org/marketing/SoftSkillswebsite0209.pdf.

80. Carl J. Schramm, "Expeditionary Economics: Spurring Growth After Conflicts and Disasters," *Foreign Affairs* 89, no. 3 (May/June 2010): 91–92, http://www.kauffman.org/uploadedFiles/ForeignAffairsExpedEcono510.pdf.

81. "Is DOD the new AID? Tasking Soldiers with Economic Development," transcript, *Ideas in Action with Jim Glassman*, October 2010, http://www.ideasinactiontv.com/episodes/2010/10/is-dod-the-new-aid-tasking-soldiers-with-economic-development.html.

82. David J. Berteau, Gregory Kiley, Hardin Lang, Matthew Zlatnik, Tara Callahan, Ashley Chandler, and Thomas Patterson, "Final Report on Lessons Learned: Department of Defense Task Force for Business and Stability Operations," Center for Strategic and International Studies, June 2010, 2, http://tfbso.defense.gov/www/Lessons_Learned_Report.pdf.

83. http://www.cnas.org/node/4054.

84. "DOD Releases Defense Reviews, 2011 Budget Proposal, and 2010 War Funding Supplemental Request—Update," news release no. 084-10, U.S. Department of Defense, Office of the Assistant Secretary of Defense (Public Affairs), February 1, 2010, http://www.defense.gov/releases/release.aspx?releaseid=13281.

85. "The USA's New Littoral Combat Ships (LCS)," *Defense Industry Daily* (August 24, 2011), http://www.defenseindustrydaily.com/the-usas-new-littoral-combat-ships-updated-01343/.

86. Magnus Nordenman, "Pentagon Bets on COIN, Against Peer Competitor," *New Atlanticist* policy and analysis blog, April 7, 2009, http://www.acus.org/new_atlanticist/pentagon-bets-coin-against-peer-competitor.

87. August Cole, "Senate Kills Funds for F-22 Fighters," *Wall Street Journal* (July 22, 2009), http://online.wsj.com/article/SB124818597270968593.html.

88. William H. McMichael, "DOD Sets Priorities with 2011 Budget, QDR," *Army Times* (February 2010), http://www.armytimes.com/news/2010/02/military_2011_budget_QDR_020110w/.

89. Todd Harrison, "The FY 2012 Defense Budget: What to Expect in an Age of Austerity," Backgrounder, Center for Strategic and Budgetary Assessments, February 2011, 5–6, http://www.csbaonline.org/wp-content/uploads/2011/02/2011.02.11-The-FY-2012-Defense-Budget-What-To-Expect-In-An-Age-of-Austerity.pdf.

90. QDR 2010, 18.

91. Noah Shachtman, "Pentagon Chief Rips Heart Out of Army's 'Future,'" Danger Room, *Wired*, April 6, 2009, http://www.wired.com/dangerroom/2009/04/gates-rips-hear/; Andrew Feickert and Nathan Jacob Lucas, "Army Future Combat System (FCS) 'Spin-Outs' and Ground Combat Vehicle (GCV): Background and Issues for Congress," Congressional Research Service, RL32888, November 30, 2009, http://www.fas.org/sgp/crs/weapons/RL32888.pdf.

92. Eric T. Olson, 2010 Posture Statement, USSOCOM, http://www.socom.mil/SOCOMHome/Documents/USSOCOM%20Posture%20Statement.pdf.

93. Jim Dorschner, "Special Delivery: Special Forces Insertion," *Jane's Defence Weekly* 46, no. 21 (May 27, 2009): 26.

94. Fritz and Hermsmeyer, "The U.S. Air Force and Stability Operations Transformation."

95. 2010 Army Posture Statement, https://secureweb2.hqda.pentagon.mil/vdas_army posturestatement/2010/aps_pages/two_critical.asp#armymodernization.

96. Statement of General James T. Conway, Commandant of the Marine Corps, before the Senate Armed Services Committee on the 2010 Posture of the United States Marine Corps, February 25, 2010, 12–14, http://armed-services.senate.gov/statemnt/2010/02%20February/Conway%2002–25–10.pdf.

97. Statement of Admiral Gary Roughead, Chief of Naval Operations, before the House Subcommittee on Defense, Committee on Appropriations, March 11, 2010, 4–5, http://www.au.af.mil/au/awc/awcgate/navy/navyposture2010.pdf.

98. Ibid., 13.

99. Ibid., 15.

100. Depending on what is calculated into the cost, a single F-22 costs between $84 million and over $300 million. An MRAP, in comparison, can cost up to $1 million, with all the parts and upgrades, though its basic price tag ranges from $400,000 to $800,000. A Chinook CH-47 helicopter costs about $35 million.

101. Suzanne C. Nielsen, "An Army Transformed: The U.S. Army's Post-Vietnam Recovery and the Dynamics of Change in Military Organizations," The Letort Papers (Carlisle Barracks, Penn.: U.S. Army War College, September 2010), 37.

102. Brigadier General Abe Abrams, "FM 7-0 *Training for Full Spectrum Operations*," powerpoint, Combined Arms Center for Training, 4, http://usacac.army.mil/cac2/archives/2009/January/FM70.asp.

4. EXPLAINING THE MILITARY'S MISSION REVOLUTION

1. Author's interview with David A. Fastabend, Washington, D.C., September 20, 2010.

2. David A. Fastabend, "FM 100-5, 1998: Endless Evolution," *Army* (May 1997): 45.

3. Vasilios Tasikas, "Developing the Rule of Law in Afghanistan: The Need for a New Strategic Paradigm," *Army Lawyer* 45 (July 2007).

4. As described in a paper published by the Marine Corps Command and Staff College: "The Directive is a monumental shift in DoD priorities and should be viewed as an

indicator of changing policies and concept of employment to meet the challenges of the post 9/11 world." Robert G. McCarthy, III, "Stability Operations: Defeating the Twenty-First Century Threat," EWS Contemporary Issues Papers, U.S. Marine Corps Command and Staff College, Quantico, Va., February 2008, 4, http://www .dtic.mil/cgi-bin/GetTRDoc?AD=ADA498221&Location=U2&doc=GetTRDoc .pdf.

5. Statement of General Charles C. Krulak, Commandant of the Marine Corps, U.S. Marine Corps, before the Senate Armed Services Committee on September 29, 1998, Concerning Posture, http://www.globalsecurity.org/military/library/congress/1998_ hr/980929ck.htm.

6. Robert D. Kaplan, "The Coming Anarchy," *The Atlantic* (February 1994), http://www .theatlantic.com/magazine/archive/1994/02/the-coming-anarchy/4670/1/.

7. Martin van Creveld, *The Transformation of War* (New York: The Free Press, 1991).

8. Ibid., 29.

9. Robert L. Pfaltzgraff Jr., "The Emerging Global Security Environment," *Annals of the American Academy of Political and Social Science* 517 (September 1991): 10.

10. Nathan Freier, *DOD Leaders, Strategists, and Operators in an Era of Persistent Unconventional Challenge* (Washington, D.C.: Center for Strategic and International Studies, June 2009), 2–3.

11. *Operations* (2008), 1-4.

12. Max Boot, "America's Destiny Is to Police the World," *Financial Times* (February 19, 2003), http://www.cfr.org/publication/5559/americas_destiny_is_to_police_the_ world.html?id=5559.

13. Andrew J. Bacevich, *American Empire* (Cambridge, Mass.: Harvard University Press, 2002), 142, 167.

14. Derek S. Reveron, *Exporting Security* (Washington, D.C.: Georgetown University Press, 2010), 49.

15. Janine Davidon, *Lifting the Fog of Peace: How Americans Learned to Fight Modern War* (Ann Arbor: University of Michigan Press, 2010).

16. Theo Farrell and Terry Terriff, eds., *The Sources of Military Change: Culture, Politics, Technology* (Boulder, Colo.: Lynne Rienner, 2002), 10.

17. Barry R. Posen, *The Sources of Military Doctrine: France, Britain, and Germany Between the World Wars* (Ithaca, N.Y.: Cornell University Press, 1984); Stephen Peter Rosen, *Winning the Next War: Innovation and the Modern Military* (Ithaca, N.Y.: Cornell University Press, 1991).

18. Janice Gross Stein, "Building Politics Into Psychology: The Misperception of Threat," *Political Psychology* 9, no. 2 (June 1988): 245–271.

19. There is an entire literature, referred to by critics as revisionist, which claims that American leaders either deliberately exaggerated or completely overestimated the extent of the threat the USSR posed to the United States. See, for example: Thomas G. Paterson, *Meeting the Communist Threat: Truman to Reagan* (New York: Oxford University Press, 1988); Willard C. Matthias, *America's Strategic Blunders: Intelligence*

Analysis and National Security, 1936–1991 (University Park, Penn.: Penn State Press, 2001), 100.

20. See, for example, J. Samuel Barkin and Bruce Cronin, "The State and the Nation: Changing Norms and the Rules of Sovereignty in International Relations," *International Organization* 48, no. 1 (Winter 1994): 107–130.

21. *U.S. National Security Strategy*, 1996, http://www.fas.org/spp/military/docops/national/1996stra.htm.

22. *International Affairs Function 150: Summary and Highlights*, Fiscal Year 2009 Budget Request, http://pdf.usaid.gov/pdf_docs/PCAAB698.pdf.

23. Ole Wæver, "Securitization and Desecuritization," in *On Security*, ed. R. Lipschutz (New York: Columbia University Press, 1995), 55.

24. Barry Buzan, "Rethinking Security After the Cold War," *Cooperation and Conflict* 32, no. 1 (March 1997).

25. Michael C. Williams, "Words, Images, Enemies: Securitization and Internal Politics," *International Studies Quarterly* 47 (2003): 513–514.

26. John Gerard Ruggie, "The Past as Prologue? Interests, Identity, and American Foreign Policy," *International Security* 21, no. 4 (Spring 1997): 103, 119. Emphasis in original.

27. Ibid., 120.

28. Kenneth N. Waltz, "Structural Realism After the Cold War," *International Security* 25, no. 1 (Summer 2000): 27.

29. Mary Kaldor, "American Power: From 'Compellance' to Cosmopolitanism?" *International Affairs* 79, no. 1 (2003): 13.

30. It has been asserted that because Osama bin Laden referred to his attacks on U.S. and Western targets as a war, Bush, in calling for a "war on terror," was simply reacting in kind. Yet a terrorist organization declaring war is very different from a state declaring war. Militias in the United States often outfit themselves in camouflage and perceive themselves as at war with the government, but the government, for its part, simply deals with them as criminals. Indeed, international terrorism had, until Bush's war on it, been distinguished from warfare precisely because it was an alternative to it, a hit-and-run tactic by nonstate actors hoping to inflict pain but with no hope of posing, in any way, an existential threat. By declaring war on terror (or on terrorism, or on terrorists . . . *which* was never clear), the Bush administration made a deliberate decision to broaden the range of potential responses the United States could use against terrorists and, more importantly, against states perceived as supporting them.

31. See, for example Nina M. Serafino and Martin A. Weiss, *Peacekeeping and Conflict Transitions: Background and Congressional Action on Civilian Capabilities*, CRS Report for Congress, Congressional Research Service, updated January 6, 2006, CRS-2. The authors cite "the widespread perception since 9/11 that global instability directly threatens U.S. security and that it is a vital U.S. interest to transform weak and failing states into stable, democratic ones."

32. *U.S. National Intelligence Strategy*, 2005, 1–2.

33. *U.S. National Security Strategy*, 2006, 15.

34. Commission on Weak States and U.S. National Security, *On the Brink: Weak States and U.S. National Security*, 2004, 6–7.

35. For a great litany of quotes about the threats posed by failed states, see Stewart Patrick, *Weak Links: Fragile States, Global Threats, and International Security* (Oxford: Oxford University Press, 2011), 3–5.

36. Harry Verhoeven, "The Self-Fulfilling Prophecy of Failed States: Somalia, State Collapse, and the Global War on Terrorism," *Journal of Eastern African Studies* 3, no. 3: 405.

37. Tony Zinni and Tony Koltz, *The Battle for Peace: A Frontline Vision of America's Power and Purpose* (New York: Palgrave MacMillan, 2006), 214.

38. David Baldwin, "Security Studies and the End of the Cold War," *World Politics* 48, no. 1 (October 1995): 118.

39. Richard N. Haass, *The Reluctant Sheriff: The United States After the Cold War* (New York: Council on Foreign Relations, 1997), 132.

40. *A New Era of Engagement . . . Agency Financial Report, Fiscal Year 2009* (Washington, D.C.: U.S. Department of State), 5.

41. *USAID Primer: What We Do and How We Do It* (Washington, D.C.: USAID, January 2006), 2, http://www.usaid.gov/about_usaid/primer.html.

42. "Management of Interagency Efforts Concerning Reconstruction and Stabilization," NSPD-44 (Washington, D.C.: The White House, December 2005).

43. Henry Kissinger, *Does America Need a Foreign Policy? Toward a Diplomacy for the Twenty-First Century* (New York: Simon & Schuster, 2001), 82.

44. C. Wright Mills, *The Power Elite* (1956; repr. New York: Oxford University Press, 2000), 222.

45. Susan B. Epstein et al., "Foreign Policy Agency Reorganization," *Foreign Policy of the United States* (Huntington, N.Y.: Nova Science Publishers, 2000), 1:49–50.

46. "International Affairs Budget 101," *U.S. Global Leadership Campaign*, http://www.usglc.org/budget-breakdown/.

47. Derek S. Reveron and Kathleen A. Mahoney-Norris, "'Military-Political' Relations: The Need for Officer Education," *Joint Force Quarterly* 52 (1st quarter 2009): 64.

48. "The Air Force in Facts and Figures," *Air Force Magazine* (May 2009): 34, http://www.airforce-magazine.com/MagazineArchive/Magazine%20Documents/2009/May%202009/0509facts_fig.pdf.

49. U.S. Census Bureau, October 13, 2009.

50. Thomas B. Edsell, "Defense Industry Embraces Democrats, Hillary By Far the Favorite," *Huffington Post* (October 17, 2007), http://www.huffingtonpost.com/2007/10/17/defense-industry-embraces_n_68927.html.

51. Chalmers Johnson and Tom Engelhardt, "Economic Death Spiral at the Pentagon," *TomDispatch.com* (February 2, 2009), http://www.tomdispatch.com/post/175029.

52. Interview with Chuck Spinney, *NOW*, transcript, January 27, 2006, http://www.pbs.org/now/printable/transcriptNoW204_full_print.html.

53. Gordon Adams, "The Politics of National Security Budgets," Stanley Foundation, February 2007, 13, http://www.stimson.org/budgeting/pdf/Politics_of_National_Security_Budgeting.pdf.

54. Remarks by Defense Secretary Gates at the Command and General Staff College, Fort Leavenworth, Kansas, May 7, 2010, http://www.defense.gov/transcripts /transcript.aspx?transcriptid=4623.

55. Adams, "The Politics of National Security Budgets," 5.

56. Cindy Williams and Gordon Adams, "Strengthening Statecraft and Security: Reforming U.S. Planning and Resource Allocation," Massachusetts Institute of Technology Security Studies Program Occasional Paper, June 2008, 54, http://www.comw .org/pda/fulltext/WilliamsAdamsOccasionalPaper6–08.pdf.

57. *Leading Through Civilian Power: The First Quadrennial Diplomacy and Development Review*, 2010, http://www.comw.org/pda/fulltext/WilliamsAdamsOccasional Paper6-08.pdf.

58. Author's interview with Erik Leklem, civilian, OSD Policy, Pentagon, September 21, 2010.

59. Phone interview with Richard Byess, USAID, DCHA/OMA, June 29, 2010.

60. Howard Berman, opening statement before the House Committee on Foreign Affairs, "Striking the Appropriate Balance: The Defense Department's Expanding Role in Foreign Assistance," 111th Cong., 1st sess., 2009, http://www.internationalrelations .house.gov/111/48139.pdf, 1–2.

61. U.S. Global Leadership Coalition, "Senior Military Leaders Urge Congress to Boost Non-Military Tools," *PR Newswire* (March 10, 2010), http://intldevelopment.ein news.com/article.php?nid=3117.

62. Howard LaFranchi, "Gates, Clinton Oppose Cuts to State Department Budget," *Christian Science Monitor* (April 23, 2010), http://www.csmonitor.com/USA/Foreign -Policy/2010/0423/Gates-Clinton-oppose-cuts-to-State-Department-budget

63. Berman, "Striking the Appropriate Balance," 1.

64. Steve Hynd, "Counterinsurgency Consensus Misguided," *New Atlanticist Policy and Analysis Blog*, Atlantic Council, March 20, 2009, http://www.acus.org/new_atlanti cist/counterinsurgency-consensus-misguided.

65. *Embassies as Command Posts in the Anti-Terror Campaign*, Senate Foreign Affairs Committee, December 15, 2006, http://www.fas.org/irp/congress/2006_rpt/embas sies.html.

66. "New Civilian Tasks for the Military," show transcript, April 11, 1993, produced by Center for Defense Information, http://www.cdi.org/adm/630/. Col. Summers continued: "It's just dangerous now to go out and seek out these outside missions and pull away from the primary mission of why the military was created, which essentially is to kill people and destroy things in the name of the United States. I mean, that's the real bottom line. Nobody really wants to talk about that, but that's really what it is. And it's the ability to do that that gives it its utility to the United States."

67. "New Civilian Tasks for the Military."

68. DODD 3000.05, 3.1.

69. Ibid., 4.3.

70. Ibid., 4.1.

71. National Defense Authorization Act of 2006, Pub. L. No. 109–163, § 1206. 119 Stat. 3136, 3456–58 (2006).

72. Nina M. Serafino, "Security Assistance Reform: 'Section 1206' Background and Issues for Congress," RS22285, Congressional Research Service, June 29, 2010, http://www.fas.org/sgp/crs/natsec/RS22855.pdf.

73. Ibid., introduction.

74. "Section 1206 Security Assistance: Briefing for Senate Foreign Relations Committee Staff," General Accounting Office, December 14, 2006, http://www.gao.gov/new.items/d07416r.pdf.

75. Ernesto Londoño, "U.S. 'Money Weapon' Yields Mixed Results," *Washington Post* (July 27, 2009), http://www.washingtonpost.com/wp-dyn/content/article/2009/07/26/AR2009072602833.html.

76. "Quarterly Report and Semi-Annual Report to the United States Congress: Section 2: Iraq Reconstruction Funding and Uses," Washington D.C.: Special Inspector General of Iraq, January 30, 2011, 21, http://www.sigir.mil/files/quarterlyreports/January2011/Report_-_January_2011.pdf#view=fit.

77. "Secretary Gates Details $154 Billion in Defense Savings Over Five Years," American Society of Military Comptrollers, January 2011, http://www.asmconline.org/2011/01/secretary-gates-details-154-billion-in-defense-savings-over-five-years/.

78. Christopher Drew and Thom Shanker, "Struggle Forecast for Pentagon and Deficit Hawks," *New York Times* (January 7, 2011), http://www.nytimes.com/2011/01/08/us/politics/08military.html?scp=2&sq=defense%20budget&st=cse.

79. Ibid.

80. Thom Shanker and Christopher Drew, "Pentagon Seeks Biggest Cuts Since Before 9/11," *New York Times* (January 6, 2011), http://www.nytimes.com/2011/01/07/us/07military.html?scp=4&sq=defense%20budget&st=cse.

81. Sandra Erwin, "Secretary Gates Budget Proposal: Good for Defense, Bad for the National Debt," *National Defense* (January 6, 2011), http://www.nationaldefensemagazine.org/blog/Lists/Posts/Post.aspx?ID=281.

82. Travis Sharp, "U.S. Defense Spending 2001–2009," Center for Arms Control and Non-Proliferation, February 20, 2008, http://armscontrolcenter.org/policy/securityspending/articles/defense_spending_since_2001/.

83. Craig Whitlock, "Pentagon to Cut Spending by $78 Billion, Reduce Troop Strength," *Washington Post* (January 7, 2011), http://www.washingtonpost.com/wp-dyn/content/article/2011/01/06/AR2011010603628.html.

84. Michael Gerson, "A War Fighter's Budget," *Washington Post* (April 10, 2009), http://www.washingtonpost.com/wp-dyn/content/article/2009/04/09/AR2009040903446.html.

85. Erwin, "Secretary Gates Budget Proposal."

86. A 2010 poll found that 73 percent of Americans fear terrorism more than a nuclear attack. The same poll found that when asked which issues are of the highest importance, 43 percent named the economy and only 11 percent named national security. "73% Fear Terrorists More Than Nuclear Attack," *Rasmussen Report* (December 27, 2010), http://www.rasmussenreports.com/public_content/politics/current_events/russia/73_fear_terrorists_more_than_nuclear_attack.

87. This is a lesson deeply engrained in the business community, and there is a huge literature, both professional and academic, on strategic adaptation and growth as requirements for institutional survival. In his book on the topic, Raymond Zammuto writes: "Organizations gain their license to exist by creating . . . valued outcomes. It is through the satisfaction of the wants and needs of members of society that society in turn legitimizes an organization's existence. . . . Organizations have to perform effectively in order to survive. Effective organizations, evolving in tandem with the larger society, modify their performance to meet changing social needs and constraints." Raymond F. Zammuto, *Assessing Organizational Effectiveness: Systems Change, Adaptation, and Strategy* (Albany, N.Y.: SUNY Press, 1982), 4. See also, for example, Alex and David Bennet, *Organizational Survival in the New World: The Intelligent Complex Adaptive System* (Burlington, Mass.: Elsevier, 2004).

88. "New Civilian Tasks for the Military," show transcript, April 11, 1993, produced by Center for Defense Information, http://www.cdi.org/adm/630/.

89. Robert M. Gates, "A Balanced Strategy: Reprogramming the Pentagon for a New Age," *Foreign Affairs* 88, no. 1 (January/February 2009): 30.

90. USAWC conference, April 2010, LTC (ret) Nathan Freier, "Why Does It Matter" Panel.

91. USAWC conference, April 2010, Dr. Deane-Peter Baker, "Rules of War" Panel.

92. USAWC conference, April 2010, Dr. Paul Kan, "Who Participates?" Panel.

5. IMPLICATIONS OF MISSION REVOLUTION

1. Rod Nordland "UN Rejects 'Militarization' of Afghan Aid," *New York Times* (February 17, 2010), http://www.nytimes.com/2010/02/18/world/asia/18aid.html; Peter Walker et al., "Italian Official Condemns Haiti Earthquake Relief as 'Vanity Parade,'" *Guardian* (January 25, 2010), http://www.guardian.co.uk/world/2010/jan/25/italy-condemns-haiti-earthquake-relief-effort; Donald F. Herr, "Changing Course: Proposals to Reverse the Militarization of U.S. Foreign Policy," International Policy Report, *CIP Online* (September 2008), http://www.ciponline.org/nationalsecurity/publications/ipr/Mil_USFP_IPR0908.pdf.

2. Ann Scott Tyson, "Gates Warns of Militarized Policy," *Washington Post* (July 16, 2008), http://www.washingtonpost.com/wp-dyn/content/article/2008/07/15/AR2008071502777.html.

3. "Is Militarization Undermining U.S. Foreign Policy Goals?" UNDP-USA conference, May 28, 2008, http://undp-usa.blogspot.com/2008/06/is-militarization-undermining-us.html.

4. General Charles F. Wald, U.S. Air Force (Ret.), paper presented at the National Security and the Threat of Climate Change Conference, Wilson Center, Environmental Change and Security Program, Washington, D.C., May 2007, http://www.wilsoncenter.org/index.cfm?topic_id=1413&fuseaction=topics.event_summary&event_id=236344.

5. The traditional operational phases are One (planning), Two (deployment), Three (employment), and Four (redeployment), though they have been presented in various formats in different service doctrines and publications, with as few as four phases and as many as seven. Phase Zero is universally understood as day-to-day "shaping" of the peacetime environment, and the final phase in all of the continuums reverts to stability operations, though they can be both kinetic and nonkinetic.

6. Thomas P. M. Barnett, *The Pentagon's New Map: War and Peace in the Twenty-First Century* (New York: Berkley Books, 2004), 299.

7. Ibid., 315.

8. Ibid., 322–323.

9. U.S. European Command, http://www.eucom.mil/english/MissionAndVision.asp.

10. U.S. Pacific Command, *United States Pacific Command Strategy: Partnership, Readiness, Presence,* April 2009, 3, http://www.pacom.mil/web/pacom_resources/pdf/pacom%20strategy%2002APR09.pdf.

11. U.S. Africa Command, http://www.africom.mil/AboutAFRICOM.asp; Elizabeth Dickinson, "Think Again: AFRICOM," *Foreign Policy* (November 17, 2009), http://www.foreignpolicy.com/articles/2009/11/17/think_again_africom?page=full.

12. Donna Miles, "SouthCom Transformation Promotes New Approach to Regional Challenges," *American Forces Press Service* (August 26, 2008), http://www.defense.gov/news/newsarticle.aspx?id=50936.

13. U.S. Southern Command, http://www.southcom.mil/PA/Facts/Mission.htm.

14. Miles, "SouthCom Transformation Promotes New Approach to Regional Challenges."

15. Ibid.

16. Lauren Ploch, "Africa Command: U.S. Strategic Interests and the Role of the U.S. Military in Africa," *Congressional Research Service* (October 2009): 8, http://assets.opencrs.com/rpts/RL34003_20091002.pdf.

17. Ward, "AFRICOM Posture Statement 2008," under "Introduction."

18. Theresa Whelan, testimony before the Subcommittee on African Affairs of the Committee on Foreign Relations of the U.S. Senate, "Exploring the U.S. Africa Command and a New Strategic Relationship with Africa," 110th Cong., 1st sess., 2007, http://www.fas.org/irp/congress/2007_hr/africom.html.

19. Ward, "AFRICOM Posture Statement 2008," under "AFRICOM Support to the Global War on Terror." Emphasis added.

20. William E. Ward, "AFRICOM Posture Statement Before the Senate and House Armed Services Committees," 2009, 7, http://www.africom.mil/pdfFiles/USAFRICOM2009PostureStatement.pdf.

21. Dickinson, "Think Again: AFRICOM."

22. U.S. Southern Command, *Command Strategy 2016*, 7, http://www.southcom.mil/Ap psSC/files/0UI0I1175252190.pdf.

23. Ibid., 14. With respect to socioeconomic and political development, see Objective 3.2, especially 3.2.d.

24. *Doctrine for the Armed Forces of the United States*, Joint Publication 1 (Washington, D.C.: U.S. Joint Chiefs of Staff, May 14, 2007), i.

25. It is worth noting that the terms "military engagement" and "peacetime military engagement" are being used differently now than even during the 1990s. Until very recently, engagement meant kinetic operations, and peacetime military engagement referred to military deployments for peacekeeping and peace enforcement. Now the terms military engagement and peacetime military engagement are being used in reference to the establishment and maintenance of military-to-military relations. See, for an example of prior use of the terminology, Carl H. Groth Jr. and Diane T. Berliner, "Peacetime Military Engagement: A Framework for Policy Criteria," report prepared for DOD by Logistics Management Institute (LMI), August 1993, http://www.dtic .mil/cgi-bin/GetTRDoc?Location=U2&doc=GetTRDoc.pdf&AD=ADA272699. For the contemporary definition and examples, see U.S. Army Field Manual 3-0, chapter 9, "Stability Operations," section 5, "Peacetime Military Engagement," http:// www.globalsecurity.org/military/library/policy/army/fm/3-0/ch9.htm#par1-1.

26. *Doctrine for the Armed Forces of the United States* (2007), I-15.

27. Elisabeth Bumiller, "Calling for Restraint, Pentagon Faces Test of Influence with Ally," *New York Times* (January 29, 2011), http://www.nytimes.com/2011/01/30/world/ middleeast/30military.html.

28. Several State Department personnel expressed support for the military's efforts via SOUTHCOM and AFRICOM, telling the author that the coordination and cooperation between the GCCs and embassies was smooth and beneficial. Their only concerns were with regard to authorities like 1206 and Security Force Assistance, which they perceived as encroaching on State Department roles. Author's interviews with State Department personnel, Foggy Bottom, September 20–21, 2010.

29. *Duncan Hunter National Defense Authorization Act for Fiscal Year 2009*, S 3001, 110th Cong., 2nd sess., (January 3, 2008), under "Restriction on Obligation of Funds for United States Southern Command Development Assistance Activities," http://frwe bgate.access.gpo.gov/cgi-bin/getdoc.cgi?dbname=110_cong_bills&docid=f:s3001enr .txt.pdf.

30. House Committee on Armed Services, *Duncan Hunter National Defense Authorization Act for Fiscal Year 2009 Report on H.R. 5658*, 110th Cong., 2nd sess., H. Rpt.110– 652, http://thomas.loc.gov/cgi-bin/cpquery/T?&report=hr652&dbname=110&, under "United States Africa Command."

31. Lauren Ploch, "AFRICOM: An Independent Review for the New Administration," remarks at a conference at the Center for Advanced Defense Studies in Washington, D.C., 2009, 54, http://www.c4ads.org/files/CADS_AFRICOM09_Transcript .pdf. One example of this is AFRICOM's invitation to the State Department's deputy

mission directors to participate in its Theater Security Working Group. This represents an "unprecedented step" in interagency collaboration, since the combatant command's policy planning process usually occurs without the participation of civilian agencies.

32. *Doctrine for the Armed Forces of the United States* (2007), V-15–V-16. These directorates are: Manpower and Personnel Directorate (J-1), Intelligence Directorate (J-2), Operations Directorate (J-3), Logistics Directorate (J-4), Plans Directorate (J-5), and the Communications System Directorate (J-6).

33. Theresa Whelan, "Why AFRICOM?" paper presented during the Tswalu Dialogue organized by the Brenthurst Foundation, 2007, 71, http://www.rusi.org/downloads/assets/Tswalu_07_WHP.pdf.

34. "Directorates and Staff," http://www.southcom.mil/AppsSC/pages/leadershipStaff.php. SOUTHCOM's directorates, following its interagency reorganization, are Chief of Staff, Commander's Action Group, Enterprise Support, Partnering Directorate, Policy and Strategy Directorate, Resources and Assessments, Security and Intelligence Directorate, and Stability Directorate.

35. Edward Marks, "Why USAFRICOM?" *Joint Forces Quarterly* 52 (2009): 149.

36. *Actions Needed to Address Stakeholder Concerns, Improve Interagency Collaboration, and Determine Full Costs Associated with the U.S. Africa Command* (Washington, D.C.: Government Accountability Office, Defense Management, 2009), 26, http://www.gao.gov/new.items/d09181.pdf.

37. Ibid., 21.

38. Ibid.

39. Ibid.

40. Nina M. Serafino, "The Department of Defense Role in Foreign Assistance: Background, Major Issues, and Options for Congress," *Congressional Research Service* (December 2008): 24, http://www.fas.org/sgp/crs/natsec/RL34639.pdf.

41. Kate Brannen, "Report: Return U.S. Security Assistance Role to State Department," *Defense News* (April 2011), http://www.defensenews.com/story.php?i=6284812; Gordon Adams and Rebecca Williams, *A New Way Forward: Rebalancing Security Assistance Programs and Authorities* (Washington, D.C.: Stimson Center, March 2011), http://www.stimson.org/images/uploads/research-pdfs/A_New_Way_Forward_20110420_1.pdf.

42. Ploch, "AFRICOM: An Independent Review for the New Administration," 8.

43. Transcript: "AFRICOM's Rationales, Roles and Progress on the Eve of Operations," House Committee on Oversight and Government Reform, Subcommittee on National Security and Foreign Affairs, July 15, 2008, Witness: Lauren Ploch, Analyst in African Affairs, Foreign Affairs, Defense, and Trade Division, Congressional Research Service, http://www.africom.mil/getArticle.asp?art=1921.

44. In 2007, some State Department personnel balked at being sent into Iraq, claiming that it was a "potential death sentence." Alex Spillius, "U.S. Diplomats Protest Forced Postings in Iraq," *Telegraph* (November 2, 2007), http://www.telegraph.co.uk/news/uknews/1568164/US-diplomats-protest-forced-postings-in-Iraq.html.

45. Eric Edelman, Transcript, Defense Writers Group, November 14, 2008, http://www
.airforce-magazine.com/DWG/Documents/2008/November%202008/111408edel
man.pdf.

46. James Traub, "Afghanistan's Civil War," *New York Times Magazine* (June 15, 2010),
http://www.nytimes.com/2010/06/20/magazine/20Afghanistan-t.html?hpw.

47. Paula Broadwell, guest columnist in Thomas E. Ricks's "Best Defense" blog, "Ignatius, Kaplan, and Klein Just Don't Get It: Petraeus Is Changing the Afghan War's
Intensity, Not Its Overall Strategy," *Foreign Policy* (October 20, 2010), http://ricks
.foreignpolicy.com/posts/2010/10/20/ignatius_kaplan_and_klein_just_don_t_get_
it_petraeus_is_changing_the_afghan_war_s_i.

48. Josh Boak, "U.S.-Funded Infrastructure Deteriorates Once Under Afghan Control,
Report Says," *Washington Post* (January 4, 2011), http://www.washingtonpost.com/
wp-dyn/content/article/2011/01/03/AR2011010302175.html.

49. Garry Reid, Deputy Assistant Secretary of Defense, Special Operations and Combating Terrorism, Statement for the Record, Senate Armed Service Subcommittee
on Emerging Threats and Capabilities, March 10, 2010, http://armed-services.senate
.gov/statemnt/2010/03%20March/Reid%2003–10–10.pdf.

50. Tim Arango, "War in Iraq Defies U.S. Timetable for End of Combat," *New York Times*
(July 2, 2010), http://www.nytimes.com/2010/07/03/world/middleeast/03iraq.html.

51. Frederick W. Kagan, "New Thinking, Old Realities," *AEI Online* (October 2006),
http://www.aei.org/outlook/25010.

52. Peter W. Chiarelli and Patrick R. Michaelis, "Winning the Peace: The Requirement
for Full-Spectrum Operations," *Military Review* (July–August 2005): 4–17, http://
www.au.af.mil/au/awc/awcgate/milreview/chiarelli.pdf.

53. Justin Naylor, "1-8 Cav Soldiers Take on New Missions," *Army Times* (March 27,
2009), http://www.army.mil/-news/2009/03/27/18850-1-8-cav-soldiers-take-on-new
-missions/.

54. Michael Hastings, "The Runaway General," *Rolling Stone* (June 22, 2010), http://
www.rollingstone.com/politics/news/17390/119236?RS_show_page=0.

55. QDR 2010, 69.

56. In one interview, a U.S. civil affairs officer told the author how disturbing it was for him
and his men to support Afghan leaders who entertained with these "dancing boys."

57. "Defining War for the 21st Century," paper presented at the Strategic Studies Institute, U.S. Army War College, Twenty-first Annual Strategy Conference, Washington, D.C., April 6–8, 2010.

58. Karen H. Seal, Thomas J. Metzler, Kristian S. Gima, Daniel Bertenthal, Shira Maguen, and Charles R. Marmar, "Trends and Risk Factors for Mental Health Diagnoses Among Iraq and Afghanistan Veterans Using Department of Veterans Affairs
Healthcare, 2002–2008," *American Journal of Public Health* 99, no. 9 (2009): 1651–1658,
http://www.medscape.com/viewarticle/715223; Thom Shanker, "Army Is Worried
About Rising Stress of Return Tours to Iraq," *New York Times* (April 6, 2008), http://
www.nytimes.com/2008/04/06/washington/06military.html.

59. John Donnelly, "More Troops Lost to Suicide," *Congress.org* (January 24, 2011), http://www.congress.org/news/2011/01/24/more_troops_lost_to_suicide; Eli Rosenberg, "Does the Military Have a Suicide Problem?" *Atlantic Wire* (January 25, 2011), http://www.theatlanticwire.com/politics/2011/01/does-the-military-have-a-suicide-problem/17919/.

60. Stacy Bannerman, "Multiple Deployments to Iraq and Afghanistan Wars May Increase Risk of Spouse Suicide," *TruthOut* (October 25, 2009), 17:49, http://www.veteransforcommonsense.org/index.php/veterans-category-articles/1454-stacy-bannerman.

61. Andrew Tilghman, "The Army's Other Crisis," *Washington Monthly* (July 2007), http://www.washingtonmonthly.com/features/2007/0712.tilghman.html. Unfortunately, in the four years since Tilghman wrote his article, troops have gone on fourth and fifth deployments to Iraq and Afghanistan.

62. Greg Jaffe, "Pentagon's Gates Keeps Single-Minded Focus in Dual Wars in Iraq and Afghanistan," *Washington Post* (May 15, 2009), http://www.washingtonpost.com/wp-dyn/content/article/2009/05/14/AR2009051404450_2.html?sub=AR.

63. Tom Vogel, "Post 9/11 Military Officers Poll Release Press Conference," U.S. Global Leadership Coalition, http://www.usglc.org/2008/07/15/post-911-military-officers-poll-release-press-conference/. This comes from a survey conducted on behalf of the Center for U.S. Global Engagement by the bipartisan polling team of Peter D. Hart Research Associates (D) and Public Opinion Strategies (R). The survey was "among 606 commissioned U.S. military officers, including 499 active duty officers and 107 officers who retired after the 9/11/2001 attacks. The survey was conducted from June 24 to 30, 2008, and included a combination of telephone and Internet interviews." For a description of the survey methodology, see http://www.usglobalengagement.org.php58.websitetestlink.com/USGLCdocs/Military_poll_highlights.pdf.

64. Thom Shanker, "Top Officer Urges Limit on Mission of Military," *New York Times* (January 12, 2009), http://www.nytimes.com/2009/01/13/washington/13military.html?_r=2&ref=world.

65. U.S. Global Leadership Coalition, "Senior Military Leaders Urge Congress to Boost Non-Military Tools," *PR Newswire* (March 10, 2010), http://intldevelopment.einnews.com/article.php?nid=3117.

66. Nina M. Serafino and Martin M. Weiss, *Peacekeeping and Conflict Transitions: Background and Congressional Action on Civilian Capabilities*, CRS Report for Congress (Washington, D.C.: Congressional Research Service, updated January 6, 2006), CRS-14.

67. Robert M. Gates, "Helping Others Defend Themselves: The Future of U.S. Security Assistance," *Foreign Affairs* 89, no. 3 (May–June 2010).

68. Serafino and Weiss, *Peacekeeping and Conflict Transitions*, CRS-8, CRS-9.

69. U.S. Department of State, Office of the Coordinator for Reconstruction and Stabilization, http://www.state.gov/s/crs/.

70. Condoleezza Rice, remarks at Georgetown School of Foreign Service, January 18, 2006, http://www.state.gov/secretary/rm/2006/59306.htm.

71. Greg Bruno, "Waiting on a Civilian Surge in Afghanistan," Council on Foreign Relations interview with John E. Herbst, then-coordinator for reconstruction and

stabilization, U.S. State Department, March 31, 2010, http://www.cfr.org/afghani
stan/waiting-civilian-surge-afghanistan/p21785.

72. The number of PRTs is volatile, so it may have changed since the writing of this book.

73. "Provincial Reconstruction Teams," Fact Sheet, Embassy of the United States, Baghdad, Iraq, September 15, 2009, http://iraq.usembassy.gov/iraq_prt/provincial-recon
struction-teams-fact-sheet.html; Robert Perito, "Embedded Provincial Reconstruction Teams," Peace Brief, United States Institute of Peace, February 2008, http://
www.usip.org/resources/embedded-provincial-reconstruction-teams.

74. Spencer Case, U.S. Army SGT, "Development in Eastern Afghanistan: Keys to Success," ISAF Public Affairs Office, June 1, 2010, http://www.isaf.nato.int/article/isaf
-releases/development-in-eastern-afghanistan-keys-to-success.html.

75. Janine Davidson, "Making Government Work: Pragmatic Priorities for Interagency
Coordination," *Orbis* 53, no. 3 (Summer 2009): 435.

76. Author's interviews with several State Department, Defense Department, and think
tank personnel, Washington, D.C., September 2010.

77. Steven Metz, "The Civilian Surge Myth," *New Republic* (October 15, 2009), http://
www.tnr.com/article/world/the-civilian-surge-myth?page=0,1.

78. Interview #51, U.S. Institute of Peace—ADST Afghanistan Experience Project, Oral His-
tories, http://www.usip.org/files/file/resources/collections/histories/afghanistan/51.pdf.

79. "U.S. Short of Diplomats for Iraq, Afghanistan Reconstruction," *AFP* (April 28, 2008),
http://afp.google.com/article/ALeqM5jtyTtMgdIcIsa-R8S_mHcKVYRhRQ.

80. Ibid.

81. Davidson, "Making Government Work," 423.

82. Karen DeYoung, "Civilians to Join Afghan Build-Up," *Washington Post* (March
19, 2009), http://www.washingtonpost.com/wp-dyn/content/article/2009/03/18/
AR2009031802313.html?hpid=topnews.

83. Curt Tarnoff, "Iraq: Reconstruction Assistance," Congressional Research Service Report, August 20, 2008, http://www.dtic.mil/cgi-bin/GetTRDoc?AD=ADA486585&
Location=U2&doc=GetTRDoc.pdf.

84. Nima Abbaszadeh et al., "Provincial Reconstruction Teams: Lessons and Recommendations," Princeton, N.J., Woodrow Wilson School of Public and International Affairs,
January 2008, 48, http://wws.princeton.edu/research/pwreports_f07/wws591b.pdf.

85. Ibid.

86. Ibid.

87. Hillary Clinton Nomination Hearings to Be Secretary of State, Hillary Rodham
Clinton, Secretary of State, Senate Foreign Relations Committee, Washington, D.C.,
January 13, 2009, http://sarajevo.usembassy.gov/washdc_20090113.html.

88. "Quadrennial Diplomacy and Development Review: Overview" (Washington, D.C.:
Department of State, 2010), http://www.state.gov/s/dmr/qddr/.

89. Tara Soneshine and Beth Cole, "A Tectonic Shift at State and USAID?" *Huffington
Post* (October 27, 2010), http://www.huffingtonpost.com/tara-sonenshine/a-tectonic
-shift-at-state_b_774946.html?ir=World.

90. QDDR, 12.

91. Warren P. Strobel, "State Department Planning to Field a Small Army in Iraq," *McClatchy Newspapers* (July 21, 2010), http://www.mcclatchydc.com/2010/07/21/97915/state-dept-planning-to-field-a.html.

92. "Diplomats Seek War Gear as Troops Exit Iraq," *Associated Press* (June 15, 2010), http://www.boston.com/news/world/middleeast/articles/2010/06/15/diplomats_seek_war_gear_as_troops_exit_iraq/.

93. Jess T. Ford, statement, "Challenges Facing the Bureau of Diplomatic Security," GAO testimony before the Subcommittee on Oversight of Government Management, the Federal Workforce, and the District of Columbia, Committee on Homeland Security and Governmental Affairs, U.S. Senate, December 9, 2009, http://www.gao.gov/new/items/d10290t.pdf.

94. Carlos Lozada, "A Sneak Peak at Hillary Clinton's New Global Strategy," *Washington Post* (October 24, 2010), http://www.washingtonpost.com/wp-dyn/content/article/2010/10/22/AR2010102203592.html.

95. Reuben E. Brigety II, testimony before the House Committee on Foreign Affairs, "Striking the Appropriate Balance: The Defense Department's Expanding Role in Foreign Assistance," 111th Cong., 1st sess., 2009, http://foreignaffairs.house.gov/111/bri031809.pdf, 2. In response to the question "What do you perceive to be the comparative advantages and disadvantages of DoD conducting foreign and security assistance," Brigety noted that while there are several advantages to the military performing these tasks, there are three main disadvantages to DoD's mission expansion: "First, the focus on the performance of programs of tactical or strategic value can mean assistance efforts are directed to places of the greatest potential threat rather than places of the greatest human need. . . . Second, the military's growing involvement in this space risks the appearance of 'militarization' of America's foreign assistance. . . . Finally, and most importantly, DoD does not possess a coherent assessment methodology for evaluating the strategic or tactical success of its assistance programs, especially in permissive environments." Rep. Howard Berman also raised similar concerns in his opening statement before the House Committee on Foreign Affairs, "Striking the Appropriate Balance: The Defense Department's Expanding Role in Foreign Assistance," 111th Cong., 1st sess., 2009, http://www.internationalrelations.house.gov/111/48139.pdf, 1–3. To be fair and accurate, civilians may perform no better at reconstruction in the absence of clear policy objectives and guidance. Their decisions may be based more on politics than progress and more on short-term goals than long-term sustainability. That being said, they are better positioned, ideally, to consider the broader scope of American interests over the long term than is the military.

96. Volker Franke, "The Peacebuilding Dilemma: Civil-Military Cooperation in Stability Operations," *International Journal of Peace Studies* 11, no. 2 (Autumn/Winter 2006), 5–25, http://www.gmu.edu/programs/icar/ijps/vol11_2/11n2FRANKE.pdf.

97. Dexter Filkins, "Afghan Offensive Is New War Model," *New York Times* (February 12, 2010), http://www.nytimes.com/2010/02/13/world/asia/13kabul.html?_r=1.

98. The International Council on Security and Development, "Operation Moshtarak: Lessons Learned," March 2010, 2, http://www.icosgroup.net/documents/operation_moshtarak.pdf.

99. Tom Bowman, "In Afghanistan, the Civil Service 'Surge' That Isn't," *Morning Edition*, National Public Radio, September 7, 2010, http://www.npr.org/templates/story/story.php?storyId=129678727.

100. Anthony H. Cordesman, "Realism in Afghanistan: Rethinking an Uncertain Case for the War," Center for Strategic and International Studies, June 16, 2010, http://csis.org/publication/realism-afghanistan-rethinking-uncertain-case-war.

101. Greg Jaffe and Leila Fadel, "U.S. Military Adopts New Role in Iraq," *Washington Post* (September 1, 2010), http://www.washingtonpost.com/wp-dyn/content/article/2010/09/01/AR2010090101126.html.

102. Michael Hastings, "The Runaway General," *Rolling Stone* (June 22, 2010), http://www.rollingstone.com/politics/news/17390/119236?RS_show_page=0.

103. *Counterinsurgency*, 1-22, 1-25.

104. Thomas E. Ricks, *The Gamble* (New York: Penguin, 2009), 162.

105. *Counterinsurgency*, 2-2. Emphasis added.

106. Robert M. Gates, "A Balanced Strategy: Reprogramming the Pentagon for a New Age," *Foreign Affairs* 88, no. 1 (January–February 2009): 28–40.

107. Hans Binnendijk and Patrick M. Cronin, eds., *Civilian Surge: Key to Complex Operations* (Washington, D.C.: National Defense University, 2009).

108. Remarks by Secretary Gates at the Command and General Staff College, Fort Leavenworth, Kansas, May 7, 2010, http://www.defense.gov/utility/printitem.aspx?print=http://www.defense.gov/transcripts/transcript.aspx?transcriptid=4623.

109. Raj Rana, "Contemporary Challenges in the Civil-Military Relationship: Complementarity or Incompatibility?" *International Review of the Red Cross* (September 2004): 586.

110. For example: "Our data suggest that reconstruction money works when projects are small, troops have a good working relationship with noncombatants, projects are chosen in consultation with local officials, programs are administered by local contractors, and a provincial reconstruction team is nearby to provide guidance." Eli Berman, Joseph H. Felter, and Jacob N. Shapiro, "Constructive COIN: How Development Can Fight Radicals," *Foreign Affairs* (June 1, 2010), http://www.foreignaffairs.com/articles/66432/eli-berman-joseph-h-felter-and-jacob-n-shapiro/constructive-coin?page=show.

6. A NEW WORLD ORDER?

1. Jennifer Morrison Taw and Jed Peters, *Operations Other Than War: Implications for the U.S. Army* (Santa Monica, Calif.: RAND Arroyo Center, 1995), 23.

2. A U.S. State Department official told the author in an interview at Foggy Bottom on September 20, 2010, that this new security agenda is unrealistic and unmanageable and will have serious negative repercussions on American foreign policy efforts.

3. Gordon Adams, "Assessing the QDR and 2011 Defense Budget," *Bulletin of the Atomic Scientists* (March 2, 2010), http://www.thebulletin.org/web-edition/columnists/gordon-adams/assessing-the-qdr-and-2011-defense-budget.

4. Michael Parenti, "The Logic of U.S. Intervention," in *Masters of War: Militarism and Blowback in the Era of American Empire*, ed. Carl Boggs (New York: Routledge, 2003), 20.

5. Representative Barney Frank and Representative Ron Paul, "Why We Must Reduce Military Spending," *Huffington Post* (July 6, 2010), http://www.huffingtonpost.com/rep-barney-frank/why-we-must-reduce-milita_b_636051.html.

6. Steven Metz and Frank Hoffman, "Restructuring America's Ground Forces: Better, Not Bigger," *Policy Analysis Brief*, Stanley Foundation, September 2007, 7, http://www.stanleyfoundation.org/resources.cfm?id=262.

7. Phoebe Marr, "Occupational Hazards," *Foreign Affairs* (July–August 2005), http://www.foreignaffairs.com/articles/60844/phebe-marr/occupational-hazards.

8. Robert H. Johnson, "Exaggerating America's Stakes in Third World Conflicts," *International Security* 10, no. 3 (Winter 1985–1986): 32–48.

9. Stewart Patrick, *Weak Links: Fragile States, Global Threats, and International Security* (Oxford: Oxford University Press, 2011), 16.

10. Benjamin O. Fordham, "A Very Sharp Sword: The Influence of Military Capabilities on American Decisions to Use Force," *Journal of Conflict Resolution* 48, no. 5 (October 2004): 636.

11. Fritz and Hermsmeyer, for example, exclaim that "The new six-phase model reflects real-world operational experience and represents a genuine transformation in Department of Defense (DOD) thinking." Oliver Fritz and Gregory A. Hermsmeyer, "The U.S. Air Force and Stability Operations Transformation." *Joint Force Quarterly* 47 (December 2007): 128–134, http://findarticles.com/p/articles/mi_m0KNN/is_47/ai_n28028077/.

BIBLIOGRAPHY

Abbaszadeh, Nima, Mark Crow, Marianne El-Khoury, Jonathan Gandomi, David Kuwayama, Christopher MacPherson, Meghan Nutting, Nealin Parker, Taya Weiss. "Provincial Reconstruction Teams: Lessons and Recommendations." Princeton, New Jersey: The Woodrow Wilson School of Public and International Affairs, January 2008. http://wws.princeton.edu/research/pwreports_f07/wws591b.pdf

Abrams, Abe. "FM 7-0 *Training for Full Spectrum Operations.*" Powerpoint presentation. Fort Leavenworth, Kansas: Combined Arms Center for Training, January 2009. http://usacac.army.mil/cac2/archives/2009/January/FM70.asp.

Actions Needed to Address Stakeholder Concerns, Improve Interagency Collaboration, and Determine Full Costs Associated with the U.S. Africa Command. Washington, D.C.: Government Accountability Office, Defense Management, 2009. http://www.gao.gov/new.items/d09181.pdf.

Adams, Gordon. "Assessing the QDR and 2011 Defense Budget." *Bulletin of the Atomic Scientists* (March 2, 2010). http://www.thebulletin.org/web-edition/columnists/gordon-adams/assessing-the-qdr-and-2011-defense-budget.

Adams, Gordon. "The Politics of National Security Budgets." Muscatine, Iowa: The Stanley Foundation, February 2007. http://www.stimson.org/budgeting/pdf/Politics_of_National_Security_Budgeting.pdf.

Adams, Gordon, and Rebecca Williams. *A New Way Forward: Rebalancing Security Assistance Programs and Authorities.* Washington, D.C.: Stimson Center, March 2011. http://www.stimson.org/images/uploads/research-pdfs/A_New_Way_Forward_20110420_1.pdf.

"Aerospace Expeditionary Force (AEF); Air and Space Expeditionary Task Force (ASETF); (Formerly Air Expeditionary Force)." Globalsecurity.org. http://www.globalsecurity.org/military/agency/usaf/aef-intro.htm.

"AFRICOM's Rationales, Roles and Progress on the Eve of Operations." House Committee on Oversight and Government Reform, Subcommittee on National Security and Foreign Affairs, July 15, 2008, Witness: Lauren Ploch, Analyst in African

Affairs, Foreign Affairs, Defense, and Trade Division, Congressional Research Service. http://www.africom.mil/getArticle.asp?art=1921.

Aiello, Thomas. "Constructing 'Godless Communism': Religion, Politics, and Popular Culture, 1954–1960." *Americana* 4, no. 1 (Spring 2005).

"The Air Force in Facts and Figures." *Air Force Magazine* (May 2009): 24–57. http://www.airforce-magazine.com/MagazineArchive/Magazine%20Documents/2009/May%202009/0509facts_fig.pdf.

"The Air Force in Facts and Figures: 2010 USAF Almanac." *Air Force Magazine* (May 2010): 36–66. http://www.airforce-magazine.com/MagazineArchive/Magazine%20Documents/2010/May%202010/0510facts_figs.pdf.

"Another Crossroads? Professional Military Education Two Decades After the Goldwater-Nichols Act and the Skelton Panel." U.S. House of Representatives, Committee on Armed Services, Subcommittee on Oversight and Investigations, April 2010, Washington, D.C. http://democrats.armedservices.house.gov/index.cfm/files/serve?File_id=d4748d4a-b358-49d7-8c9a-aa0ba6f581a6.

Arango, Tim. "War in Iraq Defies U.S. Timetable for End of Combat." *New York Times* (July 2, 2010). http://www.nytimes.com/2010/07/03/world/middleeast/03iraq.html.

"Army Doctrine Update." Combined Arms Doctrine Directorate, U.S. Army Combined Arms Center, Fort Leavenworth, Kansas, February 24, 2007. http://asc.army.mil/docs/transformation/Army_Doctrine_Update_FM501_FM30.pdf.

Army Posture Statement. Washington, D.C.: Headquarters, Department of the Army, 2010. https://secureweb2.hqda.pentagon.mil/vdas_armyposturestatement/2010/aps_pages/two_critical.asp#armymodernization.

"Aspin Criticizes Pentagon's Approach to the Use of Military Force in the Post–Cold War Era." *Jinsa Security Affairs* (October 1992): 1. http://www.securityaffairs.org/archived_site/1992/oct1992.pdf.

"ATG 101." Information Brief, Marine Air Ground Task Force Training Command (MAGTFTC) Advisor Training Group, April 11, 2011. http://www.marines.mil/unit/29palms/ATG/Documents/ATG%20101%2011%20April%202011.pdf.

Bacevich, Andrew J. *American Empire*. Cambridge, Mass.: Harvard University Press, 2002.

——. *The New American Militarism*. Oxford: Oxford University Press, 2005.

——. "The Petraeus Doctrine." *The Atlantic* (October 2008). http://www.theatlantic.com/doc/200810/petraeus-doctrine.

Baldwin, David. "Security Studies and the End of the Cold War." *World Politics* 48, no. 1 (October 1995): 117–141.

Bankus, Brent C. "We've Done This Before." *Small Wars Journal* 4 (February 2006): 33–35. http://smallwarsjournal.com/documents/swjvol4.pdf.

Bannerman, Stacy. "Multiple Deployments to Iraq and Afghanistan Wars May Increase Risk of Spouse Suicide." *TruthOut* (October 25, 2009). http://www.veteransforcommonsense.org/index.php/veterans-category-articles/1454-stacy-bannerman.

Banusiewicz, John D. "'As Iraqis Stand Up, We Will Stand Down,' Bush Tells Nation." *Armed Forces Press Service* (June 28, 2005). http://www.defenselink.mil/news/newsarticle .aspx?id=16277.

Barkin, J. Samuel, and Bruce Cronin. "The State and the Nation: Changing Norms and the Rules of Sovereignty in International Relations." *International Organization* 48, no. 1 (Winter 1994): 107–130.

Barnes, Julian E. "Defense Chief Urges Bigger Budget for State Department." *Los Angeles Times* (November 27, 2007). http://articles.latimes.com/2007/nov/27/nation/na-gates27.

Barnett, Thomas P. M. *The Pentagon's New Map: War and Peace in the Twenty-First Century.* New York: Berkley Books, 2004.

Beebe, Kenneth. "The Air Force's Missing Doctrine: How the Air Force Ignores Counterinsurgency." *Air and Space Power Journal* 20, no. 1 (Spring 2006): 30. http:// www.airpower.maxwell.af.mil/airchronicles/apj/apj06/spr06/beebe.html.

Bennet, Alex, and David Bennet. *Organizational Survival in the New World: The Intelligent Complex Adaptive System.* Burlington, Mass.: Elsevier, 2004.

Berman, Eli, Joseph H. Felter, and Jacob N. Shapiro. "Constructive COIN: How Development Can Fight Radicals." *Foreign Affairs* (June 1, 2010). http://www .foreignaffairs.com/articles/66432/eli-berman-joseph-h-felter-and-jacob-n-shapiro /constructive-coin?page=show.

Berman, Howard. "Striking the Appropriate Balance: The Defense Department's Expanding Role in Foreign Assistance." Opening statement before the House Committee on Foreign Affairs, 111th Cong., 1st sess., 2009. http://www.internation alrelations.house.gov/111/48139.pdf.

Bert, Wayne. *The Reluctant Superpower: United States' Policy in Bosnia, 1991–95.* New York: St. Martin's Press, 1997.

Berteau, David J., Gregory Kiley, Hardin Lang, Matthew Zlatnik, Tara Callahan, Ashley Chandler, and Thomas Patterson. "Final Report on Lessons Learned: Department of Defense Task Force for Business and Stability Operations." Washington, D.C.: Center for Strategic and International Studies, June 2010. http://tfbso.defense.gov/ www/Lessons_Learned_Report.pdf.

"Beyond Goldwater Nichols: U.S. Government and Defense Reform for a New Strategic Era." Phase 1 Report, Center for Strategic and International Studies. Washington, D.C.: Center for Strategic and International Studies, March 2004.

"Beyond Nation Building." Remarks as Delivered by Secretary of Defense Donald H. Rumsfeld, 11th Annual Salute to Freedom, Intrepid Sea-Air-Space Museum, New York City, Friday, February 14, 2003.

Binnendijk, Hans, and Patrick M. Cronin, eds. *Civilian Surge: Key to Complex Operations.* Washington, D.C.: National Defense University, 2009.

Binnendijk, Hans, and Stuart E. Johnson. *Transforming for Stabilization and Reconstruction Operations.* Washington, D.C.: National Defense University, 2004.

Blechman, Barry M., and Stephen S. Kaplan. *Force Without War: U.S. Armed Forces as a Political Instrument.* Washington, D.C.: Brookings Institution, 1978.

Boak, Josh. "U.S.-Funded Infrastructure Deteriorates Once Under Afghan Control, Report Says." *Washington Post* (January 4, 2011). http://www.washingtonpost.com/wp-dyn/content/article/2011/01/03/AR2011010302175.html.

Boot, Max. "America's Destiny is to Police the World." *Financial Times* (February 19, 2003). http://www.cfr.org/publication/5559/americas_destiny_is_to_police_the_world.html?id=5559.

——. Statement before the Terrorism, Unconventional Threats and Capabilities Subcommittee of the Committee on Armed Services, House of Representatives, 109th Congress, 2nd session, June 29, 2006. http://www.fas.org/irp/congress/2006_hr/soc.pdf.

Bowie, Robert R., and Richard H. Immerman. *Waging Peace.* New York: Oxford University Press, 1998.

Bowman, Tom. "In Afghanistan, the Civil Service 'Surge' That Isn't." *Morning Edition,* National Public Radio, September 7, 2010. http://www.npr.org/templates/story/story.php?storyId=129678727.

Brannen, Kate. "Report: Return U.S. Security Assistance Role to State Department." *Defense News* (April 2011). http://www.defensenews.com/story.php?i=6284812.

Breslin-Smith, Janet, and Cliff Krieger. "Strategic Drift? The Future of the National War College." *Joint Force Quarterly* 55 (4th quarter 2009): 14–20.

Brigade Combat Team. Army Field Manual (FM) 3-90.6. Washington, D.C.: Headquarters, Department of the Army, August 4, 2006.

Brigety, Reuben E. *Striking the Appropriate Balance: The Defense Department's Expanding Role in Foreign Assistance.* Testimony before the House Committee on Foreign Affairs, 111th Cong., 1st sess., 2009. http://foreignaffairs.house.gov/111/bri031809.pdf.

Broadwell, Paula. Guest columnist. "Ignatius, Kaplan, and Klein Just Don't Get It: Petraeus Is Changing the Afghan War's Intensity, Not Its Overall Strategy." In "Best Defense" blog, by Thomas Ricks. *Foreign Policy* (October 20, 2010). http://ricks.foreignpolicy.com/posts/2010/10/20/ignatius_kaplan_and_klein_just_don_t_get_it_petraeus_is_changing_the_afghan_war_s_i.

Bruno, Greg. "Waiting on a Civilian Surge in Afghanistan." Interview with John E. Herbst, then-coordinator for reconstruction and stabilization, U.S. State Department. Washington, D.C.: Council on Foreign Relations, March 31, 2010. http://www.cfr.org/afghanistan/waiting-civilian-surge-afghanistan/p21785.

"Building Language Skills and Cultural Competencies in the Military: DOD's Challenges in Today's Education Environment." U.S. House of Representatives, Committee on Armed Services, Subcommittee on Oversight and Investigations, November 2008. http://prhome.defense.gov/READINESS/DLO/files/LanguageCultureReport Nov08_HASC.pdf.

Bumiller, Elisabeth. "Calling for Restraint, Pentagon Faces Test of Influence with Ally." *New York Times* (January 29, 2011). http://www.nytimes.com/2011/01/30/world/middleeast/30military.html.

Buzan, Barry. "Rethinking Security After the Cold War." *Cooperation and Conflict* 32, no. 1 (March 1997): 5–28.

Caldwell IV, William B. "Evolution vs. Revolution: FM 3-o." Blog entry. *Small Wars Journal* (February 15, 2008). http://smallwarsjournal.com/blog/2008/02/evolution-vs-revolution-fm-3o/.

"Canada Supports Peace Operations Training in Ghana." Government of Canada. http://www.canadainternational.gc.ca/ghana/highlights-faits/PeaceOperationsTraining-OperationsPaix-March2010.aspx?lang=en.

Caraher, Leigh C. "Broadening Military Culture." In *Transforming for Stabilization and Reconstruction Operations*, ed. Hans Binnendjik and Stuart E. Johnson, 87–96. Washington, D.C.: National Defense University Press, 2004.

Case, Spencer. "Development in Eastern Afghanistan: Keys to Success." ISAF Public Affairs Office, June 1, 2010. http://www.isaf.nato.int/article/isaf-releases/development-in-eastern-afghanistan-keys-to-success.html.

Chiarelli, Peter W., and Patrick R. Michaelis. "Winning the Peace: The Requirement for Full-Spectrum Operations." *Military Review* (July–August 2005): 4–17. http://www.au.af.mil/au/awc/awcgate/milreview/chiarelli.pdf.

"Chronology of U.S. Military Actions and Wars." *American Experience*, Public Broadcasting System. http://www.pbs.org/wgbh/amex/warletters/timeline/index.html.

Civil-Military Operations. Joint Publication (JP) 3-57. Washington, D.C.: Joint Chiefs of Staff, July 2008.

Clausewitz, Carl von. *On War*. Oxford: Oxford University Press, 2007.

Clinton, Bill. Remarks by the President. National Defense University, Ft. McNair, Va., January 29, 1998.

Cole, August. "Senate Kills Funds for F-22 Fighters." *Wall Street Journal* (July 22, 2009). http://online.wsj.com/article/SB124818597270968593.html.

Command Strategy 2016. Doral, Fla.: U.S. Southern Command, 2007. http://www.southcom.mil/AppsSC/files/0UI0I175252190.pdf.

Cordesman, Anthony H. "Iraq, Grand Strategy, and the Lessons of Military History," 2004 S. T. Lee Lecture on Military History, October 19, 2004.

——. "Realism in Afghanistan: Rethinking an Uncertain Case for the War." Washington, D.C.: Center for Strategic and International Studies, June 16, 2010. http://csis.org/publication/realism-afghanistan-rethinking-uncertain-case-war.

Counterinsurgency. Army Field Manual (FM) 3-24/Marine Corps Warfighting Publication (MCWP) 3-3.5. Washington D.C.: Headquarters, Department of the Army/Headquarters,Marine Corps Combat Development Command, December 2006.

Counterinsurgency Operations. Fleet Marine Force Manual (FMFM) 8-2. Washington, D.C.: U.S. Government Printing Office, 1967. http://www.vietnam.ttu.edu/star/images/137/1370521001a.pdf.

Daalder, Ivo H. "Knowing When to Say No: The Development of U.S. Policy for Peacekeeping." In *UN Peacekeeping, American Politics, and the Uncivil Wars of the 1990s*, ed. William J. Durch, 35–67. New York: St. Martin's Press, 2006.

Dauber, Cori E. "Implications of the Weinberger Doctrine for American Military Intervention in a Post–Desert Storm Age." In *Dimensions of Western Military*

Intervention, ed. Colin McInnis and Nicholas J. Wheeler, 66–90. Portland, Oregon: Frank Cass Publishers, 2002.

Davidson, Janine. *Lifting the Fog of Peace: How Americans Learned to Fight Modern War.* Ann Arbor: University of Michigan Press, 2010.

——. "Making Government Work: Pragmatic Priorities for Interagency Coordination." *Orbis* 53, no. 3 (Summer 2009): 419–438.

Davis II, Robert T. *The Challenge of Adaptation: The U.S. Army in the Aftermath of Conflict, 1953–2000.* Long War Series, Occasional Paper 27. Fort Leavenworth, Kan.: Combat Studies Institute Press, U.S. Army Combined Arms Center, 2008. http://www.dtic .mil/cgi-bin/GetTRDoc?Location=U2&doc=GetTRDoc.pdf&AD=ADA481031.

Dean, David J. *The Air Force Role in Low-Intensity Conflict.* Maxwell Air Force Base, Ala.: Air University Press, October 1986.

"Debacle in the Desert." *Time* (May 5, 1980).

"Defense Language Transformation Roadmap." Washington, D.C.: Department of Defense, January 2005. http://www.defense.gov/news/Mar2005/d20050330roadmap.pdf.

"Defining War for the 21st Century." Paper presented at the Strategic Studies Institute, U.S. Army War College, XXI Annual Strategy Conference, Washington D.C., April 6–8, 2010.

Department of Defense Dictionary of Military and Associated Terms. Joint Publication 1-02. Washington, D.C.: Department of Defense, 2009.

Department of Defense Directive, Number 3000.05. November 28, 2005. Subject: Military Support for Stability, Security, Transition, and Reconstruction (SSRT) Operations. http://www.usaid.gov/policy/cdie/ssso6/sss_1_080106_dod.pdf.

DeYoung, Karen. "Civilians to Join Afghan Build-Up." *Washington Post* (March 19, 2009). http://www.washingtonpost.com/wp-dyn/content/article/2009/03/18/AR2009031802313 .html?hpid=topnews.

Dickinson, Elizabeth. "Think Again: AFRICOM." *Foreign Policy* (November 17, 2009). http://www.foreignpolicy.com/articles/2009/11/17/think_again_africom?page=full.

"Diplomats Seek War Gear as Troops Exit Iraq." *Associated Press* (June 15, 2010). http:// www.boston.com/news/world/middleeast/articles/2010/06/15/diplomats_seek_war_ gear_as_troops_exit_iraq/.

"Directorates and Staff." United States Southern Command. http://www.southcom.mil/ AppsSC/pages/leadershipStaff.php.

Dobbs, Michael. *Madeleine Albright: A Twentieth-Century Odyssey.* New York: Henry Holt and Company, 1999.

Doctrine for the Armed Forces of the United States. Joint Publication (JP) 1. Washington, D.C.: U.S. Joint Chiefs of Staff, May 2007.

Doctrine for the Armed Forces of the United States. Joint Publication (JP) 1. Washington, D.C.: U.S. Joint Chiefs of Staff, May 2007, incorporating Change 1, March 2009. http://www.dtic.mil/doctrine/new_pubs/jp1.pdf.

Donnelly, John. "More Troops Lost to Suicide." Congress.org, January 24, 2011. http:// www.congress.org/news/2011/01/24/more_troops_lost_to_suicide.

Dorschner, Jim. "Special Delivery: Special Forces Insertion." *Jane's Defence Weekly* 46, no. 21 (May 27, 2009): 24–31.

Drew, Christopher, and Thom Shanker. "Struggle Forecast for Pentagon and Deficit Hawks." *New York Times* (January 7, 2011). http://www.nytimes.com/2011/01/08/us/politics/08military.html?scp=2&sq=defense%20budget&st=cse.

Duncan Hunter National Defense Authorization Act for Fiscal Year 2009 Report on H.R. 5658, 110th Congress, 2nd session, H. Rpt.110–652, under "United States Africa Command." http://thomas.loc.gov/cgi-bin/cpquery/T?&report=hr652&dbname=110&.

Duncan Hunter National Defense Authorization Act for Fiscal Year 2009, S 3001, 110th Congress, 2nd session, January 3, 2008, under "Restriction on Obligation of Funds for United States Southern Command Development Assistance Activities," Section 942. http://frwebgate.access.gpo.gov/cgi-bin/getdoc.cgi?dbname=110_cong_bills&docid =f:s3001enr.txt.pdf.

Edelman, Eric. Transcript. Defense Writers Group, November 14, 2008. http://www .airforce-magazine.com/DWG/Documents/2008/November%202008/111408edel man.pdf.

Edsell, Thomas B. "Defense Industry Embraces Democrats, Hillary by Far the Favorite." *Huffington Post* (October 17, 2007). http://www.huffingtonpost.com/2007/10/17/ defense-industry-embraces_n_68927.html.

"The Eisenhower Doctrine: A Message to Congress, January 5, 1957." *The Department of State Bulletin* 36, no. 917 (January 21, 1957): 83–87, http://www.fordham.edu/halsall/ mod/1957eisenhowerdoctrine.html.

Embassies as Command Posts in the Anti-Terror Campaign. Senate Foreign Affairs Committee, December 15, 2006. http://www.fas.org/irp/congress/2006_rpt/embas sies.html.

Epstein, Susan B., Larry Q. Nowels, and Steven A. Hildreth. "Foreign Policy Agency Reorganization." In *Foreign Policy of the United States*, ed. Ernest Simone, 1:45–62. Huntington, N.Y.: Nova Science Publishers, 2000.

Esterbrook, John. "Rumsfeld: It Would Be a Short War." *CBS News* (November 15, 2002). http://www.cbsnews.com/stories/2002/11/15/world/main529569.shtml.

Erwin, Sandra. "Secretary Gates' Budget Proposal: Good for Defense, Bad for the National Debt." *National Defense* (January 6, 2011). http://www.nationaldefensemag azine.org/blog/Lists/Posts/Post.aspx?ID=281.

"Evolving the MAGTF for the 21st Century." Concept Paper. Quantico, Va.: U.S. Marine Corps, March 20, 2009. http://www.quantico.usmc.mil/MCBQ%20PAO%20 Press%20Releases/090430%20CDI%20Docs/CDI_EvolvingMAGTF21stCent.pdf.

Farrell, Theo, and Terry Terriff, eds., *The Sources of Military Change: Culture, Politics, Technology*. Boulder, Colo.: Lynne Rienner, 2002.

Fastabend, David A. "FM 100-5, 1998: Endless Evolution." *Army* 47, no. 5 (May 1997): 44–48.

Feickert, Andrew, and Nathan Jacob Lucas. "Army Future Combat System (FCS) 'Spin-Outs' and Ground Combat Vehicle (GCV): Background and Issues for Congress."

Washington, D.C.: Congressional Research Service, November 30, 2009. http://www.fas.org/sgp/crs/weapons/RL32888.pdf.

Feickert, Andrew, and Thomas K. Livingston. "U.S. Special Operations Forces (SOF): Background and Issues for Congress." Washington, D.C.: Congressional Research Service, March 28, 2011. http://www.fas.org/sgp/crs/natsec/RS21048.pdf.

Filkins, Dexter. "Afghan Offensive is New War Model." *New York Times* (February 12, 2010). http://www.nytimes.com/2010/02/13/world/asia/13kabul.html?_r=1.

"The First Quadrennial Diplomacy and Development Review (QDDR): Leading Through Civilian Power." Washington, D.C.: Department of State, 2010. http://www.state.gov/s/dmr/qddr/.

Fisher, Jim. "Troops Project Humanitarian Aid to North Africa." *American Forces Information Service* (March 7, 2011). http://www.militaryconnection.com/news%5Cmarch-2011%5Ctroops-aid-africa.html.

Ford, Jess T. "Challenges Facing the Bureau of Diplomatic Security." GAO Testimony before the Subcommittee on Oversight of Government Management, the Federal Workforce, and the District of Columbia, Committee on Homeland Security and Governmental Affairs, U.S. Senate, December 9, 2009. http://www.gao.gov/new.items/d10290t.pdf.

Fordham, Benjamin O. "A Very Sharp Sword: The Influence of Military Capabilities on American Decisions to Use Force." *Journal of Conflict Resolution* 48, no. 5 (October 2004): 632–656.

Foreign Internal Defense. Joint Publication 3-22. Washington, D.C.: Joint Chiefs of Staff, July 2010. http://www.dtic.mil/doctrine/new_pubs/jp3_22.pdf.

Frank, Barney, and Ron Paul. "Why We Must Reduce Military Spending." *Huffington Post* (July 6, 2010). http://www.huffingtonpost.com/rep-barney-frank/why-we-must-reduce-milita_b_636051.html.

Franke, Volker. "The Peacebuilding Dilemma: Civil-Military Cooperation in Stability Operations." *International Journal of Peace Studies* 11, no. 2 (Autumn/Winter 2006): 5–25. http://www.gmu.edu/programs/icar/ijps/vol11_2/11n2FRANKE.pdf.

Freier, Nathan. *DOD Leaders, Strategists, and Operators in an Era of Persistent Unconventional Challenge.* Washington, D.C.: Center for Strategic and International Studies, June 2009.

——. "The New Balance: Limited Armed Stabilization and the Future of U.S. Landpower." Strategic Studies Institute, U.S. Army War College, April 6, 2009. http://www.strategicstudiesinstitute.army.mil/pubs/display.cfm?PubID=915.

——. "Shifting Emphasis: Leaders, Strategists, and Operators in an Era of Persistent Unconventional Challenge." Center for Strategic and International Studies, September 2008. http://www.csis.org/media/csis/pubs/090305_shifting_emphasis.pdf.

Fritz, Oliver, and Gregory A. Hermsmeyer. "The U.S. Air Force and Stability Operations Transformation." *Joint Force Quarterly* 47 (December 2007): 128–134. http://findarticles.com/p/articles/mi_m0KNN/is_47/ai_n28028077/.

"Full-Spectrum Operations in Capstone Doctrine." Information Papers, 2008 Army Posture Statement. http://www.army.mil/aps/08/information_papers/transform/Full_Spectrum_Operations.html.

Garamone, Jim. "Flournoy Calls for Better Interagency Cooperation." *American Forces Press Service* (June 11, 2010). http://www.defense.gov/news/newsarticle.aspx ?id=59601.

Gates, Robert M. "A Balanced Strategy: Reprogramming the Pentagon for a New Age." *Foreign Affairs* 88, no. 1 (January/February 2009): 28–40.

———. "Helping Others Defend Themselves: The Future of U.S. Security Assistance." *Foreign Affairs* 89, no. 3 (May–June 2010): 2–7.

———. Remarks at the Command and General Staff College. Fort Leavenworth, Kan.: Command and General Staff College, May 7, 2010. http://www.defense .gov/utility/printitem.aspx?print=http://www.defense.gov/transcripts/transcript .aspx?transcriptid=4623.

Gentile, Gian P. "Let's Build an Army to Win All Wars." *Joint Force Quarterly* 52 (1st quarter 2009): 27–33.

———. "Our COIN Doctrine Removes the Enemy from the Essence of War." *Armed Forces Journal* (January 2008). http://www.armedforcesjournal.com/2008/01/3207722.

———. "A Strategy of Tactics: Population-Centric COIN and the Army." *Parameters* (Autumn 2009): 5–17. http://www.public.navy.mil/usff/documents/gentile.pdf.

Gerson, Michael. "A War Fighter's Budget." *Washington Post* (April 10, 2009). http:// www.washingtonpost.com/wp-dyn/content/article/2009/04/09/AR2009040903446 .html.

Gonzales, Daniel, John Hollywood, Jerry M. Sollinger, James McFadden, John DeJarnette, Sarah Harting, and Donald Temple. *Networked Forces in Stability Operations: 101st Airborne Division, 3/2 and 1/25 Stryker Brigades in Northern Iraq*. Santa Monica, Calif.: RAND, 2007.

Gordon, Michael R., and Bernard E. Trainor. *Cobra II: The Inside Story of the Invasion and Occupation of Iraq*. New York: Vintage, 2007.

Govern, Kevin H. "Paving the Road to the Warfighter: Preparing to Provide Legal Support on the Battlefield." *Army Lawyer*, DA PAM 27-50-350, Washington, D.C.: Headquarters, Department of the Army, March 2002.

Groth Jr., Carl H., and Diane T. Berliner. "Peacetime Military Engagement: A Framework for Policy Criteria." Report prepared for DOD by Logistics Management Institute (LMI), August 1993. http://www.dtic.mil/cgi-bin/GetTRDoc?Location=U2&doc =GetTRDoc.pdf&AD=ADA272699.

Ground Combat Operations. Marine Corps Warfighting Publication (MCWP) 3-1. Washington, D.C.: Headquarters, Department of the Marines, 1995. http://www .marines.mil/news/publications/Documents/MCWP%203-1%20Ground%20 Combat%20Operations.pdf.

H.R. 2207, Interagency Cooperation Commission Act, 111th Congress, 2009–2010. http://www.govtrack.us/congress/bill.xpd?bill=h111-2207.

Haass, Richard N. *The Reluctant Sheriff: The United States After the Cold War*. New York: Council on Foreign Relations, 1997.

Halberstam, David. *War in a Time of Peace*. New York: Scribner, 2001.

Hardesty, J. Michael, and Jason D. Ellis. "Training for Peace Operations: The U.S. Army Adapts to the Post–Cold War World." Peaceworks 12. Washington, D.C.: USIP Press, 1997.

Harrison, Todd. "The FY 2012 Defense Budget: What to Expect in an Age of Austerity." Backgrounder. Washington, D.C.: Center for Strategic and Budgetary Assessments, February 2011. http://www.csbaonline.org/wp-content/uploads/2011/02/2011.02.11 -The-FY-2012-Defense-Budget-What-To-Expect-In-An-Age-of-Austerity.pdf.

Hastings, Michael. "The Runaway General." Rolling Stone (June 22, 2010). http://www .rollingstone.com/politics/news/17390/119236?RS_show_page=0.

Heathscott, Chris. "Realistic Training Helping to Prepare Arkansas Soldiers for Afghanistan." Arkansas National Guard Public Affairs Office, May 18, 2011. http://www.dvidshub .net/news/70631/realistic-training-helping-prepare-arkansas-soldiers-afghanistan.

Henabray, Kevin. "Air Force Engagement in Expeditionary Warfare." Briefing. Washington, D.C.: Headquarters, U.S. Air Force, October 24, 2006.

Herr, Donald F. "Changing Course: Proposals to Reverse the Militarization of U.S. Foreign Policy." International Policy Report. Washington, D.C.: Center for International Policy, September 2008. http://www.ciponline.org/nationalsecurity/ publications/ipr/Mil_USFP_IPR0908.pdf.

Herring, George C. "America and Vietnam: The Unending War." Foreign Affairs 70, no. 5 (Winter 1991): 104–119.

"Hillary Clinton Nomination Hearings to Be Secretary of State." Washington, D.C.: Senate Foreign Relations Committee, January 13, 2009. http://sarajevo.usembassy .gov/washdc_20090113.html.

Hodge, Nathan. Armed Humanitarians: The Rise of the Nation Builders. New York: Bloomsbury, 2011.

Hoffman, Frank. "Striking a Balance: Posturing the Future Force for COIN and Conventional Warfare." Armed Forces Journal (July–August 2009). http://www .armedforcesjournal.com/2009/07/4099782.

Howard, Michael. Clausewitz. Oxford: Oxford University Press, 1983.

Humanitarian Assistance/Disaster Relief (HA/DR) Operations Planning. Naval Warfare Development Command (NWDC) Tactical Memo (TACMEMO) 3-07.6-05. Washington, D.C.: Headquarters, Department of the Navy, 2005. http://www.au.af .mil/au/awc/awcgate/navy/tm_3–07–6-05_navy_ha&dr_ops_plng.pdf.

Hynd, Steve. "Counterinsurgency Consensus Misguided." New Atlanticist Policy and Analysis Blog. Washington, D.C.: Atlantic Council, March 20, 2009. http://www .acus.org/new_atlanticist/counterinsurgency-consensus-misguided.

Inhofe, James. "Challenges of Military Readiness." Military Review (March–April 1999): 15–18.

"International Affairs Budget 101." U.S. Global Leadership Campaign. http://www .usglc.org/budget-breakdown/.

International Affairs Function 150: Summary and Highlights. Fiscal Year 2009 Budget Request. http://pdf.usaid.gov/pdf_docs/PCAAB698.pdf.

Interview #51, U.S. Institute of Peace: ADST Afghanistan Experience Project, Oral Histories.http://www.usip.org/files/file/resources/collections/histories/afghanistan/ 51.pdf.

Interview with Chuck Spinney. *NOW*. Public Broadcasting Service, January 27, 2006. http://www.pbs.org/now/printable/transcriptNoW204_full_print.html.

Irregular Warfare. Air Force Doctrine Document (AFDD) 2-3. Washington, D.C.: Headquarters, Department of the Air Force, 2007. http://www.fas.org/irp/doddir/ usaf/afdd2–3.pdf.

"Irregular Warfare (IW) Joint Operating Concept (JOC)." Version 1.0. Washington, D.C.: Department of Defense, September 2007. http://www.michaelyon-online .com/images/pdf/iw-joc.pdf.

"Is DOD the New AID? Tasking Soldiers with Economic Development." Transcript. *Ideas in Action with Jim Glassman*, October 2010. http://www.ideasinactiontv.com/ episodes/2010/10/is-dod-the-new-aid-tasking-soldiers-with-economic-develop ment.html.

"Is Militarization Undermining U.S. Foreign Policy Goals?" UN Development Program, USA (UNDP-USA). Blog report of a forum sponsored by the Partnership for Effective Peacekeeping, Washington, D.C., May 29, 2008. http://undp-usa.blogspot .com/2008/06/is-militarization-undermining-us.html.

Jaffe, Greg. "Pentagon's Gates Keeps Single-Minded Focus in Dual Wars in Iraq and Afghanistan." *Washington Post* (May 15, 2009). http://www.washingtonpost.com/wp -dyn/content/article/2009/05/14/AR2009051404450_2.html?sub=AR.

Jaffe, Greg, and Leila Fadel. "U.S. Military Adopts New Role in Iraq." *Washington Post* (September 1, 2010). http://www.washingtonpost.com/wp-dyn/content/article/2010/ 09/01/AR2010090101126.html.

Jean, Grace V. "Aerial Drones Going Mainstream in Naval Special Warfare." *National Defense* (May 2011). http://www.nationaldefensemagazine.org/archive/2011/May/Pages/ AerialDronesGoingMainstreamInNavalSpecialWarfare.aspx.

——. "Army Special Forces Gear up for Gray Eagle." *National Defense* (May 2011). http://www.nationaldefensemagazine.org/archive/2011/May/Pages/ArmySpecial ForcesGearUpForGrayEagle.aspx.

Jockel, Joseph T. *The Canadian Forces: Hard Choices, Soft Power*. Toronto: Canadian Institute of Strategic Studies, 1999.

Johnson, Chalmers, and Tom Engelhardt. "Economic Death Spiral at the Pentagon." *TomDispatch.com* (February 2, 2009). http://www.tomdispatch.com/post/175029.

Johnson, Robert H. "Exaggerating America's Stakes in Third World Conflicts." *International Security* 10, no. 3 (Winter 1985–1986): 32–48.

Joint Doctrine for Military Operations Other Than War. Joint Publication (JP) 3-07. Washington, D.C.: Joint Chiefs of Staff, 1995. http://www.bits.de/NRANEU/others/ jp-doctrine/jp3_07.pdf.

"Joint Doctrine Update." *Joint Force Quarterly* 53 (2nd quarter 2009): 128.

Joint Operations. Joint Publication 3-0. Washington, D.C.: Joint Chiefs of Staff, 17 September 2006, incorporating Change 2, 22 March 2010. http://www.scribd.com/doc/37553840/Joint-Ops-2010.

Joyner, James. "1.5 Million Copies of COIN Doctrine Downloaded." *Outside The Beltway* (January 6, 2007). http://www.outsidethebeltway.com/archives/15_million_copies_of_coin_doctrine_downloaded/.

Kagan, Frederick W. "New Thinking, Old Realities." *AEI Online* (October 2006). http://www.aei.org/outlook/25010.

Kaldor, Mary. "American Power: From 'Compellance' to Cosmopolitanism?" *International Affairs* 79, no. 1 (2003): 1–22.

Kaplan, Robert D. "The Coming Anarchy." *Atlantic Monthly* 273, no. 2 (February 1994): 44–65. http://www.theatlantic.com/magazine/archive/1994/02/the-coming-anarchy/4670/1/.

Kennedy, John F. Remarks to the graduating class of the U.S. Naval Academy, Annapolis, Maryland, June 7, 1961. www.jfklink.com/speeches/jfk/publicpapers/1961/jfk232_61.html.

Kilcullen, David. *The Accidental Guerrilla: Fighting Small Wars in the Midst of a Big One.* Oxford: Oxford University Press, February 2009.

Kissinger, Henry. *Does America Need a Foreign Policy? Toward a Diplomacy for the Twenty-First Century.* New York: Simon & Schuster, 2001.

Kurth, James. "Variations on the American Way of War." In *The Long War: A New History of U.S. National Security Policy Since World War II*, ed. Andrew J. Bacevich, 53–98. New York: Columbia University Press, 2007.

Labadie, S. J. "Jointness for the Sake of Jointness in 'Operation Urgent Fury.'" Naval War College, May 17, 1993.

LaFranchi, Howard. "Gates, Clinton Oppose Cuts to State Department Budget." *Christian Science Monitor* (April 23, 2010). http://www.csmonitor.com/USA/Foreign-Policy/2010/0423/Gates-Clinton-oppose-cuts-to-State-Department-budget.

Leading Through Civilian Power: The First Quadrennial Diplomacy and Development Review. Washington, D.C.: U.S. State Department and U.S. Agency for International Development, 2010. http://www.comw.org/pda/fulltext/WilliamsAdamsOccasional Paper6–08.pdf.

Letter of Instruction. U.S. Army Combat Development Command, July 11, 1966.

"Lewis, Adrian R." *The American Culture of War.* New York: Routledge, 2007.

Liddell Hart, B. H. *Strategy.* London: Faber & Faber, 1967.

Linn, Brian McAllister. *The Philippine War, 1899–1902.* Lawrence: University of Kansas Press, 2000.

Lira, Leonard. "An Integrative Approach to the Interagency Process." *InterAgency Journal* 1, no. 1 (Fall 2010): 46–55. http://thesimonscenter.org/wp-content/uploads/2010/11/IAJ-1-1-pg46–55.pdf.

Londoño, Ernesto. "U.S. 'Money Weapon' Yields Mixed Results." *Washington Post* (July 27, 2009). http://www.washingtonpost.com/wp-dyn/content/article/2009/07/26/AR2009072602833.html.

Lozada, Carlos. "A Sneak Peak at Hillary Clinton's New Global Strategy." *Washington Post* (October 24, 2010). http://www.washingtonpost.com/wp-dyn/content/article/2010/10/22/AR2010102203592.html.

"Making Peace While Staying Ready for War: The Challenges of U.S. Military Participation in Peace Operations." Congressional Budget Office, December 1999. http://www.cbo.gov/doc.cfm?index=1809&type=0&sequence=0.

"Management of Interagency Efforts Concerning Reconstruction and Stabilization." National Security Presidential Directive (NSPD) 44. Washington, D.C.: The White House, December 2005. http://www.fas.org/irp/offdocs/nspd/nspd-44.html.

Mapping the Global Future: Report of the National Intelligence Council's 2020 Project. Washington, D.C.: Government Printing Office, 2004. http://www.dni.gov/nic/NIC_globaltrend2020_s4.html.

Marine Air-Ground Task Force Civil-Military Operations. Marine Corps Warfighting Publication (MCWP) 3-33.1. Washington, D.C.: Headquarters, Department of the Marines, 2003. http://www.marines.mil/news/publications/Documents/MCWP%20 3-33.1%20Marine%20Air-Ground%20Task%20Force%20Civil_Military%20 Operations.pdf.

Marks, Edward. "Why USAFRICOM?" *Joint Force Quarterly* 52 (1st quarter 2009): 148–151.

Marr, Phebe. "Occupational Hazards," *Foreign Affairs* 84, no. 4 (July–August 2005). http://www.foreignaffairs.com/articles/60844/phebe-marr/occupational-hazards.

Matthias, Willard C. *America's Strategic Blunders: Intelligence Analysis and National Security, 1936–1991.* University Park, Pa.: Penn State Press, 2001.

McCarthy III, Robert G. "Stability Operations: Defeating the Twenty-First Century Threat." EWS Contemporary Issues Papers. Quantico, Va.: U.S. Marine Corps Command and Staff College, February 2008. http://www.dtic.mil/cgi-bin/GetTRD oc?AD=ADA498221&Location=U2&doc=GetTRDoc.pdf.

McMichael, William H. "DOD Sets Priorities with 2011 Budget, QDR." *Army Times* (February 2010). http://www.armytimes.com/news/2010/02/military_2011_budget_ QDR_020110w/.

Melanson, Richard A. *American Foreign Policy Since the Vietnam War: The Search for Consensus from Richard Nixon to George W. Bush.* 4th ed. Armonk, N.Y.: M. E. Sharpe, 2005.

McClintock, Michael. *Instruments of Statecraft.* New York: Pantheon, 1992.

Memorandum to the Members of the Special Group, NSAM 124. http://www.jfklibrary .org/Asset-Viewer/qJbe3E_H7kmxvtbyzSb8pw.aspx.

Message, 291420Z Sep 82, Commander in Chief, U.S. Southern Command (CINCSOUTH).

Metz, Steven. "The Civilian Surge Myth." *New Republic* (October 15, 2009). http://www .tnr.com/article/world/the-civilian-surge-myth?page=0,1.

Metz, Steven, and Frank Hoffman. "Restructuring America's Ground Forces: Better, Not Bigger." *Policy Analysis Brief.* Muscatine, Ia.: The Stanley Foundation, September 2007. http://www.stanleyfoundation.org/resources.cfm?id=262.

Miles, Donna. "SouthCom Transformation Promotes New Approach to Regional Challenges." *American Forces Press Service* (August 26, 2008). http://www.defense.gov/news/newsarticle.aspx?id=50936.

Mills, C. Wright. *The Power Elite.* 1956. Repr., New York: Oxford University Press, 2000.

"Military Operations: Impact of Operations Other Than War on the Services Varies." Report to the Chairman, Subcommittee on Readiness and Military Management Support, Committee on Armed Services, U.S. Senate, Washington, D.C., United States General Accounting Office, 1999, GAO/NSIAD-99-69. http://www.gao.gov/archive/1999/ns99069.pdf.

Military Operations in Low Intensity Conflict. Field Manual (FM) 100-20/AFP 3-20. Washington, D.C.: Headquarters, Departments of the Army and Air Force, 1990. http://www.globalsecurity.org/military/library/policy/army/fm/100-20/10020ch1.htm#s_9.

Military Operations Other Than War. Air Force Doctrine Document (AFDD) 2-3. Washington, D.C.: Headquarters, Department of the Air Force, 2000. http://www.dtic.mil/doctrine/jel/service_pubs/afd2_3.pdf.

"Misinformation about 'Gladio/Stay Behind' Networks Resurfaces." *America.gov* (January 30, 2006). http://www.america.gov/st/pubs-english/2006/January/2006012 0111344atlahtnevelo.3114282.html.

"Misreading History?" *Endgame on Frontline.* Public Broadcasting Service, June 19, 2007. http://www.pbs.org/wgbh/pages/frontline/endgame/themes/misreading.html.

"Mission and Vision." United States European Command. http://www.eucom.mil/english/MissionAndVision.asp.

Morschauser, Robert D. "The Brigade Combat Team: Stability and Security Force Assistance Operations." Strategy Research Project, U.S. Army War College, Carlisle Barracks, Penn., February 2010.

Nagl, John A. *Learning to Eat Soup with a Knife: Counterinsurgency Lessons from Malaya and Vietnam.* Chicago: University of Chicago Press, 2003.

——. "Let's Win the Wars We're In." *Joint Force Quarterly* 52 (1st quarter 2009): 20–26.

National Defense Authorization Act for Fiscal Year 2006, Public Law. No. 109-163. http://www.dod.gov/dodgc/olc/docs/PL109–163.pdf.

A National Security Strategy of Engagement and Enlargement. Washington, D.C.: The White House, 1996. http://www.fas.org/spp/military/docops/national/1996stra.htm.

The National Security Strategy of the United States of America. Washington, D.C.: The White House, 2006. http://www.dami.army.pentagon.mil/site/dig/documents/NationalSecurityStrategy-MAR06.pdf.

Naval Humanitarian Assistance Missions. Experimental Tactic (EXTAC) 1011. Washington, D.C.: Headquarters, Department of the Navy, 1996. http://pksoi.army.mil/doctrine_concepts/documents/UN%20Guidelines/Service%20Doctrine/ex1011%20Naval%20HA%20Msns.pdf.

Naval Warfare. Naval Doctrine Publication (NDP) 1. Washington, D.C.: Headquarters, Department of the Navy, 1994. http://www.dtic.mil/doctrine/jel/service_pubs/ndp1.pdf.

Naval Warfare. Naval Doctrine Publication (NDP) 1. Washington, D.C.: Headquarters, Department of the Navy, 2010. http://usnwc.edu/Academics/Maritime-Staff-Operators-Course/documents/NDP-1-Naval-Warfare-(Mar-2010)_Chapters2-3.aspx.

Naylor, Justin. "1-8 Cav Soldiers Take on New Missions." *Army Times* (March 27, 2009). http://www.army.mil/-news/2009/03/27/18850-1-8-cav-soldiers-take-on-new-missions/.

Naylor, Sean D. "More Than Door Kickers." *Armed Forces Journal* 143, no. 8 (March 2006): 28–30.

Nelson, Richard W. "The Multinational Force in Beirut." In *The Multinational Force in Beirut, 1982–1984*, ed. Anthony McDermott and Kjell Skjelsbaek, 95–100. Board of Regents of the State of Florida, 1991.

Neustadt, Richard E., and Ernest R. May. *Thinking in Time: The Uses of History for Decision Makers*. New York: The Free Press, 1986.

"New Civilian Tasks for the Military." Transcript. Washington, D.C.: Center for Defense Information, April 11, 1993. http://www.cdi.org/adm/630/.

A New Era of Engagement . . . Agency Financial Report, Fiscal Year 2009. Washington, D.C.: U.S. Department of State, 2009.

Nielson, Suzanne C. "An Army Transformed: The U.S. Army's Post–Vietnam Recovery and the Dynamics of Change in Military Organizations." The Letort Papers. Carlisle Barracks, Penn.: U.S. Army War College, September 2010.

Nordenman, Magnus. "Pentagon Bets on COIN, Against Peer Competitor." *New Atlanticist Policy and Analysis Blog* (April 7, 2009). http://www.acus.org/new_atlanticist/pentagon-bets-coin-against-peer-competitor.

Nordland, Rod. "UN Rejects 'Militarization' of Afghan Aid." *New York Times* (February 17, 2010). http://www.nytimes.com/2010/02/18/world/asia/18aid.html.

Nunez, Joseph R. "Canada's Global Role: A Strategic Assessment of its Military Power." *Parameters* (Autumn 2004): 75–93.

"OD Releases Defense Reviews, 2011 Budget Proposal, and 2010 War Funding Supplemental Request—Update." News Release no. 084-10. U.S. Department of Defense, Office of the Assistant Secretary of Defense (Public Affairs), February 1, 2010. http://www.defense.gov/releases/release.aspx?releaseid=13281.

Office of the Coordinator for Reconstruction and Stabilization Web site, U.S. Department of State. http://www.state.gov/s/crs/.

O'Hanlon, Michael. "Transformation Reality Check." *Armed Forces Journal* 144, no. 8 (March 2007). http://www.armedforcesjournal.com/2007/03/2515135/.

Olsen, Howard, and John Davis. *Training U.S. Army Officers for Peace Operations: Lessons from Bosnia*. Washington, D.C.: U.S. Institute for Peace Press, October 1999.

Olson, Eric. U.S. Special Operations Command (USSOCOM) Posture Statement. 2010. http://www.socom.mil/SOCOMHome/Documents/USSOCOM%20Posture%20Statement.pdf.

On the Brink: Weak States and U.S. National Security. Washington, D.C.: Commission on Weak States and U.S. National Security, Center for Global Development, 2004. http://www.cgdev.org/doc/weakstates/Full_Report.pdf.

Operation Moshtarak: Lessons Learned. London: International Council on Security and Development, March 2010. http://www.icosgroup.net/2010/report/operation -moshtarak-lessons-learned/.

Operation Urgent Fury." *Globalsecurity.org.* http://www.globalsecurity.org/military/ops/ urgent_fury.htm.

Operations. Air Mobility Command Instruction (AMCI) 10-403. Washington, D.C.: Department of the Air Force, February 22, 2007.

Operations. U.S. Army Field Manual 100-5. Washington, D.C.: Headquarters, Department of the Army, June 1993.

Operations. U.S. Army Field Manual (FM) 3-0. Washington, D.C.: Headquarters, Department of the Army, 2001. http://www.dtic.mil/doctrine/jel/service_pubs/ fm3_0a.pdf.

Operations. U.S. Army Field Manual (FM) 3-0. Washington, D.C.: Headquarters, Department of the Army, 2008.

Operations Against Guerrilla Units. Fleet Marine Force Manual (FMFM) 8-2. Washington, D.C.: U.S. Government Printing Office, 1964. http://www.vietnam.ttu .edu/star/images/107/1070916001a.pdf.

Operations and Organization. Air Force Doctrine Document (AFDD)(I). Washington, D.C.: Headquarters, Department of the Air Force, 2007. http://www.fas.org/irp/ doddir/usaf/afdd2.pdf.

O'Rourke, Ronald. "Navy Irregular Warfare and Counterterrorism Operations: Background and Issues for Congress." Washington, D.C.: Congressional Research Service, April 11, 2011. http://www.fas.org/sgp/crs/natsec/RS22373.pdf.

Ostrom Jr., Charles W., and Brian L. Job. "The President and the Political Use of Force." *American Political Science Review* 80, no. 2 (June 1986): 541–566.

Parenti, Michael. "The Logic of U.S. Intervention." In *Masters of War: Militarism and Blowback in the Era of American Empire,* ed. Carl Boggs, 19–36. New York: Routledge, 2003.

Parrish, Karen. "Special Operations Faces Soaring Demands, Commander Says." *American Forces Press Service* (February 8, 2011). http://www.defense.gov/news/news article.aspx?id=62737.

Paschall, Rod. "Low-Intensity Conflict Doctrine: Who Needs It?" *Parameters* 15, no. 3 (Autumn 1985): 33–45.

Paterson, Thomas G. *Meeting the Communist Threat: Truman to Reagan.* New York: Oxford University Press, 1988.

Patrick, Stewart. *Weak Links: Fragile States, Global Threats, and International Security.* Oxford: Oxford University Press, 2011.

"Peace Operations: Effect of Training, Equipment, and Other Factors on Unit Capability." Chapter Report, GAO/NSIAD-96-14, October 1995. http://www.fas .org/man/gao/nsiad-96-014.htm.

"Peacekeeping: National Defence." In May Report of the Auditor General of Canada. 1996. http://www.oag-bvg.gc.ca/internet/English/parl_oag_199605_07_e_5038.html.

Perito, Robert. "Embedded Provincial Reconstruction Teams." Peace Brief, Washington, D.C.: United States Institute of Peace, February 2008. http://www.usip.org/resources/embedded-provincial-reconstruction-teams.

Pfaltzgraff Jr., Robert L. "The Emerging Global Security Environment." *Annals of the American Academy of Political and Social Science* 517 (September 1991): 10–24.

Ploch, Lauren. "Africa Command: U.S. Strategic Interests and the Role of the U.S. Military in Africa." CRS Report, Washington, D.C.: Congressional Research Service, October 2009. http://assets.opencrs.com/rpts/RL34003_20091002.pdf.

——. "AFRICOM: An Independent Review for the New Administration." Remarks at AFRICOM Conference. Washington, D.C.: Center for Advanced Defense Studies, 2009. http://www.c4ads.org/files/CADS_AFRICOM09_Transcript.pdf.

Posen, Barry R. *The Sources of Military Doctrine: France, Britain, and Germany Between the World Wars.* Ithaca, N.Y.: Cornell University Press, 1984.

Powell, Colin L., *My American Journey.* New York: Ballantine Books, 1996.

——. "U.S. Forces: Challenges Ahead." *Foreign Affairs* 71 (Winter 1992/1993): 32–45. http://www.pbs.org/wgbh/pages/frontline/shows/military/force/powell.html.

Priest, Dana. *The Mission: Waging War and Keeping Peace with America's Military.* New York: W. W. Norton, 2004.

"Provincial Reconstruction Teams." Fact Sheet, Embassy of the United States, Baghdad, Iraq, September 15, 2009. http://iraq.usembassy.gov/iraq_prt/provincial-reconstruction-teams-fact-sheet.html.

Quadrennial Defense Review Report. Washington, D.C.: Department of Defense, 1997. http://www.fas.org/man/docs/qdr/sec3.html.

Quadrennial Defense Review Report. Washington, D.C.: Department of Defense, 2006.

Quadrennial Defense Review Report. Washington, D.C.: Department of Defense, February 2010. http://www.defense.gov/qdr/images/QDR_as_of_12Feb10_1000.pdf.

"Quarterly Report and Semi-Annual Report to the United States Congress: Section 2: Iraq Reconstruction Funding and Uses." Washington D.C.: Special Inspector General of Iraq, January 30, 2011. http://www.sigir.mil/files/quarterlyreports/January2011/Report_-_January_2011.pdf#view=fit.

Rana, Raj. "Contemporary Challenges in the Civil-Military Relationship: Complementarity or Incompatibility?" *International Review of the Red Cross.* Cambridge: ICRC and Cambridge University Press, September 2004.

Reid, Garry. Statement for the Record. Washington, D.C.: Senate Armed Service Subcommittee on Emerging Threats and Capabilities, March 10, 2010. http://armed-services.senate.gov/statemnt/2010/03%20March/Reid%2003–10-10.pdf.

Remarks by Defense Secretary Gates at the Command and General Staff College, Fort Leavenworth, Kan,, May 7, 2010. http://www.defense.gov/transcripts/transcript.aspx?transcriptid=4623.

"Report to Congress on the Implementation of DoD Directive 3000.05 *Military Support for Stability, Security, Transition, and Reconstruction (SSTR) Operations.*" Secretary of Defense, Washington, D.C., April 1, 2007.

Reveron, Derek S. *Exporting Security*. Washington, D.C.: Georgetown University Press, 2010.

Reveron Derek S., and Kathleen A. Mahoney-Norris. "'Military-Political' Relations: The Need for Officer Education." *Joint Force Quarterly* 52 (1st quarter 2009): 61–66.

Rice, Condoleezza. Remarks at Georgetown School of Foreign Service, January 18, 2006. http://www.state.gov/secretary/rm/2006/59306.htm.

Ricks, Thomas E. *Fiasco: The American Military Adventure in Iraq*. New York: Penguin, 2006.

———. *The Gamble*. New York: Penguin, 2009.

Rosello, Victor M. "Soft Skills for Twenty-First Century Land Dominance." Landpower Essay 09-1. Arlington, Va.: Association of the U.S. Army, Institute of Land Warfare, January 2009. http://www3.ausa.org/marketing/SoftSkillswebsite0209.pdf.

Rosen, Stephen Peter. *Winning the Next War: Innovation and the Modern Military*. Ithaca, N.Y.: Cornell University Press, 1991.

Rosenberg, Eli. "Does the Military Have a Suicide Problem?" *Atlantic Wire* (January 25, 2011). http://www.theatlanticwire.com/politics/2011/01/does-the-military-have-a-suicide-problem/17919/.

Ruggie, John Gerard. "The Past as Prologue? Interests, Identity, and American Foreign Policy." *International Security* 21, no. 4 (Spring 1997): 89–125.

"Rumsfeld Foresees Swift Iraq War." *BBC News* (February 7, 2003). http://news.bbc.co.uk/2/hi/middle_east/2738089.stm.

Saunders, Richard M. "Military Force in the Foreign Policy of the Eisenhower Presidency." *Political Science Quarterly* 100, no. 1 (Spring 1985): 97–116.

Schadlow, Nadia. "War and the Art of Governance." *Parameters* (Autumn 2003): 85–94.

Schlegel, Charles. Mission Briefing. 435th Contingency Response Group, 2009. http://www.jeaddc.com/2009PresentationsPosted/435%20CRG%20Overview.pdf.

Schramm, Carl J. "Expeditionary Economics: Spurring Growth After Conflicts and Disasters." *Foreign Affairs* 89, no. 3 (May–June 2010): 89–99. http://www.kauffman.org/uploadedFiles/ForeignAffairsExpedEcono510.pdf.

Seal, Karen H., Thomas J. Metzler, Kristian S. Gima, Daniel Bertenthal, Shira Maguen, and Charles R. Marmar. "Trends and Risk Factors for Mental Health Diagnoses Among Iraq and Afghanistan Veterans Using Department of Veterans Affairs Healthcare, 2002–2008." *American Journal of Public Health* 99, no. 9 (2009): 1651–1658. http://www.medscape.com/viewarticle/715223.

"Secret Report Urges New Afghanistan Policy." *Politico* (February 3, 2009). http://www.cbsnews.com/stories/2009/02/03/politics/politico/main4771546.shtml.

"Secretary Gates Details $154 Billion in Defense Savings Over Five Years." American Society of Military Comptrollers, January 2011. http://www.asmconline.org/2011/01/secretary-gates-details-154-billion-in-defense-savings-over-five-years/.

"Section 1206 Security Assistance: Briefing for Senate Foreign Relations Committee Staff." Washington, D.C.: U.S. General Accounting Office, December 14, 2006. http://www.gao.gov/new.items/d07416r.pdf.

Sellers, John S. "The Weinberger Doctrine: Useful Compass or Flawed Checklist?" Thesis. School of Advanced Airpower Studies, June 2001. http://www.dtic.mil/cgi -bin/GetTRDoc?AD=ADA407811&Location=U2&doc=GetTRDoc.pdf.

"Senior Military Leaders Urge Congress to Boost Non-Military Tools," *PR Newswire*. Washington, D.C.: U.S. Global Leadership Coalition, March 10, 2010. http://intlde velopment.einnews.com/article.php?nid=3117.

Serafino, Nina M. "The Department of Defense Role in Foreign Assistance: Background, Major Issues, and Options for Congress." CRS Report. Washington, D.C.: Congressional Research Service, December 2008. http://www.fas.org/sgp/crs/ natsec/RL34639.pdf.

——. "Security Assistance Reform: 'Section 1206' Background and Issues for Congress." CRS Report. Washington, D.C.: Congressional Research Service, June 29, 2010. http://www.fas.org/sgp/crs/natsec/RS22855.pdf.

Serafino, Nina M., and Martin A. Weiss. *Peacekeeping and Conflict Transitions: Background and Congressional Action on Civilian Capabilities*. CRS Report for Congress. Washington, D.C.: Congressional Research Service, updated January 6, 2006.

"73% Fear Terrorists More Than Nuclear Attack." *Rasmussen Report* (December 27, 2010). http://www.rasmussenreports.com/public_content/politics/current_events/ russia/73_fear_terrorists_more_than_nuclear_attack.

Shachtman, Noah. "Pentagon Chief Rips Heart Out of Army's 'Future.'" Danger Room. *Wired* (April 6, 2009). http://www.wired.com/dangerroom/2009/04/gates-rips-hear/.

Shalikashvili, John. *NewsHour* transcript. September 25, 1997.

——. "Shalikashvili: Focus Remains on Warfighting, Not Peacekeeping." *Defense Daily* (September 2, 1994).

Shanker, Thom. "Army Is Worried About Rising Stress of Return Tours to Iraq." *New York Times* (April 6, 2008). http://www.nytimes.com/2008/04/06/washington/06military. html.

——. "Plan to Shift Military Spending Faces Skepticism." *New York Times* (May 11, 2009). http://www.nytimes.com/2009/05/11/world/asia/11gates.html?adxnnl=1&ref =politicss&adx.

——. "Top Officer Urges Limit on Mission of Military." *New York Times* (January 12, 2009). http://www.nytimes.com/2009/01/13/washington/13military.html?_r=2&ref =world.

Shanker, Thom, and Christopher Drew. "Pentagon Seeks Biggest Cuts Since Before 9/11." *New York Times* (January 6, 2011). http://www.nytimes.com/2011/01/07/us/07military .html?scp=4&sq=defense%20budget&st=cse.

Shape, Response, Prepare Now—A Military Strategy for a New Era. National Military Strategy of the United States. Washington, D.C.: Joint Chiefs of Staff, 1997. http:// www.au.af.mil/au/awc/awcgate/nms/.

Sharp, Travis. "U.S. Defense Spending 2001–2009." Washington, D.C.: The Center for Arms Control and Non-Proliferation, February 20, 2008. http://armscontrolcenter .org/policy/securityspending/articles/defense_spending_since_2001/.

Shaw, Robert C. "Integrating Conventional and Special Operations Forces." *Military Review* 77, no. 4 (July/August 1997): 37–41.

Shinseki, Eric. "Shinseki: Division Readiness Problems Due to Deployments," *Defense Daily* (November 12, 1999).

"6th Special Operations Squadron." Fact Sheet, Hurlburt Field, Fla.: U.S. Air Force, February 24, 2011. http://www2.hurlburt.af.mil/library/factsheets/factsheet.asp?id=3496.

Small Wars Council. On-line discussion forum of the *Small Wars Journal*, "Military Transition Teams (MTTs) in Iraq." http://council.smallwarsjournal.com/showthread.php?t=4260.

Small Wars Manual. U.S. Marine Corps, Washington, D.C.: U.S. Government Printing Office, 1940. http://www.scribd.com/doc/8218892/Small-Wars-Manual-1940-Edition.

Soneshine, Tara, and Beth Cole. "A Tectonic Shift at State and USAID?" *Huffington Post* (October 27, 2010). http://www.huffingtonpost.com/tara-sonenshine/a-tectonic-shift-at-state_b_774946.html?ir=World.

Special Forces Unconventional Warfare. Field Manual 3-05.201. Washington, D.C.: Headquarters, Department of the Army, September 2007. http://www.fas.org/irp/doddir/army/fm3–05–130.pdf.

Special Operations. Joint Publication (JP) 3-05. Washington, D.C.: Joint Chiefs of Staff, April 2011. http://www.dtic.mil/doctrine/new_pubs/jp3_05.pdf.

Spillius, Alex. "U.S. Diplomats Protest Forced Postings in Iraq." *Telegraph* (November 2, 2007). http://www.telegraph.co.uk/news/uknews/1568164/US-diplomats-protest-forced-postings-in-Iraq.html.

Stability Operations. U.S. Army Field Manual (FM) 3-07. Washington, D.C.: U.S. Department of the Army, October 6, 2008. http://usacac.army.mil/cac2/Repository/FM307/FM3–07.pdf.

"Stability Operations: Where We Are and the Road Ahead." Symposium Report, December 13–14, 2004, sponsored by the U.S. Army Peacekeeping and Stability Operations Institute, the U.S. Department of State, and the U.S. Institute of Peace at Carlisle Barracks, Penn.

Stability Operations and Support Operations, FM 3–07 (FM 100–20). Washington, D.C.: Headquarters, Department of the Army, February 2003.

"Stand Up and Be Counted: The Continuing Challenge of Building the Iraqi Security Forces." U.S. House of Representatives, Committee on Armed Services, Subcommittee on Oversight and Investigations, June 25, 2007. http://democrats.armedservices.house.gov/index.cfm/files/serve?File_id=2bfb0934–1745–4c80–8e21–205915e97cfb.

Statement of Admiral Gary Roughead, Chief of Naval Operations, before the House Subcommittee on Defense, Committee on Appropriations, March 11, 2010. http://www.au.af.mil/au/awc/awcgate/navy/navyposture2010.pdf.

Statement of General Bryan D. Brown, Commander U.S. Special Operations Command, Before the House Armed Services Committee Subcommittee on Terrorism, Unconventional Threats and Capabilities, on the current manning, equipping, and readiness challenges facing special operations forces, January 31, 2007. http://www.docstoc

.com/docs/51014850/HEARING-Before-the-House-Armed-Services-Committee-Subcommittee-on.

Statement of General Charles C. Krulak, Commandant of the Marine Corps, U.S. Marine Corps, before the Senate Armed Services Committee on 29 September 1998, Concerning Posture. http://www.globalsecurity.org/military/library/congress/1998_hr/980929ck.htm.

Statement of General James T. Conway, Commandant of the Marine Corps, before the Senate Armed Services Committee on the 2010 Posture of the United States Marine Corps, February 25, 2010. http://armed-services.senate.gov/statemnt/2010/02%20 February/Conway%2002-25-10.pdf.

Stein, Janice Gross. "Building Politics into Psychology: The Misperception of Threat." *Political Psychology* 9, no. 2 (June 1988): 245–271.

Strobel, Warren P. "State Department Planning to Field a Small Army in Iraq." *McClatchy Newspapers* (July 21, 2010). http://www.mcclatchydc.com/2010/07/21/97915/state -dept-planning-to-field-a.html.

"A Strong But Risky Show of Force." *Time* (May 26, 1975).

Tarnoff, Curt. "Iraq: Reconstruction Assistance." CRS Report. Washington, D.C.: Congressional Research Service, August 20, 2008. http://www.dtic.mil/cgi-bin/Ge tTRDoc?AD=ADA486585&Location=U2&doc=GetTRDoc.pdf.

Tasikas, Vasilios. "Developing the Rule of Law in Afghanistan: The Need for a New Strategic Paradigm." *Army Lawyer* (July 2007): 45–60.

Taw, Jennifer. *Interagency Coordination in Operations Other Than War: Implications for the U.S. Army.* Santa Monica, Calif.: RAND, 1997.

Taw, Jennifer M., David Persselin, and Maren Leed. *Meeting Peace Operations Requirements While Maintaining MTW Readiness.* Santa Monica, Calif.: RAND, 1998.

Taw, Jennifer M., and Jed Peters. *Operations Other Than War: Implications for the U.S. Army.* Santa Monica, Calif.: RAND, 1995.

Tilghman, Andrew. "The Army's Other Crisis." *Washington Monthly* (July 2007). http:// www.washingtonmonthly.com/features/2007/0712.tilghman.html.

Training for Full Spectrum Operations. Army Field Manual (FM) 7-0. Washington, D.C.: Headquarters, Department of the Army, 2008.

Training Units and Developing Leaders for Full Spectrum Operations. Army Field Manual (FM) 7-0. Washington, D.C.: Headquarters, Department of the Army, 2011.

Transformation Through Innovation and Integration: The National Intelligence Strategy of the United States. Washington, D.C.: Office of the Director of National Intelligence, 2005. http://www.dni.gov/publications/NISOctober2005.pdf.

Traub, James. "Afghanistan's Civil War," *New York Times Magazine* (June 15, 2010). http:// www.nytimes.com/2010/06/20/magazine/20Afghanistan-t.html?hpw.

2009 Army Posture Statement, submitted to the Committees and Subcommittees of the U.S. Senate and the House of Representatives, 1st Session, 111th Congress, May 7, 2009. http://www.army.mil/aps/09/2009_army_posture_statement_web .pdf.

"2006 and Beyond: What the U.S. Army Is Doing." *Torchbearer National Security Report.* Association of the United States Army, March 2006. http://www.ausa.org/publica tions/torchbearercampaign/tnsr/Documents/TBear_March_06_optimized.pdf.

Tyson, Ann Scott. "Gates Warns of Militarized Policy." *Washington Post* (July 16, 2008). http://www.washingtonpost.com/wp-dyn/content/article/2008/07/15/AR2008 071502777.html.

"U.S. Army/U.S. Marine Corps Counterinsurgency Center." Pamphlet. http://usacac .army.mil/CAC2/coin/repository/COIN_Center_Pamphlet.pdf.

"U.S. Short of Diplomats for Iraq, Afghanistan Reconstruction." *Agence France-Press* (April 28, 2008). http://afp.google.com/article/ALeqM5jtyTtMgdIcIsa-R8S_ mHcKVYRhRQ.

Ucko, David H. *The New Counterinsurgency Era: Transforming the U.S. Military for Modern Wars.* Washington, D.C.: Georgetown University Press, 2009.

United States Africa Command Web site. http://www.africom.mil/AboutAFRICOM.asp.

United States Pacific Command Strategy: Partnership, Readiness, Presence. Hawaii: United States Pacific Command, April 2009. http://www.pacom.mil/web/pacom_resources/ pdf/pacom%20strategy%2002APR09.pdf.

United States Southern Command Web site. http://www.southcom.mil/PA/Facts/ Mission.htm.

United States Special Operations Command Web site. http://www.socom.mil/ SOCOMHome/Pages/USSOCOM.aspx.

"The USA's New Littoral Combat Ships (LCS)." *Defense Industry Daily* (August 24, 2011). http://www.defenseindustrydaily.com/the-usas-new-littoral-combat-ships -updated-01343/.

USAID Primer: What We Do and How We Do It. Washington, D.C.: U.S. Agency for International Development, January 2006. http://www.usaid.gov/about_usaid/primer .html.

"The Uses of Military Power." Remarks Prepared for Delivery by the Hon. Caspar W. Weinberger, Secretary of Defense, to the National Press Club, Washington, D.C., Wednesday, November 28, 1984. http://www.pbs.org/wgbh/pages/frontline/shows/ military/force/weinberger.html.

USIP Interview #45. Afghanistan Experience Project 1. http://www.usip.org/files/file/ resources/collections/histories/afghanistan/45.pdf.

USMC Professional Knowledge: Gained from Operational Experience in Vietnam, 1965–1966. NAVMC 2614, Washington, D.C.: U.S. Government Printing Office, 1967.

van Creveld, Martin. *The Transformation of War.* New York: The Free Press, 1991.

Verhoeven, Harry. "The Self-Fulfilling Prophecy of Failed States: Somalia, State Collapse and the Global War on Terrorism." *Journal of Eastern African Studies* 3, no. 3 (November 2009): 405–425.

Vogel, Tom. "Post 9/11 Military Officers Poll Release Press Conference." Washington, D.C.: U.S. Global Leadership Coalition, July 15, 2008. http://www.usglc .org/2008/07/15/post-911-military-officers-poll-release-press-conference/.

Wæver, Ole. "Securitization and Desecuritization." In *On Security*, ed. Ronnie D. Lipschutz, 46–86. New York: Columbia University Press, 1995.

Wald, Charles F. Paper presented at the National Security and the Threat of Climate Change Conference. Washington, D.C.: Wilson Center, Environmental Change and Security Program, May 2007. http://www.wilsoncenter.org/index.cfm?topic_id=1413&fuseaction=topics.event_summary&event_id=236344.

Walker, Peter, and agencies. "Italian Official Condemns Haiti Earthquake Relief as 'Vanity Parade.'" *Guardian* (January 25, 2010). http://www.guardian.co.uk/world/2010/jan/25/italy-condemns-haiti-earthquake-relief-effort.

Wallace, William S. "FM 3-0 Operations: The Army's Blueprint." *Military Review* (March–April 2008): 2–7. http://cgsc.contentdm.oclc.org/cdm/singleitem/collection/p124201coll1/id/237/rec/10.

——. "Full Spectrum Operations: FM 3-0: Resetting the Capstone of Army Doctrine." *Army* 58, no. 3 (March 2008): 35–38. http://www3.ausa.org/webint/DeptArmyMagazine.nsf/byid/TEUE-7BRSQC/$File/Wallace.pdf?OpenElement.

Waltz, Kenneth N. "Structural Realism After the Cold War." *International Security* 25, no. 1 (Summer 2000): 5–41.

Ward, William E. "United States Africa Command." Statement before the Senate Armed Services Committee and the House Armed Services Committee, Washington, D.C.: U.S. Congress, March 17–18, 2009. http://www.africom.mil/pdfFiles/USAFRICOM2009PostureStatement.pdf.

Whelan, Theresa. "Exploring the U.S. Africa Command and a New Strategic Relationship with Africa." Testimony before the Subcommittee on African Affairs of the Committee on Foreign Relations of the U.S. Senate, 110th Congress, 1st sess., 2007. http://www.fas.org/irp/congress/2007_hr/africom.html.

——. "Why AFRICOM?" Paper presented during the Tswalu Dialogue organized by the Brenthurst Foundation, Johannesburg, South Africa, 2007. http://www.rusi.org/downloads/assets/Tswalu_07_WHP.pdf.

Whitlock, Craig. "Pentagon to Cut Spending by $78 Billion, Reduce Troop Strength." *Washington Post* (January 7, 2011). http://www.washingtonpost.com/wp-dyn/content/article/2011/01/06/AR2011010603628.html.

Williams, Cindy, and Gordon Adams. "Strengthening Statecraft and Security: Reforming U.S. Planning and Resource Allocation." Massachusetts Institute of Technology Security Studies Program Occasional Paper, Boston, Massachusetts. Massachusetts Institute of Technology, June 2008. http://www.comw.org/pda/fulltext/WilliamsAdamsOccasionalPaper6-08.pdf.

Williams, Michael C. "Words, Images, Enemies: Securitization and Internal Politics." *International Studies Quarterly* 47, no. 4 (2003): 511–531.

Wolf, Julie. "The Invasion of Grenada." *Reagan, The American Experience*, Public Broadcasting System. http://www.pbs.org/wgbh/amex/reagan/peopleevents/pande07.html.

BIBLIOGRAPHY

Wood, Owen. "Canada: The World's Peacekeeper." *CBC News* (October 30, 2003). http://www.cbc.ca/news/background/cdnmilitary/worldspeacekeeper.html.

Wood, Todd R. "The Maneuver Enhancement Brigade and Its Role in Stability Operations." *Maneuver Support* (Summer 2009): 26–30. http://www.wood.army.mil/engrmag/Maneuver%20Support%20Magazine/PDFs%20for%20Summer%202009/Wood.pdf.

Woodward, Bob. *Plan of Attack*. New York: Simon & Schuster, 2006.

Wulffe, Matt. *Robert Rogers' Rules for the Ranging Service: An Analysis*. Westminster, Md.: Heritage Books, 2009.

Yates, Lawrence A. *The U.S. Military's Experience in Stability Operations, 1789–2005*. Global War on Terrorism Occasional Paper 15. Fort Leavenworth, Kan.: Combat Studies Institute Press, 2006.

Zammuto, Raymond F. *Assessing Organizational Effectiveness: Systems Change, Adaptation, and Strategy*. Albany: State University of New York Press, 1982.

Zinni, Anthony. Speech to the U.S. Naval Institute and the Marine Corps Association. 2003.

Zinni, Tony, and Tony Koltz. *The Battle for Peace: A Frontline Vision of America's Power and Purpose*. New York: Palgrave MacMillan, 2006.

INDEX